Study Guide for the Second Edition of *Technical Analysis*

The Complete Resource for Financial Market Technicians

Study Guide for the Second Edition of *Technical Analysis*

The Complete Resource for Financial Market Technicians

Charles D. Kirkpatrick II, CMT
Julie R. Dahlquist, Ph.D., CMT

Vice President, Publisher: Tim Moore
Associate Publisher and Director of Marketing: Amy Neidlinger
Executive Editor: Jim Boyd
Editorial Assistant: Pamela Boland
Operations Specialist: Jodi Kemper
Marketing Manager: Megan Graue
Cover Designer: Chuti Prasertsith
Managing Editor: Kristy Hart
Project Editor: Betsy Harris
Copy Editor: Charlotte Kughen
Proofreader: Debbie Williams
Interior Designer: Gary Adair
Senior Compositor: Gloria Schurick
Manufacturing Buyer: Dan Uhrig

This book is sold with the understanding that neither the author nor the publisher is engaged in rendering legal, accounting, or other professional services or advice by publishing this book. Each individual situation is unique. Thus, if legal or financial advice or other expert assistance is required in a specific situation, the services of a competent professional should be sought to ensure that the situation has been evaluated carefully and appropriately. The author and the publisher disclaim any liability, loss, or risk resulting directly or indirectly, from the use or application of any of the contents of this book.

FT Press offers excellent discounts on this book when ordered in quantity for bulk purchases or special sales. For more information, please contact U.S. Corporate and Government Sales, 1-800-382-3419, corpsales@pearsontechgroup.com. For sales outside the U.S., please contact International Sales at international@pearsoned.com.

Company and product names mentioned herein are the trademarks or registered trademarks of their respective owners.

ISBN-10: 0-13-309260-7
ISBN-13: 978-0-13-309260-8

Pearson Education LTD.
Pearson Education Australia PTY, Limited.
Pearson Education Singapore, Pte. Ltd.
Pearson Education Asia, Ltd.
Pearson Education Canada, Ltd.
Pearson Educación de Mexico, S.A. de C.V.
Pearson Education—Japan
Pearson Education Malaysia, Pte. Ltd.

Library of Congress Cataloging-in-Publication Data

Kirkpatrick, Charles D.
  Study guide for the second edition of Technical analysis : the complete resource for financial market technicians / Charles D. Kirkpatrick II, Julie R. Dahlquist.
       p. cm.
   ISBN 978-0-13-309260-8 (pbk. : alk. paper)
  1. Technical analysis (Investment analysis) 2. Investment analysis. I. Dahlquist, Julie R., 1962- II. Kirkpatrick, Charles D. Technical analysis. III. Title.
   HG4529 .K564 2011 Study guide
   332.63'2042–dc23
                                   2012026299

Contents

About the Authors

Charles D. Kirkpatrick II, CMT, is

- President, Kirkpatrick & Company, Inc., Kittery, Maine—a private corporation specializing in technical research; Editor and Publisher of the *Market Strategist* newsletter.

- Past Adjunct Professor of Finance, Brandeis University International School of Business, Waltham, Massachusetts.

- Past Director and Vice President, Market Technicians Association Educational Foundation, New York, New York—a charitable foundation dedicated to encouraging and providing educational courses in technical analysis at the college and university level.

- Past Editor, *Journal of Technical Analysis*, New York, New York—the official journal of technical analysis research.

- Past Director, Market Technicians Association, New York, New York—an association of professional technical analysts.

- Author of *Beat the Market: Invest by Knowing What Stocks to Buy and What Stocks to Sell* and *Time the Markets: Using Technical Analysis to Interpret Economic Data.*

In his life in the stock and options markets, Mr. Kirkpatrick has been a hedge fund manager, investment advisor, advisor to floor and desk traders and portfolio managers, institutional stock broker, options trader, desk and large-block trader, lecturer and speaker on aspects of technical analysis to professional and academic groups, expert legal witness on the stock market, owner of several small businesses, owner of an institutional brokerage firm, and part owner of a CBOE options trading firm. His research has been published in Barron's and elsewhere. In 1993 and in 2001, he won the Charles H. Dow Award for excellence in technical research, and in 2009, he won the MTA Annual Award for his contributions to technical analysis. Educated at Phillips Exeter Academy, Harvard College (A.B.) and the Wharton School of the University of Pennsylvania (M.B.A.), he was also a decorated combat officer with the 1st Cavalry Division in Vietnam. He currently resides in Maine with his wife, Ellie, and their various domestic animals.

Julie R. Dahlquist, Ph.D., CMT, received her B.B.A. in economics from University of Louisiana at Monroe, her M.A. in Theology from St. Mary's University, and her Ph.D. in economics from Texas A&M University. Currently, she is a senior lecturer, Department of Finance, at the University of Texas at San Antonio College of Business. Dr. Dahlquist is a recipient of the Charles H. Dow Award for excellence and creativity in technical analysis and is a frequent presenter at national and international conferences. She is the coauthor (with Richard Bauer) of *Technical Analysis of Gaps: Identifying Profitable Gaps for Trading* and *Technical Market Indicators: Analysis and Performance.* Her research has appeared in the *Financial Analysts Journal, Journal of Technical Analysis, Managerial Finance, Applied Economics, Working Money, Financial Practices and Education, Active Trader,* and in the *Journal of Financial Education.* She serves as Editor of *The Journal of Technical Analysis* and is on the Board of the Market Technicians Association Educational Foundation. She resides in San Antonio with her husband, Richard Bauer, and their two children, Katherine and Sepp.

CHAPTER 1
Introduction to Technical Analysis

In its basic form, technical analysis is the study of prices in freely traded markets with the intent of making profitable trading or investment decisions. Consider the basic assumptions presented by Robert D. Edwards and John Magee in their classic book *Technical Analysis of Stock Trends:*

► Stock prices are determined solely by the interaction of demand and supply.

► Stock prices tend to move in trends.

► Shifts in demand and supply cause reversals in trends.

► Shifts in demand and supply can be detected in charts.

Many technical analysts have learned their trade from the mentors with whom they have worked. Numerous individuals who are interested in studying technical analysis today, however, do not have access to such a mentor. Thus, we wrote *Technical Analysis: The Complete Resource for Financial Market Technicians*. Our intent in writing the book was to provide the student of technical analysis with a systematic study of the field. Whether you are a novice college student or an experienced practitioner, our book provides a coherent and comprehensive summation of the body of knowledge that has developed in the field over the past 150 years. We have written this study guide to accompany the second edition of *Technical Analysis*. Its purpose is to assist students studying technical analysis for college coursework or professional examinations in organizing, reviewing, and measuring their comprehension of the subject matter.

Each chapter begins with a set of chapter objectives. These objectives provide concrete outcomes regarding topics you should understand and skills you should gain as you work your way through the chapter.

Next, we provide a summary of the chapter content. These chapter summaries present the major topics within a chapter, but they do not provide all the detailed information regarding those topics. You can think of them as a roadmap of the material, guiding you to the major stops you should make to discover more specifics regarding the material. For example, when you read the definition of a simple moving average in a chapter summary, this should spur you to recall the information in the chapter about how a shorter simple moving average adjusts more quickly to a change in trend than does a longer simple moving average.

Active learning is important whenever you are studying a subject such as technical analysis. You should study with pencil and paper in hand. Writing notes about new concepts as you come across them helps ensure that you understand the material and increases retention. We encourage you to interact with the material as much as possible. One of the best strategies for doing this is the time-tested method of outlining as you read. We suggest that you create an outline for each chapter as you read it. The headings and the subheadings within the chapters provide a guideline for points within your outline. Creating outlines helps you see how different parts of technical analysis fit together and provides an excellent method of organizing the material and your thoughts. In addition, as you go back to study and review the material later, you will find that your outlines provide quick reference to important points and guide you to the places in the textbook should you need to read more.

A thorough understanding of the vocabulary within a discipline is a prerequisite for comprehension of the material. In every chapter, we provide a section entitled "Key Concepts and Vocabulary" which contains vocabulary and concepts with which you might be unfamiliar. If you do not understand these terms, you will have difficulty with the material in the chapter. Some of these are technical terms, unique to the discipline of technical analysis. Others are terms with which you might be familiar in other contexts, but they have specific meaning within the field of technical analysis. We suggest that you keep a running list of definitions to form a glossary of terms to help you study or that you make flash cards with these terms.

Some of the material within the textbook requires the technician to make specific calculations. Other material requires the technician to be able to recognize quickly and easily particular patterns. Therefore, in some chapters we have provided a section entitled "Practice and Application." This section provides an opportunity for you to interact with the material, working through calculations or sketching chart patterns. In doing these tasks, you move from a familiarity with the material to a working knowledge of the material.

Each chapter in *Technical Analysis: The Complete Resource for Financial Market Technicians* concludes with a series of end-of-chapter review questions. This study guide provides sample solutions for each of these questions. We would like to emphasize that it is through thinking about and constructing answers to the end-of-chapter questions that understanding occurs. In that sense, the "answer" to the question is not as important as the mental process of responding to the question. Although it might be tempting to jump straight to the answers and try to "learn" them, we strongly encourage you to construct your own answers first.

In some cases, the questions ask you to use market data when forming an answer. For these questions in particular, the final answer is not as important as the process of analyzing the data. For these questions, your answer might differ from the sample solution we have provided. First, if you are using a different period or a different security than what we have used to construct the sample response, your answer will be different. Second, even if you use the same security and period we consider, your answer might differ slightly. Different data sources differ slightly in their reporting of data; something as simple as differences in the number of decimal places reported can lead to a slightly different numerical answer in the end. Over time, these differences become magnified, as databases adjust historical prices not only for errors but for stock splits and dividends.

Finally, at the end of each chapter we provide a "self-test." These self-tests are comprised of multiple-choice questions and are designed to enable you to assess your knowledge and comprehension of the subject matter. These questions are similar to questions you might encounter on Level 1 and Level 2 examinations for the Market Technician Association's Chartered Market Technician (CMT) professional designation program. We designed these questions to give you a quick summary of your comfort level with the material in that chapter. These questions do not cover all the material in the chapter, and knowing the answers to these particular questions does not ensure thorough understanding of the material. Thus, these questions are not meant for "study;" they are meant for assessing your knowledge. A score of less than 80% on one of these self-tests is an indication that you need to spend more time studying the chapter to master the material contained in it. The answers to the self-test questions appear at the end of this study guide.

Learning any skill takes practice, practice, practice. Technical analysis is no different. Because technical analysis is the study of financial markets, the more involved you are with the financial markets on a daily basis, the more meaningful and productive your study of technical analysis will be. Watching the stock market and examining charts on a daily basis help you gain a familiarity with price behavior and enhance your ability to recognize traditional chart patterns. As with all things in life, the more you put into your study, the more you will get out of it.

CHAPTER 2

The Basic Principle of Technical Analysis—The Trend

Chapter Objectives

By the end of this chapter, you should be able to

► Define the term *trend*

► Explain why determining the trend is important to the technical analyst

► Distinguish between primary, secondary, short-term, and intraday trends

► Discuss some of the basic beliefs upon which technical analysis is built

Chapter Summary

How Does the Technical Analyst Make Money?

In order to make money using technical methods, remember:

► "The trend is your friend"—play the trend.

► Don't lose—control risk.

► Manage your money—avoid ruin.

What Is a Trend?

A **trend** is a directional movement of prices. For a trend to be useful, it must remain in effect long enough to be identified and still be playable. An **uptrend** is a rising trend; it occurs when prices reach higher peaks and higher troughs. A **downtrend** occurs when prices reach lower troughs and lower peaks. A **sideways** trend, or flat trend, occurs when prices trade in a range, moving up and down, but remaining at the same level on average.

How Are Trends Identified?

Analysts often use moving averages to identify trends. Trends can also be identified by drawing lines between extreme points on price graphs. Another, but less practical, method of determining trends is using linear least-squares regression.

Why Do Markets Trend?

Price is the result of the interaction of supply and demand. A change in price is, therefore, due to a change in supply or demand. Rather than focusing on the indeterminable reasons why supply and demand might be changing, the technical analyst watches prices themselves for evidence of change.

What Trends Are There?

The **fractal nature of trends** refers to the fact that trends act similarly over different length periods. Long, medium, or very short periods produce trends with the same characteristics and patterns. Technical analysts divide trends into several broad categories: the **primary trend** (measured in months or years), the **secondary trend** or **intermediate trend** (measured in weeks or months), the **short-term trend** (measured in days), and the **intraday trend** (measured in minutes or hours).

What Other Assumptions Do Technical Analysts Make?

The basic underlying theory of technical analysis is that markets trend. In addition, technical analysts assume:

▶ Price is determined by the interaction of supply and demand

▶ Price discounts everything

▶ Prices are nonrandom

▶ Prices form recognizable patterns

▶ Price patterns are fractal

▶ Prices reflect emotions, such as fear and greed, and emotional feedback causes "bubbles" and "panics."

Key Concepts and Vocabulary

A number of terms and concepts that might be new to you appear in this chapter. As you read this chapter, pay close attention to the following terms and concepts. Write down a definition or explanation for each.

Trend

Uptrend

Downtrend

Sideways trend

Fractal nature of trends

Primary trend

Secondary trend

Intraday trend

Short-term trend

Practice and Application

The idea that stock prices trend is central to the practice of technical analysis. Identifying an uptrend, a downtrend, and a sideways trend is an important skill for the technical analyst. Use the space below to sketch a graph representing each of these three major categories of trends.

Trend	Sketch	Notes
Uptrend		

Trend	Sketch	Notes
Downtrend		
Sideways Trend		

End-of-Chapter Review Questions

1. *Explain why the notion that prices trend is central to the practice of technical analysis.*

   Money is made by buying a security at the beginning of an uptrend at a low price, riding the trend, and selling the security when the trend ends at a high price. The change in price during the trend is what enables the trader to profit.

2. *The earlier an uptrend can be spotted, the more money an investor can make by "riding the trend." Explain why recognizing a trend too late reduces potential profits for the investor.*

   Because price is increasing in an uptrend, the sooner you spot the uptrend the cheaper the price at which you can buy the stock (in relation to the future higher prices), and you will experience a larger price appreciation. Suppose, for example, a stock has been trading at $5 per share and then begins trending upward to $20 per share. The analyst who immediately recognizes this will gain $15 per share. However, investors who do not spot the trend until later, when the price reaches $11, will realize only a $9 per-share gain.

3. *The sooner an investor recognizes that a trend has changed, the more profitable the inves-tor's trading will be. Explain why early recognition of trend reversals influences the investor's profitability.*

Assume you have spotted an upward trend in a stock and have purchased the stock. As the uptrend continues, your profit increases. However, when the trend reverses, the stock price stops increasing and begins decreasing. For maximum profit, you want to spot this reversal as soon as possible to exit the position. The sooner you sell the stock after the reversal, the higher your profits will be.

4. *Newton's first law of motion is inertia—an object in motion will remain in motion in the same direction unless acted upon by an unbalanced force. How does this physics principle serve as an analogy for the notion of trends in technical analysis?*

Technical analysts believe that when price has been moving in a particular direction that directional movement in price will continue. If a stock price is increasing (an uptrend exists), we would expect this uptrend to continue until something occurs to end the upward motion. As long as buyers are stronger in the market than sellers, the price will go up. When buying weakens and selling strengthens, the upward price movement will end.

5. *Define primary, secondary, short-term, and intraday trends.*

For identification purposes, technical analysts have divided trends into several broad cat-egories. These are the primary trend (measured in months or years), the secondary or inter-mediate trend (measured in weeks or months), the short-term trend (measured in days), and the intraday trend (measured in minutes or hours).

6. *Gather monthly data for the DJIA from 1965 until the present. One publicly available source for this data can be found electronically at http://finance.yahoo.com using the ticker symbol ^DJI. Under "quotes," choose the "historical prices" options. At this point, you will be able to choose a monthly data option and download the data into a spreadsheet.*

   a. *Graph the monthly data for the DJIA for the 1965 through 1980 time period. Was the market in an uptrend, downtrend, or sideways trend during that time? Explain your answer.*

**DJIA January 1965-December 1980
Monthly**

During the 1965–1980 period, the market was in a sideways trend. The DJIA oscillated between approximately 700 and 1000 points, with no clear upward or downward trend.

b. *Graph the monthly data for the DJIA for the 1980 through 1990 period. Was the market in an uptrend, downtrend, or sideways trend during that time? Explain your answer.*

DJIA January 1980-December 1990

The graph shows a clear upward trend between 1980 and 1990. Although not every month resulted in positive returns to investors, investors who were invested for the entire period would have experienced almost a three-fold increase in their net worth.

c. *Graph the monthly data for the DJIA for the 1990 through 2000 time period. Was the market in an uptrend, downtrend, or sideways trend during that time? Explain your answer.*

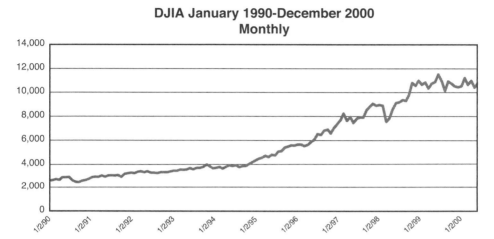

DJIA January 1990-December 2000 Monthly

The graph for the DJIA from 1990–2000 shows a strong uptrend. Over the period, the DJIA rose from about 2,600 to 11,000. The DJIA approximately doubled from 1990 through 1996 and then doubled again from 1996 through 1999.

d. *Graph the monthly data for the DJIA from 2000 until the present. Has the market been in an uptrend, downtrend, or sideways trend? Explain your answer.*

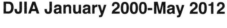

DJIA January 2000-May 2012

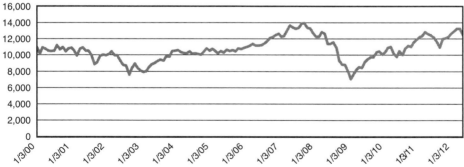

The chart is for data through May 2012. Your chart might appear different if your ending period is different. Since 2000, the market has been in a sideways trading range. The market has experienced a great deal of volatility; the DJIA lost approximately 50% of its value from its 2007 high to its 2009 low. However, there has been no consistent, strong directional trend in the market over the period.

e. *Comparing the four charts that you have generated, what conclusions do you draw about historical market trends?*

During certain periods, it is easy for investors to ride the trend and profit. During the 1980s and 1990s, investors who owned stocks saw substantial gains. In a strong uptrend a "buy and hold" strategy can be extremely profitable. However, in other periods a "buy and hold" strategy will not be very profitable. For example, investors who entered the market in 1965 would find that their net worth had not really increased by 1980 if they were practicing a "buy and hold" strategy. They would have experienced some gains and some losses over the period, but they would have found themselves just about at their starting point. Investors who entered the market in 2000 and held their positions until May of 2012 would have made a small return, but experienced a wild ride to do so.

7. *Choose a one-year period during each of the 1965–1980, 1980-1990, 1990–2000 and 2000–present periods. Download daily DJIA data from the Yahoo! Finance Web site for each of these three one-year periods. Graph the daily data for each of these three periods. What types of trends do you see in these daily data graphs? Comparing these daily graphs to the monthly graphs during the same periods, what similarities and what differences do you find?*

Individual graphs differ depending on the year chosen. The following graph represents the daily levels of the DJIA for 1975. Remember that the overall market trend for 1965–1980 was sideways. The following graph is a snapshot of a portion of that period. The first half of 1975 showed a strong upward trend in the DJIA, with approximately a 40% gain. The second half of the year showed a sideways trading range.

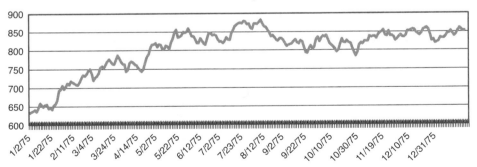

DJIA January-December 1975
Daily

The following chart represents daily moves in the DJIA during 1985. The overall trend in the graph is upward. However, most of the upward movement occurred in the first month and in the last couple of months of the year. February through September was relatively flat, with the DJIA at about the same level in mid-September as it was in February. Remember that the 1980–1990 period saw strong upward movement in the DJIA; the upward trend in 1985 contributed to the upward trend of the overall period. The following graph highlights, however, that the upward movement did not occur in a straight line, and investors did not gain every month during that period.

DJIA January-December 1985
Daily

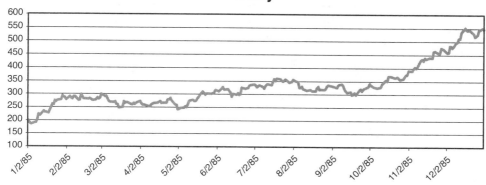

The following chart is a daily chart of the DJIA for the year 1995. The chart shows a strong uptrend. Remember that the market was in a long-term uptrend, with the DJIA doubling between 1995 and 1998.

DJIA January-December 1995
Daily

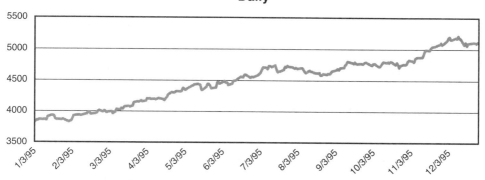

Daily data for the DJIA for 2005 is displayed in the following chart. The DJIA oscillated in a trading range for the year with no clear directional trend. Since 2000, the market has experienced this type of sideways movement.

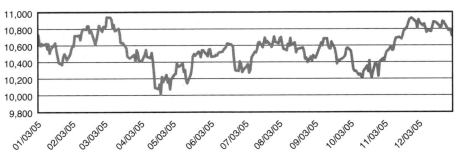

DJIA January-December 2005
Daily

Self-Test

1. *Which of the following best describes an uptrend?*

    a. A movement of prices characterized by higher and higher peaks and lower and lower troughs

    b. A movement of prices characterized by lower and lower peaks and higher and higher troughs

    c. A movement of prices characterized by higher and higher peaks and higher and higher troughs

    d. A movement of prices characterized by higher and higher peaks with no troughs

2. *The secondary trend*

    a. Is measured in weeks or months.

    b. Is always in the same direction as the primary trend.

    c. Is of no importance to the technical analyst.

    d. Is determined by fundamental factors rather than supply and demand.

3. *Which of the following is NOT a basic assumption made by technical analysts?*

    a. Prices trend.

    b. Prices are random.

    c. Patterns are fractal.

    d. Price is determined by supply and demand.

4. *Technical analysts divide trends into broad categories including*

   a. Primary, secondary, and short-term trends.

   b. Main, subordinate, and intraday trends.

   c. Primary, fractal, and emotional trends.

   d. Supply, demand, and behavioral trends.

5. *A _____ occurs when price moves up and down within a range, but remains, on average, at the same level.*

   a. Fractal trend

   b. Secondary trend

   c. Primary trend

   d. Sideways trend

6. *Long and short periods tend to produce trends with the same characteristics and patterns due to the*

   a. Fractal nature of trends.

   b. Random nature of prices.

   c. Secondary trend acting counter to the primary trend.

   d. Dominance of supply over demand in determining prices.

7. *Which of the following would you be most likely to hear a technical analyst say?*

   a. "Price movement is random."

   b. "The primary trend should be ignored so that the investor can concentrate on the secondary trend."

   c. "Price is determined by demand rather than by supply."

   d. "Human decisions are affected by two basic emotions: fear and greed."

8. *According to technical analysts, stock prices are determined by _____ and _____.*

   a. Randomness; fractal motion

   b. Fear; randomness

   c. Supply; demand

   d. Demand; long-term trend

9. *Alex creates a stock chart using weekly data for a stock over the past five years. He tells you that he is trying to determine if the stock is in an uptrend. Given the information Alex is using, you can conclude that he is most interested in determining the _____ for the stock.*

   a. Primary trend

   b. Secondary trend

   c. Short-term trend

   d. Fractal trend

10. *Technical analysts*

    a. Only consider short-term trends and ignore longer-term price movement.

    b. Place great emphasis on understanding the determinants of supply and demand.

    c. Believe the stock prices are determined by demand rather than by supply.

    d. Assume that recognizable patterns in stock prices repeatedly occur.

CHAPTER 3
History of Technical Analysis

Chapter Objectives

By the end of this chapter, you should be familiar with

▶ The history of financial markets and exchanges

▶ The creation of market indices by Charles Dow

▶ The development of technical analysis in the United States over the past century

▶ The impact that academic theory and fundamental stock market analysis have had on the development and use of technical analysis

▶ The impact that data availability and computer power have had on the development of technical analysis

Chapter Summary

Early Financial Markets and Exchanges

Markets have existed for thousands of years, and exchanges have existed since at least the fourteenth century. Technical analysis has probably been used, in some form, for centuries.

Modern Technical Analysis

Charles Dow (1851–1902) is considered the father of modern technical analysis. He introduced the use of stock market indexes to measure the performance of the stock market. During the 1920s and early 1930s, Wyckoff was a newsletter writer; Ayers created the advance-decline line; Schabaker began identifying chart patterns using the terms "triangle," "pennant," and "head-and-shoulders;" and Gann focused on the commodity markets. In 1948, Edwards and Magee published *Technical Analysis of Stock Trends*. Granville developed the concept of on-balance-volume and promoted the use of a 200-day moving average during the 1950s. Momentum became an important concept during the 1960s. By the 1970s, computer use increased the accuracy of charts and enabled analysts to calculate ratios and oscillators more quickly. Wilder developed the relative strength index (RSI), the Directional Movement concept, the Parabolic System, and the Average True Range. Donchian promoted the use of 10-day and 20-day moving average crossovers as well as channel breakouts, and Zweig promoted the use of the put-call ratio. The technological advances allowed for the development of moving-average envelopes and the Moving-Average Convergence/Divergence (MACD) oscillator. Nison introduced Japanese candlestick charting to the western financial markets in the late 1980s.

Current Advances in Technical Analysis

The Efficient Markets Hypothesis is being questioned and new lines of inquiry, such as behavioral finance, are focusing on the psychology of market participants. Falling commissions, the increased speed of communication, and computer technology have led to more interest in technical analysis.

Self-Test

1. *Who is considered the father of modern technical analysis?*

    a. Edward Magee

    b. Charles Dow

    c. Graham Dodd

    d. Leonard Ayers

2. *What was the first company in the U.S. to publish stock prices publicly on a consistent basis?*

    a. Dow Jones Company

    b. Standard and Poors

    c. Graham and Dodd Securities

    d. The Henry Poor Company

3. *Behavioral finance*

    a. Is based upon the efficient markets hypothesis.

    b. Was introduced to the Japanese in the late 1800s.

    c. Is concerned with the behavior of prices rather than the emotions of buyers and sellers.

    d. Is concerned with the psychology of market participants.

4. *Which of the following has led to the advancement of technical analysis in the past few decades?*

    a. Falling commissions, increased speed of communication, and increased computational speed

    b. Rising transactions costs and adherence to the efficient markets hypothesis

    c. Rising transactions costs and ease of index calculation

    d. Ease of index calculation, availability of public data, and adherence to the efficient market hypotheses

5. *Which of the following is a chronological list of technical analysts, beginning with the analyst publishing work earliest?*

    a. Dow, Hamilton, Magee, Wilder

    b. Dow, Wilder, Appel, Magee

    c. Magee, Dow, Hamilton, Ayers

    d. Edwards, Magee, Graham, Dodd

6. *Which of the following is a TRUE statement regarding the development of technical analysis?*

    a. Classic chart patterns, such as the head and shoulders and the double top, first appeared in the literature in the early 1700s.

    b. Charles Dow was heavily influenced by the introduction of Japanese candlestick charts to the U.S. markets.

    c. Charles Dow based his work heavily on the writings of Edwards and Magee.

    d. Charles Dow introduced the use of indexes to measure the stock market in the late 1800s.

7. *Japanese candlestick charts were*

    a. Introduced into the U.S. by Steve Nison in the late 1980s.

    b. First written about by Charles Dow and later developed in the Japanese markets.

    c. The main type of chart used in the U.S. during the 1920s and early 1930s.

    d. Developed after computer power was great enough to calculate complex mathematical models rapidly.

8. *Which of the following is a TRUE statement?*

   a. Although technical analysis works well for short-term trading, the basic principles do not work for longer time periods.

   b. Although the basic principles of technical analysis are valid for short and long time periods, the indicators and methods utilized for these horizons often have their own characteristics.

   c. Technical analysis works well for the stock market, but the principles are not valid in the commodities markets due to the unique instruments traded.

   d. Although emotions played an important role in determining stock prices in the early 1900s, this is no longer the case.

9. *The Relative Strength Index was*

   a. Created by Welles Wilder in the 1970s.

   b. Created by Charles Dow as a precursor to the Dow Jones Index.

   c. Developed by Graham and Dodd in response to the increased availability of corporate data.

   d. Developed in the Japanese markets and brought to the Western markets in the 1980s.

10. *Those who study behavioral finance*

   a. Developed the Efficient Markets Hypothesis.

   b. Have found instances of predictable investor behavior.

   c. Are concerned with the behavior, rather than the emotions or psychology, of market participants.

   d. Believe that all stock price movement is random.

CHAPTER 4
The Technical Analysis Controversy

Chapter Objectives

After studying this chapter, you should have a good understanding of

▶ The basic principles of the Random Walk Hypothesis (RWH)

▶ The historical distribution of stock market returns

▶ The basic principles of the Efficient Markets Hypothesis (EMH)

▶ The pragmatic criticisms of technical analysis

▶ How technical analysts respond to critics

Chapter Summary

Do Markets Follow a Random Walk?

A **random walk** occurs when future price movement cannot be predicted by observing past price movement. If prices move in a random fashion, then no underlying patterns can exist in stock prices.

Sornette has studied periods in the stock market when successive losses, referred to as **drawdowns**, have occurred. He estimates that the probability of two or more extremely large drawdowns occurring back-to-back is out in the stratosphere if stock returns are truly random. Pointing to time periods when these back-to-back events have occurred, Sornette suggests stocks do not follow a random walk. Lo and MacKinlay have also challenged the assumption of randomness based on the characteristics of the distribution of stock return fluctuations.

Can Past Patterns Be Used to Predict the Future?

Even if stock prices do not follow a random walk, past patterns may not be helpful in predicting future market movements. Markets are constantly being affected by new information that might cause too much variability in the underlying pattern for knowledge of the pattern to be exploited.

What About Market Efficiency?

The **Efficient Markets Hypothesis (EMH)** states that at any given time, security prices fully reflect all available information. The profit motive of investors creates efficient markets; if the price of a security deviates from its true value, arbitrageurs compete to bring the price to the proper level.

The implication of this hypothesis is that if current prices fully reflect all information, the market price of a security is a good estimate of its intrinsic value, and no investment strategy can be used to outperform the market.

Financial markets are characterized by **asymmetric information**, a situation in which one party of a transaction has information the other party does not have. All information is not instantly and accurately disseminated to all market players. When market players receive information, they must interpret the information, which is a difficult, complex process.

The EMH assumes that investors act rationally, but results in the field of behavioral finance point to issues such as herding, overconfidence, overreaction, psychological accounting, and miscalibration of probabilities. Advocates of the EMH claim that, though irrational players can sometimes affect prices, prices are quickly brought back to their true value by rational arbitrageurs.

Arbitrage is the simultaneous purchasing and selling of the same security in two different markets at different prices. Arbitrage is not always possible because it depends on a substitutable alternative and sufficient liquidity for the arbitrageur to get into and out of a position.

Behavioral Finance and Technical Analysis

Behavioral finance appears to contradict the EMH and has become the theoretical basis for technical analysis. Unlike the EMH, which is based upon deductive reasoning, behavioral finance is based upon inductive reasoning. This inductive reasoning process is based upon observing real-world events and looking for patterns.

Pragmatic Criticisms of Technical Analysis

Technical analysis is not simply for short-term traders: studying price action can be useful for long-term decision-making. As technical analysis tools become more widely used they may become less effective, leading to old rules not working as well in the future. Although some criticize technical analysis because it requires subjective judgment, the same can be said for other forms of investment analysis.

Key Concepts and Vocabulary

A number of terms and concepts that might be new to you appear in this chapter. As you read through this chapter, pay close attention to the following terms and concepts. Write down a definition or explanation for each.

Random walk

Efficient Markets Hypothesis

Arbitrage

Drawdown

Behavioral finance

Equilibrium

Liquidity

Deductive logic

Inductive logic

Rational

Fat tails

End-of-Chapter Review Questions

1. *You walk into a room where some friends have been playing a coin toss game. They ask you to guess whether the coin will land on heads or tails on the next toss. Does the fact that your friends have knowledge about how many head and tails have already occurred in the game give them any advantage over you in guessing whether a coin will land on heads or tails on the next coin toss? Explain.*

   In this case, there is no advantage because each outcome has a 50-50 chance. For example, assume you flip a coin once, and it lands on heads. Observing that the coin landed on heads does not help predict what the outcome will be the next time the coin is flipped. Each flip of the coin is an independent event, and the outcome of one flip of the coin has no effect on the outcome of any other flip. Given its independence, counting how many outcomes resulted in heads or tails would not help you figure out the next outcome.

2. *Supporters of the Random Walk Hypothesis claim that stock prices have no "memory." What do they mean by this claim?*

   Supporters of the Random Walk Hypothesis claim that stock prices have no memory. By this, they mean that the stock's price today is not correlated with the stock's price yesterday. The stock's price today is based upon today's information and is not affected by yesterday's price. Stock prices are not impacted by the "memory" of yesterday's price. To the supporters of the Random Walk Hypothesis, no knowledge of past stock prices will help predict future stock prices.

3. *What does the term "fat tails" mean? How do fat tails differ from the tails that would occur in a normal distribution?*

Mandelbrot (1963) first noticed this phenomenon of fat tails, called a "leptokurtic distribution," in stock market returns in the early 1960s. Fat tails occur when one or more events cause stock prices to deviate extraordinarily from the mean. In a normal distribution, as you move farther from the mean the tails get thinner and thinner, asymptotically approaching the X axis. This indicates that the further away an observation is from the mean (more extreme) the less likely it is to occur. With "fat tails" the tails do not flatten out as much as in a normal distribution; thus, the extreme observations are more likely to occur than they would in a normal distribution.

4. *If the probability of a 10% decline in stock prices occurring on any particular day is 1 in 1,000 and stock returns are random, explain why the probability of having a 10% decline in stock prices on two consecutive days is only 1 in 1,000,000.*

If the probability of a one-day decline of 10% in the stock market is approximately 1 in 1,000, a 10% drop would occur once every four years (approximately 1,000 trading days) on average. Consequently, if stock returns are independent, then the probability of two consecutive daily drops of 10% would be the product of the probability of the two independent events occurring, or 1/1,000 multiplied by 1/1,000 which equals 1 in 1,000,000.

5. *What are some of the problems associated with information that bring the EMH into question?*

According to the EMH, new information is immediately and completely reflected in security prices. This hypothesis is based on the assumptions that all investors receive new information instantly and react rationally to the information. Another assumption is that arbitrageurs immediately and always act to adjust any deviations in the price back to its new value.

However, empirical evidence demonstrates that immediate and complete reactions to new information do not occur. Information is not disseminated instantly to all market players. Information can be costly for investors to attain. Interpreting and acting upon the information can be difficult and costly for investors to do. The EMH assumes that arbitrage brings prices back to equilibrium if investors are reacting irrationally. In many cases, arbitrage is not easy or practical. Appropriate investment vehicles do not always exist for the arbitrageur. There may not be sufficient liquidity for the arbitrageur to get into (and out of) a position.

Self-Test

1. *Suppose that DAL had a return today of 0.7%. If stock prices follow a random walk,*

    a. You would expect tomorrow's return to be negative.

    b. You would expect tomorrow's return to be 0.7%.

    c. You would expect tomorrow's return to be greater than 0.7%.

    d. Knowing today's return does not give you any information about what tomorrow's return might be.

2. *If the probability of a 3% decline in stock prices occurring on any particular day is 1 in 100 and stock returns are random, what is the probability of having a 3% decline in stock prices on two consecutive days?*

    a. One in 50

    b. One in 200

    c. One in 10,000

    d. The probably cannot be calculated if stock prices are random.

3. *The tails of a normal distribution*

    a. Get thinner and thinner, approaching zero.

    b. Get thicker and thicker, approaching infinity.

    c. Remain constant.

    d. Have no predictable shape or pattern.

4. *Which of the following would result in "fat tails"?*

    a. Stock prices follow a random walk.

    b. Stock prices do not deviate much from their mean for an extended period of time.

    c. Stock prices have no "memory," resulting in erratic, unpredictable behavior.

    d. One or more events cause stock prices to deviate extraordinarily from the mean.

5. *Which of the following is an example of arbitrage?*

    a. Aaron buys an asset in one market and simultaneously sells the asset at a higher price in another market.

    b. Florence buys a stock and then sells it as soon as it is downgraded by analysts.

    c. David buys the stock in two different companies, thinking that one or the other of the companies will land a big defense contract from the government.

    d. Tricia buys the stock of companies that have returns occurring in fat tails.

6. *A plot of actual historical stock returns*

   a. Is characterized by fat tails.

   b. Shows strong and convincing evidence that stock prices follow a random walk.

   c. Perfectly matches that of the bell-shaped curve.

   d. Shows that the normal distribution describes stock returns, allowing analysts to predict stock price movements.

7. *Which of the following does the Efficient Markets Hypothesis assume?*

   a. Stock returns follow a normal distribution with fat tails.

   b. At any point in time, all available information is reflected in stock prices.

   c. Past price data, but not past volume data, is an effective indicator of future price movement.

   d. Because both price and volume data follow a normal distribution, they are important factors in forming expectations of future price movements.

8. *In order for arbitrage to bring prices immediately to their intrinsic value*

   a. Stock prices must follow a random walk.

   b. Short-term traders must outnumber long-term investors in the market.

   c. Fat tails must exist in the distribution of stock returns.

   d. Sufficient liquidity must exist for arbitrageurs to get into and out of the market.

9. *Which of the following is a TRUE statement?*

   a. Technical analysis is used by short-term traders, but not by long-term investors.

   b. As technical rules that worked in the past become popular, they may cease to work.

   c. Fundamental analysis relies upon objective analysis while technical analysis relies upon subjective analysis.

   d. Existence of fat tails in the distribution of stock returns is an indication that stock prices follow a random walk.

10. *Believers in the Random Walk Hypothesis would say that*

   a. A trading strategy could appear to be profitable, but the success would be attributed to luck rather than the system really working.

   b. Stock trading systems based on price data outperform systems based on volume data.

   c. The existence of arbitrageurs make otherwise efficient markets inefficient.

   d. Investors do not immediately and fully react to new information as it becomes available, which results in random and arbitrary price movements.

CHAPTER 5

An Overview of Markets

Chapter Objectives

After studying this chapter, you should be familiar with

- ▶ The market characteristics required for investors to use technical analysis
- ▶ The types of markets in which technical analysis can be used
- ▶ The differences between informed, uninformed, and liquidity market players
- ▶ The differences between price-weighted, market capitalization weighted, and equally weighted averages

Chapter Summary

In What Types of Markets Can Technical Analysis Be Used?

Direct search markets and brokered markets are usually not subject to technical analysis. Dealer markets and auction markets in which liquid, substitutable assets are traded are often subject to technical analysis.

Types of Contracts

In the **cash** or **spot market**, contracts result in the immediate exchange of the agreed upon items. The **derivative market** is comprised of financial contracts that "derive" their values from some other investment vehicle. Futures, options, and swaps are common types of derivatives. The **futures market** is comprised of contracts in which the buyer and seller agree to trade at specific terms at a specific future date. A **call option** gives the owner the right to buy an asset at a particular price, known as the strike price, before the option expiration date. A **put option** gives the owner the right to sell an asset at the strike price before the option expiration date.

How Does a Market Work?

A market is comprised of different players who make buy and sell decision based upon their interpretation of different sets of information. So long as there is a balance between those who want to buy and those who want to sell, price oscillates within a relatively small zone. If buyers overwhelm sellers, the price goes up; if sellers overwhelm buyers, the price falls.

Who Are the Market Players?

Academia has divided market participants into three categories: informed, noise, and liquidity players. **Informed players** are believed to interpret new information rationally and adjust the market price of a security to its equilibrium value immediately. **Noise players**, or the public, cause random activity around the equilibrium price. **Liquidity players** participate in the market for reasons other than investment or trading.

How Is the Market Measured?

The Dow Jones averages are **price-weighted averages**; a given percentage change in a high-priced stock has a greater effect on the Dow averages than does the same percentage change in a low-priced stock. The S&P500 Index, the NYSE composite index, the NASDAQ composite index, and the Russell Indexes are **market capitalization weighted indexes**; each of the stocks contained in these indexes is weighted by its market value. Stocks with a large number of shares outstanding and a high price have a proportionate influence on these market capitalization weighted averages. **Equally weighted**, also known as **geometric** or **unweighted**, **indexes** use an equal weighting for all stocks included in the index, regardless of price or market value.

Key Concepts and Vocabulary

A number of terms and concepts that might be new to you appear in this chapter. As you read through this chapter, pay close attention to the following terms and concepts. Write down a definition or explanation for each.

Fungibility	Derivative	Equally weighted average
Direct-search market	Underlying	Limit day
Brokered market	Counterparty risk	Exchange-traded fund (ETF)
Dealer market	Noise	
Auction market	Noise players	Cash market
Bid price	Liquidity players	Futures market
Ask price	Price-weighted average	Option market
Bid-ask spread	Market capitalization weighted average	
Circuit breakers		

Practice and Application

Calculate the percentage price change for the three stocks, Alpha, Beta, and Gamma, in the following chart for Days 2–6. The formula for a percentage price change is

$$\% \text{ Price Change for Day 2} = \frac{(\text{Day 2 Price} - \text{Day 1 Price})}{\text{Day 1 Price}} \times 100$$

Company	Alpha		Beta		Gamma	
Number of Shares Outstanding	2,500,000		3,000,000		10,000,000	
	Price	*% Change*	*Price*	*% Change*	*Price*	*% Change*
Day 1	40		85		53	
Day 2	43		86		51	
Day 3	41		88		52	
Day 4	38		85		53	
Day 5	41		88		52	
Day 6	42		86		53	

Calculate the Market Cap for each stock for Days 1–6. The formula for calculating market cap is

Market Cap Day 1 = Day 1 Price × Number of Shares Outstanding

Company	Alpha		Beta		Gamma	
Number of Shares Outstanding	2,500,000		3,000,000		10,000,000	
	Price	*Market Cap*	*Price*	*Market Cap*	*Price*	*Market Cap*
Day 1	40		85		53	
Day 2	43		86		51	
Day 3	41		88		52	
Day 4	38		85		53	
Day 5	41		88		52	
Day 6	42		86		53	

Calculate a price-weighted average for each day. The formula for a price-weighted average of three stocks is

$$\text{Price Weighted Average} = \frac{\text{Price of Alpha} + \text{Price of Beta} + \text{Price of Gamma}}{3}$$

Also, calculate the percentage change in the price weighted average using the following formula:

$$\% \text{ Change in Price Weighted Average for Day 2} = \frac{(\text{Price Weighted Avg for Day 2} - \text{Price Weighted Avg for Day 1})}{\text{Price Weighted Avg for Day 1}} \times$$

Company	Alpha	Beta	Gamma		
Number of Shares Outstanding	2,500,000	3,000,000	10,000,000	*Price-Weighted Average*	*% Change in Price-Weighted Average*
	Price	*Price*	*Price*		
Day 1	40	85	53		
Day 2	43	86	51		
Day 3	41	88	52		
Day 4	38	85	53		
Day 5	41	88	52		
Day 6	42	86	53		

Calculate a market cap weighted index for each of the days. To begin, calculate the market cap for Day 1 as

Market Cap Day 1 = Market Cap Alpha + Market Cap Beta + Market Cap Gamma

For each day, calculate the index as

$$\text{MktCap Index for Day N} = \frac{\text{MktCap Alpha Day N} + \text{MktCap Beta Day N} + \text{MktCap Gamma Day N}}{\text{Market Cap Day 1}} \times 100$$

Also, calculate the % change in the market cap index for Days 2–6 using the following formula:

$$\% \text{ change in MktCap Index for Day 2} = \frac{\text{MktCap Index for Day 2} - \text{MktCap Index for Day 1}}{\text{MktCap Index for Day 1}} \times 100$$

Company	Alpha	Beta	Gamma			
Number of Shares Outstanding	2,500,000	3,000,000	10,000,000	*Market Cap*	*Market Cap Index*	*% Change in Market Cap Index*
	Price	*Price*	*Price*			
Day 1	40	85	53			
Day 2	43	86	51			
Day 3	41	88	52			
Day 4	38	85	53			
Day 5	41	88	52			
Day 6	42	86	53			

Calculate an unweighted index for each day. Begin by calculating a holding period return (HPR) for each of the stocks for Days 2–6 using the formula:

$$\text{HPR Day 2} = 1 + \frac{\text{Day 2 Price} - \text{Day 1 Price}}{\text{Day 1 Price}}$$

The unweighted index value for Day 1 is 100. For each subsequent day, calculate the unweighted index value as

Unweighted Index Day N = (Day N HPR for Alpha $\times$ Day N HPR for Beta $\times$ Day N HPR for Gamma)$^{1/3}$ $\times$ 100

Day 2 has been completed for you as an example.

Company	Alpha		Beta		Gamma			
Number of Shares Outstanding	2,500,000		3,000,000		10,000,000		$\prod HPR^{1/3}$	Index Value
	Price	HPR	Price	HPR	Price	HPR		
Day 1	40		85		53			100
Day 2	43	1.08	86	1.01	51	0.96	1.0153	101.5299
Day 3	41		88		52			
Day 4	38		85		53			
Day 5	41		88		52			
Day 6	42		86		53			

Here are solutions to use to check your answers:

Company	Alpha	Beta	Gamma	Price-Weighted Average	% Change in Price-Weighted Average	Market Cap Alpha	Market Cap Beta
Number of Shares Outstanding	2,500,000	3,000,000	10,000,000				
	Price	Price	Price				
Day 1	40	85	53	59.33		100,000,000	255,000,000
Day 2	43	86	51	60.00	1.12%	107,500,000	258,000,000
Day 3	41	88	52	60.33	0.56%	102,500,000	264,000,000
Day 4	38	85	53	58.67	-2.76%	95,000,000	255,000,000
Day 5	41	88	52	60.33	2.84%	102,500,000	264,000,000
Day 6	42	86	53	60.33	0.00%	105,000,000	258,000,000

Company									
Number of Shares Outstanding	Market Cap Gamma	Market Cap Index	% Change in Market Cap Index	HPR Alpha	HPR Beta	HPR Gamma	$\prod HPR^{1/3}$	Index Value	
Day 1	530,000,000	100.00						100	
Day 2	510,000,000	98.93	-1.07%	1.08	1.01	0.96	1.0153	101.5299	
Day 3	520,000,000	100.17	1.26%	0.95	1.02	1.02	0.9983	99.8261	
Day 4	530,000,000	99.44	-0.73%	0.93	0.97	1.02	0.9699	96.9921	
Day 5	520,000,000	100.17	0.74%	1.08	1.04	0.98	1.0310	103.1012	
Day 6	530,000,000	100.90	0.73%	1.02	0.98	1.02	1.0067	100.6741	

End-of-Chapter Review Questions

1. *For technical analysis to be used, the asset being traded must be substitutable. Explain what "fungibility" means and why fungible assets are a prerequisite for technical analysis.*

   Fungibility is the interchangeability of financial assets on identical terms. For example, shares of IBM stock are fungible; if someone owes me a share of IBM stock, I don't care which share of IBM stock I receive. One share of IBM stock is not more or less valuable than the next. Contrast this with a Van Gogh painting. A purchaser of a particular Van Gogh painting wants to receive the particular painting purchased; other Van Gogh paintings may not have the same monetary value and are not substitutable. Fungibility is a prerequisite for technical analysis. If I am watching the price movement of IBM stock, I can expect those prices to be the same prices at which I can buy and sell shares of IBM, even if the identical shares are not the ones that have been traded. In contrast, seeing that someone just paid $10 million for a particular Van Gogh painting does not mean that I could sell a painting I own for $10 million because the two paintings are not substitutable.

2. *For technical analysis to be used, the market in which the security is trading must be sufficiently liquid. Explain what "liquid" means in this context and why liquidity is a prerequisite for technical analysis.*

   A market is "liquid" when buyers and sellers can easily be found at any time. In other words, a liquid market is one in which there is a significant amount of volume being traded on a daily basis and a significant number of buyers and sellers. For example, the U.S. Treasury bill market is highly liquid. An investor wanting to sell U.S. Treasury bills can easily find a buyer and liquidate the position. Liquidity is important to the technical analyst because it allows for positions to be entered into and exited from easily when the analyst chooses.

3. *Explain the differences among "informed," "uninformed," and "liquidity" market participants.*

   The "uninformed" market participants are known as "noise players" or the "public." Most mutual fund managers, pension fund managers, traders, and technical analysts are considered also to be in this category, even if they are professionals. The "informed" investor is what has historically been referred to as the "professional or smart money investor": professional speculators, position traders, hedge fund managers, professional arbitrageurs, and insiders are considered to be in this category. Liquidity players are individuals who are participating in the market for some reason other than investment or trading. For example, a liquidity player may be an estate that needs to liquidate securities to pay taxes.

4. *Classify each of the following market participants as an informed, uninformed, or liquidity player, and explain the reasons for your classification:*

   a. *Raymond is 18 years old and ready to begin college. His parents are selling shares of MSFT and KO to pay the tuition bill.*

      Liquidity player—Raymond's parents are not making a decision to sell the shares based on any analysis of the companies or the stock. They are selling the shares simply to raise cash.

b. *Sandra just read a* Wall Street Journal *article about how successful Wal-Mart has been at managing costs. Impressed by what she read, she calls her broker and puts in an order to buy 100 shares of WMT.*

Uninformed trader—Sandra is making a decision to buy shares of Wal-Mart based on reports that she has heard. The information that she is using to base her decision on has been widely disseminated; however, it may not be correct. Or, Sandra's interpretation of this information may not be correct.

c. *Michelle, the CEO of Led Computers, purchases 5,000 shares of LED.*

Informed trader—As the CEO of the company, Michelle has a lot of information about the true financial health of the company.

5. *Explain what is meant by an index being price weighted. In a price-weighted average, would you expect a $10 stock or a $50 stock to be more important? Why?*

In a price-weighted index, the prices for each of the component stocks are added together, and the sum is divided by a divisor that has changed over the years to account for splits and stock dividends in each of the component stocks. A $50 stock is more important than a $10 stock in a price-weighted index. If both of the stocks increase by 10%, the $50 stock increases by $5 and the $10 stock increases by $1. A $5 increase brings the average price in the index up more than a $1 increase would.

6. *Explain how to compute a market-weighted average.*

The prices for each of the component stocks are multiplied by their shares outstanding and then added together, and the sum is divided by a divisor that has changed over the years to account for splits and stock dividends in each of the component stocks.

7. *Explain how to calculate an unweighted average index.*

This index is calculated by averaging the percentage price changes of each of the stocks included in the group. To begin, calculate the holding period return (HPR) for each day for each of the stocks using the following formula:

$$\text{HPR Day 2} = 1 + \frac{\text{Day 2 Price} - \text{Day 1 Price}}{\text{Day 1 Price}}$$

The unweighted index value for each day is then calculated by multiplying the HPRs for each stock for the day together and taking the nth root of that product (where n equals the number of stocks included in the index). This value is then multiplied by 100 to get the index level for the day.

8. *The following table contains six daily closing prices for four stocks.*

    a. *Calculate the daily percentage change in price for each stock.*

    b. *Calculate a price-weighted average for Days 1–6.*

    c. *Calculate a market-weighted average for Days 1–6.*

    d. *Calculate an unweighted average index for Days 1–6.*

e. Compute the daily percentage change for the price-weighted, market-weighted, and unweighted average indices.

f. Explain the differences in the results among the three types of indices.

Company	BCD		EFG		HIJ		KLM	
Number of Shares Outstanding	2,000,000		3,000,000		7,000,000		9,000,000	
	Price	% Change	Price	% Change	Price	% Change	Price	% Change
Day 1	60		85		53		16	
Day 2	63		88		52		19	
Day 3	60		91		51		15	
Day 4	61		85		53		16	
Day 5	58		87		50		17	
Day 6	60		88		53		18	

a.

Company	BCD		EFG		HIJ		KLM	
Number of Shares Outstanding	2,000,000		3,000,000		7,000,000		9,000,000	
	Price	% Change	Price	% Change	Price	% Change	Price	% Change
Day 1	60		85		53		16	
Day 2	63	5.00%	88	3.53%	52	−1.89%	19	18.75%
Day 3	60	−4.76%	91	3.41%	51	−1.92%	15	−21.05%
Day 4	61	1.67%	85	−6.59%	53	3.92%	16	6.67%
Day 5	58	−4.92%	87	2.35%	50	−5.66%	17	6.25%
Day 6	60	3.45%	88	1.15%	53	6.00%	18	5.88%

b.

Company	BCD		EFG		HIJ		KLM		
Number of Shares Outstanding	2,000,000		3,000,000		7,000,000		9,000,000		Price-Weighted Average
	Price	*% Change*	*Price*	*% Change*	*Price*	*% Change*	*Price*	*% Change*	
Day 1	60		85		53		16		53.50
Day 2	63	5.00%	88	3.53%	52	−1.89%	19	18.75%	55.50
Day 3	60	−4.76%	91	3.41%	51	−1.92%	15	−21.05%	54.25
Day 4	61	1.67%	85	−6.59%	53	3.92%	16	6.67%	53.75
Day 5	58	−4.92%	87	2.35%	50	−5.66%	17	6.25%	53.00
Day 6	60	3.45%	88	1.15%	53	6.00%	18	5.88%	54.75

c.

	BCD		EFG		HIJ		KLM		
Number of Shares Outstanding	2,000,000		3,000,000		7,000,000		9,000,000		Market Cap Weighted Average
	Price	*% Change*	*Price*	*% Change*	*Price*	*% Change*	*Price*	*% Change*	
Day 1	60		85		53		16		100.00
Day 2	63	5.00%	88	3.53%	52	−1.89%	19	18.75%	100.32
Day 3	60	−4.76%	91	3.41%	51	−1.92%	15	−21.05%	100.64
Day 4	61	1.67%	85	−6.59%	53	3.92%	16	6.67%	100.00
Day 5	58	−4.92%	87	2.35%	50	−5.66%	17	6.25%	97.61
Day 6	60	3.45%	88	1.15%	53	6.00%	18	5.88%	101.43

d.

	BCD		EFG		HIJ		KLM	
Number of Shares Outstanding	2,000,000		3,000,000		7,000,000		9,000,000	
	Price	HPR	Price	HPR	Price	HPR	Price	HPR
Day 1	60		85		53		16	
Day 2	63	1.05	88	1.04	52	0.98	19	1.19
Day 3	60	0.95	91	1.03	51	0.98	15	0.79
Day 4	61	1.02	85	0.93	53	1.04	16	1.07
Day 5	58	0.95	87	1.02	50	0.94	17	1.06
Day 6	60	1.03	88	1.01	53	1.06	18	1.06

	ΠHPR	ΠHPR$^{1/4}$	Index Value
Day 1			100
Day 2	1.2665	1.0608	106.0849
Day 3	0.7626	0.9345	99.13386
Day 4	1.0527	1.0129	100.4141
Day 5	0.9755	0.9938	99.79299
Day 6	1.1744	1.0410	103.8853

e.

Number of Shares Outstanding	Price-Weighted Average	Price-Weighted Average Return	Market Cap Weighted Average	Market Cap Weighted Average Return	Unweighted Index	Unweighted Index Return
Day 1	53.5		100		100	
Day 2	55.5	0.0374	100.3185	0.0032	106.0849	0.0608
Day 3	54.25	−0.0225	100.6369	0.0032	99.13386	−0.0655
Day 4	53.75	−0.0092	100	−0.0063	100.4141	0.0129
Day 5	53	−0.0140	97.61147	−0.0239	99.79299	−0.0062
Day 6	54.75	0.0330	101.4331	0.0392	103.8853	0.0410

f. A major difference in the three types of indexes can be seen on Day 4. On Day 4, three of the four stocks increase in price. Only EFG falls in price. However, EFG is the highest priced stock; therefore, the price decline in EFG on Day 4 is significant enough for the price weighted index to indicate that the market was down for the day. Even though EFG has fewer shares outstanding than HIJ or KLM, the high price gives EFG a relatively high market capitalization—almost twice that of KLM. Thus, EFG's large percentage decline, coupled with its high market capitalization, are enough to lead to a negative return in the market cap weighted average. The unweighted index, which assumes an equal amount of money is invested in each of the four stocks, does not weight EFG as heavily as does the price-weighted or market cap–weighted indexes; the unweighted index return is positive on Day 4.

9. *Choose five stocks that are included in the DJIA. Download the daily closing prices for these five stocks for the past 30 days from the Yahoo! Finance Web site at http://finance.yahoo. com.*

   a. *Compute and graph a daily price-weighted index for these five stocks over the past month. What was the return on the index over the 30-day period?*

   b. *Find the number of shares outstanding for these five companies. Using this information, calculate a market-weighted index for the 30-day period. Graph the index and compute the return on this index over the past month.*

   c. *Construct and graph an unweighted average index for this five-stock portfolio. Compute the rate of return on this index for the 30-day period.*

   d. *Compare and contrast the graphs that you created and the 30-day returns you calculated.*

   e. *How do you explain the differences among the graphs and the return calculations?*

Answers to this question vary depending on the five stocks you pick and the time frame of your analysis. In this response we used data from five stocks—TRV, UTX, VZ, WMT, and DIS—from January 3 through February 14, 2012, which were the first 30 trading days in that year. We obtained the daily adjusted closing price through Yahoo! Finance. (If you attempt to replicate our results, your numbers may be a bit different because Yahoo! Finance adjusts previous prices whenever dividends are paid or a stock splits.)

   a. The price-weighted index is calculated by adding the prices of the five stocks together and dividing the sum by five. The daily price-weighted index return is calculated using the formula ([Index level for the day − Index level for the previous day]/Index level for the previous day)×100. The index level and the daily index returns are as follows:

Date	TRV	UTX	VZ	WMT	DIS	Price-Weighted Index	Price-Weighted Index Return
1/3/2012	58.57	74.24	38.71	59.52	38.31	53.87	
1/4/2012	58.33	74.62	38.2	58.91	38.85	53.78	−0.163%
1/5/2012	58.9	73.91	37.94	58.63	39.5	53.78	−0.011%
1/6/2012	58.92	73.48	37.83	58.21	39.91	53.67	−0.197%
1/9/2012	59.26	73.68	37.87	58.39	39.75	53.79	0.224%
1/10/2012	59.67	75.6	38.07	58.25	39.63	54.24	0.844%
1/11/2012	59.47	76.27	38.39	58.61	38.7	54.29	0.081%
1/12/2012	59.37	76.8	38.41	58.71	38.73	54.40	0.214%
1/13/2012	58.94	75.65	38.41	58.75	38.4	54.03	−0.687%
1/17/2012	59.26	76.6	38.51	59.05	38.48	54.38	0.648%
1/18/2012	59.46	77.16	38.5	59.21	39.02	54.67	0.533%
1/19/2012	59.87	76.75	38.49	59.8	39.44	54.87	0.366%
1/20/2012	61.15	76.26	38.46	60.2	39.31	55.08	0.375%
1/23/2012	59.86	76.42	37.9	60.1	39.25	54.71	−0.672%
1/24/2012	57.58	77.34	37.3	60.57	39.25	54.41	−0.545%
1/25/2012	58.72	77.21	37.2	60.65	39.56	54.67	0.478%
1/26/2012	58.28	76.97	36.85	60.16	39.35	54.32	−0.633%
1/27/2012	57.63	77.18	36.73	59.9	39.25	54.14	−0.339%
1/30/2012	57.69	77.17	37.12	60.48	38.99	54.29	0.281%
1/31/2012	57.88	77.91	37.17	60.54	38.9	54.48	0.350%
2/1/2012	58.84	79.77	37.31	61.35	39.33	55.32	1.542%
2/2/2012	58.96	79.57	37.07	61.11	38.91	55.12	−0.354%
2/3/2012	59.69	80.59	37.35	61.2	40	55.77	1.165%
2/6/2012	58.9	80.11	37.64	61.05	40.46	55.63	−0.240%
2/7/2012	59.31	79.82	37.43	60.87	40.98	55.68	0.090%
2/8/2012	59.42	81.28	37.43	60.8	41.27	56.04	0.643%
2/9/2012	59.46	83.3	37.43	61.13	41.53	56.57	0.946%
2/10/2012	58.95	83.03	37.2	61.07	41.45	56.34	−0.407%
2/13/2012	58.57	84.4	37.63	60.97	41.79	56.67	0.589%
2/14/2012	58.73	84.16	37.54	61.39	41.6	56.68	0.021%

A graph of the price-weighted index looks like this:

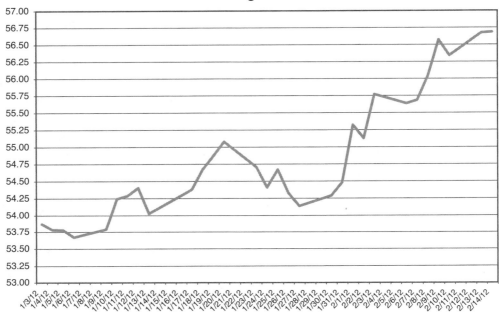

Price-Weighted Index

b. The number of shares outstanding for TRV, UTX, VZ, WMT, and DIS at the beginning of 2012 were 389 million, 911 million, 2.84 billion, 3.4 billion, and 1.79 billion, respectively. To calculate the market-weighted average, we first calculate the market capitalization for each of the five stocks on January 3 by multiplying the number of shares outstanding for the stock by the closing price of that stock. We then sum the market capitalizations and get a total of 471.2957 billion. Next, we set the base of the index to 100 by dividing 471.2957 billion by 471.2957 billion and then multiplying the result by 100. The sum of the market capitalizations for the five stocks for the subsequent days were divided by the initial day's market capitalization of 471.2957 billion and then multiplied by 100 to get each day's index level. To calculate the return for the market-weighted average index, we subtract the previous day's index level from the current day's index level and divide this difference by the previous day's level and multiply the result by 100.

Date	Market Cap Weighted Index	Market Cap Weighted Index Return
1/3/2012	100.00	
1/4/2012	99.51	−0.489%
1/5/2012	99.31	−0.203%
1/6/2012	99.01	−0.297%
1/9/2012	99.17	0.162%
1/10/2012	99.55	0.382%
1/11/2012	99.77	0.213%
1/12/2012	99.96	0.190%
1/13/2012	99.60	−0.354%
1/17/2012	100.12	0.519%
1/18/2012	100.56	0.439%
1/19/2012	101.09	0.531%
1/20/2012	101.32	0.230%
1/23/2012	100.82	−0.501%
1/24/2012	100.78	−0.033%
1/25/2012	100.97	0.183%
1/26/2012	100.24	−0.720%
1/27/2012	99.93	−0.310%
1/30/2012	100.49	0.558%
1/31/2012	100.68	0.197%
2/1/2012	101.96	1.262%
2/2/2012	101.45	−0.496%
2/3/2012	102.35	0.892%
2/6/2012	102.44	0.081%
2/7/2012	102.36	−0.079%
2/8/2012	102.71	0.343%
2/9/2012	103.44	0.711%
2/10/2012	103.13	−0.296%
2/13/2012	103.68	0.533%
2/14/2012	103.82	0.138%

A chart of the market cap-weighted index looks like this:

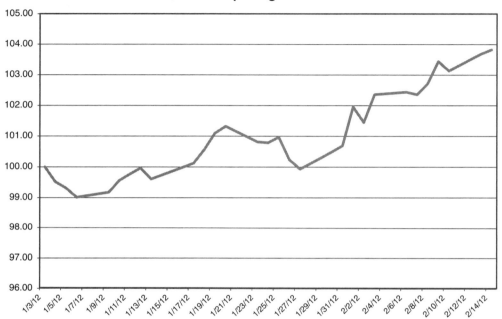

Market Cap Weighted Index

c. The unweighted index is calculated as follows:

Date	TRV	TRV Ret	UTX	UTX Ret	VZ	VZ Ret	WMT	WMT Ret	DIS	DIS Ret	Product of Returns	Fifth Root of Product of Returns	Index	% Ret of Index
1/3/2012	58.57		74.24		38.71		59.52		38.31				100	
1/4/2012	58.33	0.996	74.62	1.005	38.2	0.987	58.91	0.990	38.85	1.014	0.991	0.998	99.829	-0.17%
1/5/2012	58.9	1.010	73.91	0.990	37.94	0.993	58.63	0.995	39.5	1.017	1.005	1.001	100.103	0.27%
1/6/2012	58.92	1.000	73.48	0.994	37.83	0.997	58.21	0.993	39.91	1.010	0.995	0.999	99.895	-0.21%
1/9/2012	59.26	1.006	73.68	1.003	37.87	1.001	58.39	1.003	39.75	0.996	1.009	1.002	100.172	0.28%
1/10/2012	59.67	1.007	75.6	1.026	38.07	1.005	58.25	0.998	39.63	0.997	1.033	1.007	100.651	0.48%
1/11/2012	59.47	0.997	76.27	1.009	38.39	1.008	58.61	1.006	38.7	0.977	0.996	0.999	99.925	-0.72%
1/12/2012	59.37	0.998	76.8	1.007	38.41	1.001	58.71	1.002	38.73	1.001	1.008	1.002	100.165	0.24%
1/13/2012	58.94	0.993	75.65	0.985	38.41	1.000	58.75	1.001	38.4	0.991	0.970	0.994	99.397	-0.77%
1/17/2012	59.26	1.005	76.6	1.013	38.51	1.003	59.05	1.005	38.48	1.002	1.028	1.006	100.555	1.16%
1/18/2012	59.46	1.003	77.16	1.007	38.5	1.000	59.21	1.003	39.02	1.014	1.027	1.005	100.542	-0.01%
1/19/2012	59.87	1.007	76.75	0.995	38.49	1.000	59.8	1.010	39.44	1.011	1.022	1.004	100.439	-0.10%
1/20/2012	61.15	1.021	76.26	0.994	38.46	0.999	60.2	1.007	39.31	0.997	1.017	1.003	100.347	-0.09%
1/23/2012	59.86	0.979	76.42	1.002	37.9	0.985	60.1	0.998	39.25	0.998	0.964	0.993	99.261	-1.08%
1/24/2012	57.58	0.962	77.34	1.012	37.3	0.984	60.57	1.008	39.25	1.000	0.966	0.993	99.302	0.04%
1/25/2012	58.72	1.020	77.21	0.998	37.2	0.997	60.65	1.001	39.56	1.008	1.025	1.005	100.490	1.20%
1/26/2012	58.28	0.993	76.97	0.997	36.85	0.991	60.16	0.992	39.35	0.995	0.967	0.993	99.332	-1.15%
1/27/2012	57.63	0.989	77.18	1.003	36.73	0.997	59.9	0.996	39.25	0.997	0.982	0.996	99.628	0.30%
1/30/2012	57.69	1.001	77.17	1.000	37.12	1.011	60.48	1.010	38.99	0.993	1.015	1.003	100.290	0.66%
1/31/2012	57.88	1.003	77.91	1.010	37.17	1.001	60.54	1.001	38.9	0.998	1.013	1.003	100.257	-0.03%
2/1/2012	58.84	1.017	79.77	1.024	37.31	1.004	61.35	1.013	39.33	1.011	1.070	1.014	101.371	1.11%
2/2/2012	58.96	1.002	79.57	0.997	37.07	0.994	61.11	0.996	38.91	0.989	0.979	0.996	99.569	-1.78%
2/3/2012	59.69	1.012	80.59	1.013	37.35	1.008	61.2	1.001	40	1.028	1.064	1.012	101.241	1.68%
2/6/2012	58.9	0.987	80.11	0.994	37.64	1.008	61.05	0.998	40.46	1.012	0.997	0.999	99.948	-1.28%
2/7/2012	59.31	1.007	79.82	0.996	37.43	0.994	60.87	0.997	40.98	1.013	1.008	1.002	100.151	0.20%
2/8/2012	59.42	1.002	81.28	1.018	37.43	1.000	60.8	0.999	41.27	1.007	1.026	1.005	100.519	0.37%
2/9/2012	59.46	1.001	83.3	1.025	37.43	1.000	61.13	1.005	41.53	1.006	1.038	1.007	100.741	0.22%
2/10/2012	58.95	0.991	83.03	0.997	37.2	0.994	61.07	0.999	41.45	0.998	0.979	0.996	99.582	-1.15%
2/13/2012	58.57	0.994	84.4	1.017	37.63	1.012	60.97	0.998	41.79	1.008	1.028	1.006	100.560	0.98%
2/14/2012	58.73	1.003	84.16	0.997	37.54	0.998	61.39	1.007	41.6	0.995	1.000	1.000	99.996	-0.56%

A chart of the unweighted index looks like this:

Unweighted Index

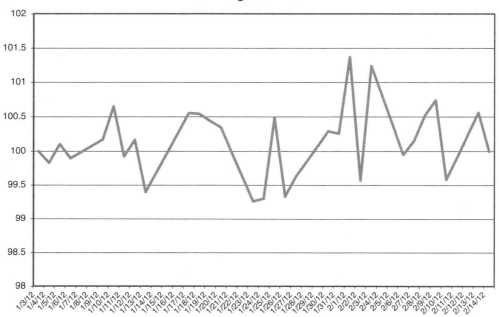

d. The following chart plots the returns as measured by the price-weighted, market cap–
weighted, and unweighted indexes. The three indexes show a similar, but not identical, pattern of returns. Some days, in particular, the difference is quite noticeable.
Look, for example, at the returns for January 5, 2012. The price-weighted and market
cap–weighted indexes both show a negative return for the day, but the unweighted-
average index return is positive. On January 5, two stocks, TRV and DIS, had positive
returns; UTX, VZ, and WMT had negative returns. As the highest priced stock in the
sample, UTX has a disproportionate effect on the price-weighted index. Because VZ
and WMT have such large market caps, representing more than 66% of the five-stock
portfolio, their negative moves on January 5 have a disproportionate effect on the
market cap–weighted index. The unweighted index shows a positive return for the day,
even though three out of the five stocks had negative returns. TRV had a 1% return
and DIS had a 1.7% return; these returns were high enough to more than offset the
small negative returns of –1%, –0.7%, and –0.5% for UTX, VZ, and WMT, respectively.

Returns for Different Indexes

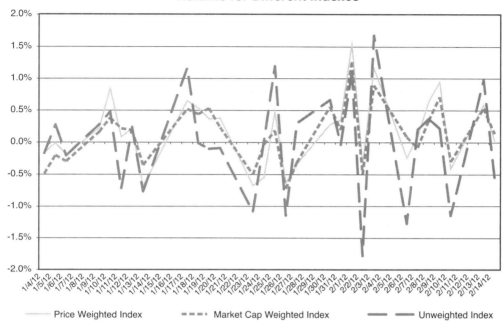

—— Price Weighted Index	▪▪▪▪ Market Cap Weighted Index	—— —— Unweighted Index

e. Another day that highlights the difference in the weighting schemes is February 1, 2012. All five stocks experienced positive returns, leading to positive returns for all three indexes. UTX, the highest priced of the five stocks, gained the most that day, which had a larger impact on the price-weighted index than it did on the other two indexes.

Self-Test

1. *Bill Branton, the CFO of Bio Pharmaceuticals, sold 1,000 shares of the company's stock today in order to pay for his son's college tuition. Mr. Branton would be considered*

    a. A noise player.

    b. A liquidity player.

    c. An uninformed player.

    d. An indexed player.

2. *Which of the following assumptions would be consistent with the creation of a price-weighted index?*

   a. An individual invests $1,000 in each stock in the index.

   b. An individual invests money in proportion to the market capitalization of each stock in the index.

   c. An individual purchases 1 share of each stock in the index.

   d. An individual purchases proportionately more shares of low priced stocks than of high priced stocks.

	Shares Outstanding	Price
Stock A	20 million	$3.00
Stock B	20 million	$5.00
Stock C	50 million	$3.00
Stock D	50 million	$4.50

3. *Using the table above, a 10% increase in the price of which stock would have the greatest effect on a price-weighted index?*

   a. Stock A

   b. Stock B

   c. Stock C

   d. Stock D

4. *Using the table above, a 10% increase in the price of which stock would have the greatest effect on a market cap–weighted index?*

   a. Stock A

   b. Stock B

   c. Stock C

   d. Stock D

5. *Which of the following is a list of synonyms?*

   a. Equally weighted average, geometric average, unweighted index

   b. Noise player, liquidity player, informed player

   c. Counterparty risk, liquidity risk, fungibility risk

   d. Spot market, forward market, futures market

6. *The Dow Jones Industrial Average is*

   a. A market capitalization weighted average.

   b. An equally weighted index.

   c. An unweighted index.

   d. A price-weighted index.

7. *Maddie is considering purchasing 100 shares of ABC. She is concerned about whether or not she will be able to sell the shares quickly and easily should she decide to change her position. Maddie is concerned about the _____ of the stock.*

   a. Liquidity

   b. Forward market

   c. Futures market

   d. Counterparty risk

8. *The _____ is an example of a dealer market, and the dealer's profit margin is known as the _____.*

   a. Forward market; forward premium

   b. NASDAQ, bid-ask spread

   c. NYSE; fungibility premium

   d. Cash market; spot premium

9. *Which of the following is a TRUE statement?*

   a. Technical analysis is useful in understanding the auction markets for paintings because the high and well-publicized prices of rare pieces of art lead to a high market capitalization.

   b. The auction market for U.S. Treasury bills cannot be analyzed using technical analysis due to the government regulation surrounding the pricing of these instruments.

   c. Technical analysis is not useful for analyzing the U.S Treasury bill market because the securities are highly liquid and easily substitutable, making it difficult for an analyst to track a specific security.

   d. Technical analysis is not useful in understanding the auction markets for paintings because a painting is unique and not substitutable for another painting.

10. *Midwest Airlines wants to hedge against rising oil prices using a derivative security. The risk Midwest Airlines faces that the party on the other side of the contract may fail to deliver is known as _____.*

    a. Counterparty risk

    b. Hedging risk

    c. Speculative risk

    d. Underlying risk

CHAPTER 6
Dow Theory

Chapter Objectives

By the end of this chapter, you should know

▶ A brief history of the development of Dow Theory and the major contributors to this development

▶ The three Dow Theory hypotheses presented by Rhea

▶ The theorems of Dow Theory

▶ The three types of trends—primary, secondary, and minor—of Dow Theory

▶ The concept of confirmation in Dow Theory

▶ The role of volume in Dow Theory

▶ The criticisms of Dow Theory

Chapter Summary

Charles H. Dow was the founder of the Dow-Jones financial news service, the founder and first editor of *The Wall Street Journal*, and the first to create an index to measure the overall price movement of U.S. stocks. A. C. Nelson was the first to use the term "Dow Theory" in describing Dow's ideas. William Peter Hamilton succeeded Dow as editor of *The Wall Street Journal* and wrote editorials using the tenets of Dow Theory. Robert Rhea refined Dow Theory, presenting three hypotheses:

1. The primary trend is inviolate.

2. The averages discount everything.

3. Dow Theory is not infallible.

Dow Theory Theorems

One theorem of Dow Theory is that the ideal market picture consists of an uptrend, top, downtrend, and bottom. A second theorem is that economic rationale should be used to explain stock market action. A third theorem is that prices trend. Three interrelated trends exist: the primary, secondary, and minor. The primary trend is the longest, representing the overall, broad long-term movement of security prices. The secondary trend is an intermediate-term trend that runs counter to the primary trend. The minor trend is shorter-term and unpredictable.

Dow Theory introduced the concept of "confirmation." Confirmation occurs when an average confirms another average's high or low; for example, when the industrial and railroad averages reached new highs and new lows together. Volume was used as a secondary confirmation of trend.

Criticisms of the Dow Theory

A lag exists between the actual turn in the primary trend and the recognition of the change in trend, resulting in investors acting after, rather than before, market tops and bottoms. Within Dow Theory, the trends are not strictly defined.

Key Concepts and Vocabulary

As you go through this chapter, pay close attention to the following vocabulary. Be sure that you can define each of the terms.

Primary trend

Secondary trend

Minor trend

Confirmation

End-of-Chapter Review Questions

1. *What were the three hypotheses of Dow Theory presented by Rhea? How is each of these hypotheses relevant for the modern investor?*

   The primary trend is inviolate: Investors should focus on the primary trend, which can't be manipulated. Price might be manipulated in the shorter-term, but the long-term trend prevails.

   The averages discount everything: Prices are the result of people acting on their knowledge, interpretation of information, and expectations. Thus, the price of a stock represents more than simply the available knowledge about an individual company. The averages foretell the shape of industry and give investors a better understanding about the health of the economy.

Dow Theory is not infallible: There is not a magic formula for profit. Although you can use careful and unbiased study of the market averages to interpret the likelihood of the markets continuing or reversing in direction, there is no guaranteed rule to follow. Study and lack of emotional reaction are keys to success.

2. *Describe what the Dow Theory ideal market pattern of an uptrend, top, downtrend, and bottom looks like.*

In Dow Theory, the ideal market picture consists of an uptrend, top, downtrend, and bottom as shown in the following diagram. These trends will be interspersed with retracements and consolidations.

Dow Theory Ideal Market Picture

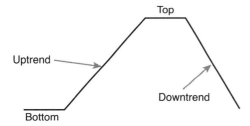

The market picture is only a depiction of the ideal form. While the real market never looks exactly like this, the picture provides a generalized model of the stock market's price behavior over time.

3. *Why did Dow think there was an important economic relationship between the stocks of industrial companies and the stocks of railroads? How do you think this general relationship between economic activity and sectors of the economy might be seen and measured in today's economy?*

According to Rhea, Dow believed that industrial stocks represented the trend of industry profits and prospects and that railroad stocks represented railroads' profits and prospects. Dow thought the profits and prospects for both of these sectors must be in accord with each other. For example, industry might be producing goods, but if railroads are not shipping the goods then industry must slow down. The increased production by the industries would simply result in their increasing inventories if the goods produced are not shipped.

Dow used a railroad average to measure the transporting of goods as rail was a major mode of transportation at the turn of the 20th century. Today, the railroad average has been changed to the transportation average to represent airlines, truckers, and other means of shipping goods. In addition to transporting goods, services can also be transported. For example, travel-related companies, such as theme parks and hotels, depend on customers being transported to them.

4. *What are the three major trends in Dow Theory? Which is the most important? Why?*

There are three major trends in Dow Theory. First, there is the primary trend. The primary trend is the broad market trend which might last several years. A bull market is a strong primary uptrend and a bear market is a broad downward trend. Second is the secondary reaction, which usually lasts from three weeks to many months. For example, during a primary bull market, a general decline over several months would be a secondary reaction. Third is the daily fluctuation known as the minor trend.

The primary trend is the most important because it represents the overall, broad, long-term movement of security prices. It is the general direction of movement in the market. In a bull market, the general trend is upward. Although there are secondary reactions in which investors experience losses, these reactions are short-lived. For long-run profitability it is more important to be in the position of the long-term movement of the market. The market is not necessarily logical in its movements from day to day, and, therefore, you should ignore the minor trend.

5. *Dow Theory teaches that, while the investor is foregoing potential profit, the investor should avoid trying to make money by attempting to predict the secondary trend. Why did Dow and his followers think that trading with the secondary trend was too risky?*

To be able to anticipate or recognize secondary reactions would increase profit by taking advantage of smaller market swings, but Dow believed this exercise was too dangerous. The primary trend and secondary trend reversal have similar characteristics, making it difficult to distinguish the two. Determining exactly when a secondary trend is beginning and ending is impossible. Instead of trying to garner some profit during those time periods and risk being wrong, it is better to be trading in the overall, long-run direction of the market.

6. *How would Dow and his followers react to the modern-day practice of day trading? According to Dow Theory, what trend are these day traders following?*

Dow, Hamilton, and Rhea would likely be horrified with the practice of day trading. Day traders are trying to capture profits by trading in the direction of the minor trend. Dow and his followers thought that trying to trade with the minor trend was too risky. They saw prices as more random and unpredictable as the time horizon shrinks. Although they did not believe that the long-term trend could be manipulated, they were concerned that the minor trend could be; thus, investors should avoid trading with the minor trend.

7. *What is meant by the term confirmation in Dow Theory?*

Dow thought economic rationale should be used in explaining moves in stock prices. Confirmation was the consideration of the industrial and railroad averages together. Confirmation in the Dow Theory occurs when both the industrial and railroad averages reach new highs or new lows together on a daily closing basis. Thus, one average is "confirming" the movement of the other. If industrials were rising, Dow wanted to make sure that the goods being produced were actually being transported (and sold) to customers. Higher production should result in increased transportation activity; if not, firms are simply increasing inventories.

8. *What role does volume play in Dow Theory?*

Volume is used as a secondary confirmation of trend. Excessively high market prices that are accompanied by less volume on rallies and more activity on declines usually suggest an overbought market. Conversely, extremely low prices with low-volume declines and increased volume on rallies suggest an oversold market.

9. *According to Dow Theory, what signals would an investor watch for that would indicate a reversal in the primary trend?*

First an investor would look for a failure of confirmation from the industrial and transportation indexes. During a primary uptrend, a failure of the industrial and transportation indexes to make new highs after a secondary reaction would alert the trader to a potential end of the primary up trend. For secondary confirmation, the investor would watch volume. Rallies occurring on low volume and declines occurring on higher volume would be further indication of an end of the primary uptrend.

10. *One of the criticisms of Dow Theory is that it calls market reversals long after they occur. Explain why Dow Theory makes these market calls late. What are the trade-offs that investors make with a system that tends to make late calls of market reversals?*

In an ideal world, a trader would want to buy at the moment an uptrend begins and sell when price peaks and the trend reverses. In the real world, however, expecting to pick the exact beginning and the exact ending of a trend is impossible. Dow Theory tends to make late calls because there is a lag between the actual turn in the primary trend and the recognition of the change in trend. Dow Theory does not recognize a change in trend until after it has occurred and has been confirmed. Thus, investors get into the market after an uptrend begins and exit after the peak in prices. These investors pay a little more for the stock than they would have if they had bought at the bottom. In addition, they sell the stock after the trend has ended for a price lower than the peak price. Dow Theory does not attempt to predict trend changes to try to enter positions at the moment the trend does change. Trying to pick the exact moment of the trend change would result in errors in judgment, high turnover, and increased transaction costs.

Self-Test

1. *Who is considered the father of modern technical analysis?*

   a. Charles Dow

   b. William Peter Hamilton

   c. Robert Rhea

   d. Alfred Cowles III

2. *Which of the following is NOT a hypothesis of Dow Theory as presented by Robert Rhea?*

   a. The primary trend is inviolate.

   b. The averages discount everything.

   c. Stocks follow a random walk.

   d. Dow Theory is not infallible.

3. *Dow introduced the concept of confirmation by comparing the*

   a. Transportation average to the growth in GDP.

   b. Volume on the NYSE to the growth in GDP.

   c. Transportation average to fuel prices.

   d. Industrial average to the transportation average.

4. *In Dow Theory, the perfect market picture consists of*

   a. An uptrend, retracements, a bottom, and consolidation.

   b. A bottom, consolidation, and an uptrend.

   c. A bottom, an uptrend, a top, and a downtrend.

   d. An uptrend and a downtrend, separated by a period of secondary consolidation and minor retracements.

5. *A theorem in Dow Theory is that*

   a. Economic rationale should be used to explain stock market action.

   b. Investors should follow the theory accurately and precisely, because studying the market and making any adjustments leads to emotional decision making.

   c. Investors should focus on minor trends because it is easier to predict what will happen in the economy during the next few months rather than during the next few years.

   d. Investors should focus on minor trends because Dow Theory is not infallible, and in case the investor is wrong, the minor trend will change sooner than the major trend.

6. *According to Dow Theory, which of the following describes the phases of a primary bull market?*

   a. Reviving confidence, response to increased corporate earnings, and prices rise on increased hopes and expectations

   b. Abandonment of hope, response to increased GDP growth, and response to increased corporate profits

   c. Prices rise on increased hopes, confidence revives, expectations increase, and corporate earnings increase

   d. Decreased volume, increased demand, higher expectations, and increased prices

7. *Which of the following is a TRUE statement within the Dow Theory?*

   a. Although being able to recognize the secondary trend can increase profit capabilities, Dow thought it was too dangerous to attempt.

   b. Dow thought that most profit potential came from trading the minor trends.

   c. According to Dow, the most profitable trading strategies occurred when the secondary trend cycled over to a minor trend.

   d. According to Dow, the most profitable time to trade was when the primary, secondary, and minor trends were all in the same direction, confirming each other.

8. *With Dow Theory,*

   a. There is a lag between the turn in the primary trend and the recognition of the change in trend, resulting in an investor acting after market tops and bottoms.

   b. There is a lag between the turn in the primary trend and recognition of the change in trend, resulting in an investor acting after market tops and before market bottoms.

   c. Any change in primary trend is immediately signaled by changes in volume, allowing an investor to buy at market bottoms and sell at market tops.

   d. Because the transportation average is used to confirm the industrial average, an investor can confidently trade secondary and minor trends rather than waiting for market tops and bottoms.

9. *In Dow Theory, when there is a primary bull market and either the industrial or transportation average fails to reach new highs during a secondary advance*

   a. The minor trend may be gaining strength.

   b. The primary trend may be reversing.

   c. The minor trend may be reversing.

   d. Investors should take advantage of the buying opportunity.

10. *To confirm a primary trend in today's economy, analysts often look for*

   a. Confirmation between the Standard and Poor's 500, representing highly capitalized companies, and the Russell 2000, representing small companies.

   b. Confirmation between the utility index and the transportation index to determine the influence of energy prices on the economic outlook.

   c. A differential in volume between the industrial average and the transportation average to determine investor psychology and buyer strength in the two markets.

   d. Confirmation between Dow's original railroad average and the new transportation average to measure market stability.

CHAPTER 7

Sentiment

Chapter Objectives

After studying this chapter, you should

▶ Understand what the term *sentiment* means

▶ Understand the concept of contrary opinion

▶ Be familiar with methods for measuring sentiment of uninformed and informed market players

Chapter Summary

Market sentiment refers to the psychology or emotions of market participants. Investor psychology is influenced by and is an influence on market activity. When investors are hopeful and optimistic, they buy stocks; this buying causes stock prices to rise, resulting in even more optimism. When investors are pessimistic and fearful, they sell stocks, driving prices lower; falling stock prices increases the fear level among investors.

What Is Sentiment?

Sentiment is defined as the net amount of any group of market players' optimism or pessimism reflected in any asset or market price at a particular time. When prices reflect emotional extremes, a reversal is usually due.

Market Players and Sentiment

The interactions between informed and uninformed players determine prices. The uninformed players are ruled by their emotions and biases. The majority of the market players are uninformed players. They tend to be optimistic after a market rise and buy, creating market peaks. After a market downturn, they are pessimistic and sell, creating market bottoms. Informed market players tend to act in a way contrary to the majority, selling at the top and buying at the bottom.

How Does Human Bias Affect Decision Making?

Researchers have found that people tend to conform to their group, because taking a position opposite of that of the group is difficult. People gain confidence by extrapolating past trends and, thus, tend to switch their opinions slowly. People feel secure in accepting the opinions of experts. "Representation" suggests that people recognize patterns that do not actually exist.

Understanding the links between emotions, investment behavior, and security prices can help the investor spot market extremes. Successful investors also are aware how their own biases may affect their investment decisions.

How Is Sentiment of Uninformed Players Measured?

Sentiment indicators are data series that indicate how much prices are at an excessively emotional level. Uninformed market players are usually wrong at major market turns; knowing what these players are doing helps us know what not to do. Traditionally, odd lot statistics were reliable indicators of the sentiment of uninformed, small investors. Today, listed options data are a better measure of public speculation. The more call buyers relative to put buyers, the more optimistic are the speculators. Volatility is also used to analyze the behavior of the uninformed market players. An increase in volatility often indicates that market players are becoming more anxious and nervous. Declining volatility is associated with investor complacency. Volatility in the Standard & Poor's 500 options, the NASDAQ composite, and the S&P100 Index are represented by VIX, VXN, and VXO, respectively. These measures are based on implied, rather than historical, volatility.

Another sentiment measure of market players is polls asking investors or commentators if they are bearish or bullish. The Advisory Service Sentiment survey, produced by Investors Intelligence Inc., determines the percentage of newsletter advisors who are bullish or bearish by reading independent investment-advisory newsletters. The American Association of Individual Investors compiles a daily poll from its membership on what they believe the stock market will do over the next six months. The Consensus Bullish Sentiment Index draws from a mix of brokerage house analysts and independent advisory services. Market Vane Corporation polls 100 leading commodity-trading advisors daily. The Sentix Sentiment Index is a weekly poll of German investors, whereas the Consumer Confidence Index is based on the expectations of U.S. consumers.

Other sentiment measures are based on movement of money within the markets. A buying climax occurs when a stock makes a new 52-week high but then closes below the previous week's close, whereas a selling climax occurs when a stock makes a new 52-week low and then closes above the previous week's close. At market bottoms, mutual funds are tending to hold a high level of cash and the ratio of money market assets to total stock market valuation tends to be high. When investors expect the market to rise, the ratio of assets held by the Rydex bull funds relative to the Rydex bear funds increases. Margin debt was a reliable indicator of uninformed investor optimism in the past, but is no longer an accurate gauge of market sentiment. Market peaks tend to be associated with a high NASDAQ to NYSE volume ratio, and market lows tend to be associated with a low ratio.

How Is the Sentiment of Informed Players Measured?

Informed players are those who are most likely to make the correct market decisions. One way to determine insider sentiment is to watch the action of insiders. This can be done by watching the sell/buy ratio of insiders and observing secondary offerings. Large block trades tend to be transacted on behalf of professionals; the ratio of blocks traded on upticks to those on downticks is an indicator of professional interest in owning stocks. The Commitments of Traders, or COT, reports published by the Commodity Futures Trading Commission (CFTC) gives some idea of informed versus uninformed trader sentiment.

Sentiment in Other Markets

The put/call volume ratio for Treasury bond futures is used as a proxy for speculation in the Treasury bond market. Treasury bond primary dealers, in anticipation of customer demands, tend to have the most long positions at tops and the most short positions at bottoms. The lengthening of the average maturity of their portfolios by money market mutual fund managers tends to be associated with increased short-term interest rates.

Key Concepts and Vocabulary

A number of terms and concepts that might be new to you appear in this chapter. As you read through this chapter, pay close attention to the following terms and concepts. Write down a definition or explanation for each.

Sentiment

Uninformed players

Informed players

Representation

Crashes

Bubbles

Call option

Put option

Volatility

Put/call ratio

Contrarian strategy

Implied volatility

Climax

End-of-Chapter Review Questions

1. *How would you define the term sentiment as it relates to the financial markets?*

   Sentiment is defined as the net amount of optimism or pessimism reflected in any asset or market price at a particular time. Sentiment refers to the feelings or emotions of market participants. As investors feel fearful or pessimistic, they tend to sell securities; as they feel hopeful and confident, they buy securities.

2. *Warren is searching for a good trading rule to follow. He says, "I would be just as happy to get information from someone who always makes the wrong investment decision as someone who always makes the right investment decision to use in devising my trading strategy." Explain why Warren would find it helpful to have information about someone's bad trading decisions.*

   If Warren finds someone who always makes the right investment decision, he knows that following that person's strategy should be profitable. If Warren finds someone who is always wrong, he also knows how to invest—exactly opposite of this individual. For example, if the always-wrong investor says "I am going long," Warren knows to go short. Warren would use the bad trader's decisions as a contrarian indicator.

3. *Explain why extremely high investor optimism is associated with market peaks.*

   The more optimistic investors are about the future of the market, the more they will buy stocks. At extremely high levels of optimism, investors have placed all available cash into the market. In fact, extremely optimistic investors often purchase stocks on margin. The only way for price to keep rising is for demand for stocks to keep increasing. However, when investors are fully invested, there is no new money coming into the market to continue fueling the price increases. As there is no more fuel to keep stock prices rising, the stock market reaches a peak.

4. *Sandra thinks Microsoft (MSFT) is currently overpriced, while Tony thinks MSFT is underpriced. Which of these two investors would be more likely to buy a put, and which one would be more likely to buy a call? Explain your answer.*

   Sandra, who thinks MSFT is overpriced, would buy a put option. A put option is the right to sell the stock at a certain price, known as the strike price, over a set time period. The put acts as an insurance policy against a fall in MSFT for Sandra; it enables her to guarantee a certain price at which she will be able to sell MSFT should the price fall.

   Tony, who thinks MSFT is currently underpriced and is likely to increase in price, would purchase a call option. Buying a call would give Tony the right to buy MSFT at the strike price over a set time period. The call option gives Tony the ability to lock in a price for MSFT should he choose to purchase the stock. If Tony is correct and the price of MSFT rises, he can exercise his option and purchase MSFT at the strike price.

5. *You hear a report that the ratio of put-to-call volume is extremely high. How would you interpret this high put/call ratio? What would you conclude about investor sentiment given this high ratio? What investment strategy would you want to follow given this high ratio?*

Because call options represent traders who believe the stock market will rise, and puts represent traders who believe that the stock market will fall, the ratio of puts to calls represents the relative demand for options by "bears" and "bulls" respectively. A high put/call ratio means that there are more people who are fearful that the market is going to fall than there are people who are optimistic about the market. Because the put/call ratio is a measure of the sentiment of uninformed players, it is a contrarian strategy. Thus, a high put/call ratio suggests a high level of fear among uninformed players and suggests that the market is close to a bottom.

6. *Explain what is meant by a contrarian investment strategy. What are some market signs that the contrarian investor might watch for?*

A contrarian investment strategy means trading contrary, or in the opposite direction, of the majority of market players. At a market peak, investment sentiment is overly optimistic: at this point a contrarian strategy would be to sell because the majority is buying. A contrarian would look for a sign of extremely optimistic, uninformed-player sentiment, such as a low put/call ratio or high margin debt to begin selling securities.

At a market bottom, investment sentiment is extremely fearful and pessimistic. Because of this pessimism, most investors are selling, but the contrarian would spot a market bottom and begin purchasing securities. A contrarian would look for signs of extreme pessimism, such as a high put/call ratio and a high money market mutual fund asset to stock mutual fund asset ratio.

7. *What information might polls give you about sentiment? What are some sources of poll data, and what general conclusions can you make about how to use poll data?*

Polls measure the sentiment of market participants by asking the players if they are bearish or bullish. Polls can give you some idea of the public mood within a certain sample of time. Poll results are contrarian indicators because they express optimism at market tops and pessimism at market bottoms. Thus, polls gather information and measure the sentiment of the uninformed investors. Some sources of poll data include Investor's Intelligence's Advisory Service Sentiment survey, AAII's daily membership poll, the Consensus Bullish Sentiment Index, the Sentix Index, and the Consumer Confidence Index. Overall, there has been mixed evidence that such polls really help investors to predict future market behavior. Thus, it may give a general idea of how the market is currently acting, but investors must be cautious when using these poll results.

8. *What type of relationship is generally seen between news reporting and market sentiment?*

The media is in the business of selling news to those who are interested. When the stock market is high because of overly optimistic investors, the media is likely to report on the strength of the market rather than the dangers that the market might decline. Thus, the news reports are often a reflection of the sentiment of the majority of investors. A plethora of positive news stories regarding the market is often a sign that the market is at a high and a turning point is near. These news stories serve as a contrarian indicator.

Self-Test

1. *Which of the following is a TRUE statement?*

    a. Although investor psychology is influenced by the market, investor psychology does not influence market activity.

    b. Investor psychology is not influenced by the market, but investor psychology does influence market activity.

    c. Investor psychology is influenced by market activity, and investor psychology is an influencer of market activity.

    d. Because markets are efficient, investor psychology is not an important component to consider when analyzing market activity.

2. *When investors are pessimistic and fearful,*

    a. They begin buying stocks, hoping to lock-in today's prices.

    b. They sell stocks.

    c. They put more money into stock mutual funds and less money into money market funds.

    d. They tend to buy call options on stocks.

3. *Uninformed players tend to be*

    a. Optimistic after a market rise and buy, creating market tops.

    b. Suspicious after a market rise and start selling, creating market tops.

    c. Correct at market turns, but incorrect during market trends.

    d. Correct in the bond market, but incorrect in the stock market.

4. *At market tops,*

    a. Informed players tend to buy, knowing that the uninformed players are most optimistic.

    b. Informed players are optimistic and uninformed players are pessimistic.

    c. Heavy volume is caused by both informed and uninformed players buying simultaneously.

    d. Informed players tend to sell, while the uninformed are most optimistic.

5. *Emotional excess can lead to an extraordinary rise in prices known as a* _____, *or to an extraordinary decline in prices known as a* _____.

    a. Bubble; crash

    b. Peak; contrarian trend

    c. Spike; contrarian trend

    d. Sentiment peak; crowd-motivated bottom

6. *Which of the following would be an indication that speculators are optimistic?*

    a. High balances in money market mutual funds relative to stock mutual funds

    b. A low number of odd lot trades

    c. A high ratio of call buyers relative to put buyers

    d. A low amount of margin debt

7. *Increased secondary offerings*

    a. Warn that the market may be at a peak.

    b. Are an indication of increased buying by informed players.

    c. Are an indication of increased selling by uninformed players.

    d. Suggest that the market has reached a bottom and that a new uptrend may be beginning.

8. *Which of these would most likely be an indication that the market is at a high and a change in trend is likely to occur soon?*

    a. A high put/call ratio

    b. *BusinessWeek*, *The Economist*, *Newsweek*, and *Barron's* all running front page stories about how the strongest bull market of the decade is likely to continue

    c. A significant drop in the number of secondary offerings

    d. Relatively high volume on the NYSE relative to the NASDAQ

9. *Which of the following best describes the concept behind contrarian investing?*

    a. Whenever the uninformed players become more active in the market, stock prices will fall.

    b. To catch unexploited profits left behind by uninformed market players, traders should trade opposite of the primary market trend.

    c. Uninformed and informed players always trade in opposite directions; a trader should determine whether the uninformed or the informed players are dominant in the market and trade with the dominant side.

    d. Whenever the uninformed players become significantly one-sided in their expectations about the future course of stock price, the market will move in the opposite direction to their expectations.

10. *The Consumer Confidence Index is*

    a. Considered a contrarian indicator because when the index has shown that consumers are overly pessimistic, the stock market has tended to rise.

    b. Considered a measure of informed market players because it measures the consumers' knowledge about their own financial conditions.

    c. Measured by surveying businesses throughout the U.S. and Europe to gauge the amount of purchasing activity occurring in different sectors of the economy.

    d. Not useful in measuring investment sentiment in that it measures the optimism of households rather than that of investors.

CHAPTER 8

Measuring Market Strength

Chapter Objectives

By the end of this chapter, you should

- ▶ Understand the importance of measuring internal market strength

- ▶ Understand what is meant by "market breadth"

- ▶ Be familiar with how the advance-decline line measures market breadth

- ▶ Be familiar with how up and down volumes relate to market strength

- ▶ Be familiar with how new high and new low statistics measure market strength

- ▶ Be familiar with the relationship between the number of stocks above their historical moving average and market strength

Chapter Summary

Confirmation occurs when prices and a market internals indicator are moving in the same direction. When a market indicator does not support the direction of price movement, the analyst has a strong warning that the trend may be in the process of reversing. This lack of confirmation is referred to as a **divergence**.

Market Breadth

An **advance** occurs when on a given day a stock closes at a higher price than it did the previous day. A **decline** occurs when the stock closes at a lower price than it did the previous day. A stock that closes at the exact price it closed the previous day is called **unchanged**. The advance/decline data is called the **breadth** of the market. Breadth indicators measure the internal strength of the market by considering how all stocks are gaining or losing in price.

The breadth line, also known as the advance-decline line, is calculated as

$$\text{Breadth Line Value}_{\text{Day T}} = (\text{\# of Advancing Stocks}_{\text{Day T}} - \text{\# of Declining Stocks}_{\text{Day T}}) + \text{Breadth Line Value}_{\text{Day T-1}}$$

A **negative divergence** occurs when the averages are reaching new price highs and the breadth line is not. This signals weak market internals and is a clue that the market uptrend might soon end.

The Haurlan Index is calculated as the number of advances minus the number of declines on a particular day, smoothed with a three-day exponential moving average. The McClellan Oscillator is

McClellan Oscillator = (19-day EMA of advances – declines) – (39-day EMA of advances – declines)

Some other breadth difference measures include the McClellan Ratio-Adjusted Oscillator, the McClellan Summation Index, the Plurality Index, the Absolute Breadth Index, and the Unchanged Issues Index.

As the number of issues being tracked changes, indicators based on differences between advances and declines are affected. Indicators based on the ratios between various configurations of advances, declines, and unchanged address this issue. The advance-decline ratio is calculated by dividing the number of advances by the number of declines.

Up and Down Volume Indicator

Daily up volume is total volume trading in advancing stocks, and down volume is total volume trading in declining stocks. Using volume, rather than simply the number of shares traded, places more emphasis on stocks that are actively traded. The Arms Index, a ratio of two ratios, is calculated as

$$\text{Arms Index} = \frac{\dfrac{\text{Advances}}{\text{Declines}}}{\dfrac{\text{Up Volume}}{\text{Down Volume}}}$$

A higher level of the Arms Index indicates that although the number of shares advancing is rising, it is doing so on relatively low volume.

Net New Highs and Net New Lows

During a strong rise in the stock market, you would want to see a number of stocks reaching new 52-week highs. During market declines, you would expect to see more stocks making 52-week lows. You can simply look at the difference between the number of new highs and the number of new lows: a larger number of new highs than new lows suggests market strength. The High Low Logic Index takes the lesser of two ratios: the number of weekly new highs to total issues or the number of weekly new lows to total issues. A low index level suggests a strongly trending market.

Using Moving Averages

The number of stocks above or below their 30-week moving average can give an indication of whether the market is overbought or oversold. This is a contrary indicator, in that when more than 70% of the stocks are trading higher than their 30-week moving average, the market is probably overbought.

Key Concepts and Vocabulary

A number of terms and concepts that might be new to you appear in this chapter. As you read through this chapter, pay close attention to the following terms and concepts. Write down a definition or explanation for each.

Divergence

Confirmation

Negative divergence

Positive divergence

Breadth

Double divergences

Oscillator

Equity line

Thrust

End-of-Chapter Review Questions

1. *Explain what the term* market breadth *means.*

   Market breadth is a measure of how many stocks are participating in a stock market move. Measuring breadth tells the analyst whether an increase in the market index is characterized by a large price increase in a few stocks or a smaller price increase in the majority of the market stocks.

2. *Explain what the term* divergence *means.*

   Divergence occurs when a market indicator does not confirm the direction of price movement. Suppose, for example, market prices are rising, reaching a new high. An indicator can be used to confirm this trend. If the indicator also reaches a new high, confirmation exists. If the indicator fails to make a new high, divergence occurs, signaling a potential change in market direction.

3. *An analyst appearing on the financial news made the following statement:*

   "Since the recent run-up in the S&P500 has been accompanied by weak internals, I do not have much confidence that the uptrend in the S&P500 will continue much longer."

   Explain what this analyst means by weak internals. What types of statistics has the analyst been looking at to determine that the market internals were weak?

   The analyst has seen an increase in the value of the S&P500, but does not have confidence that this uptrend will continue. The analyst has seen increases in stock prices, as measured by the S&P500 but is not seeing strength in the broad market that would push these prices higher. The analyst may consider several different statistics. Market breadth may indicate that though the S&P500 is rising, there are more stocks declining in price than rising. This would indicate that the market rise is powered by a few stocks making significant gains rather than a majority of the stocks rising together. The analyst might be looking at the number of stocks advancing relative to declining, the volume advances relative to declines, the number of new highs relative to new lows, or the number of stocks at relatively high or low prices relative to a price moving average.

4. *Explain how looking at new highs and new lows can help an analyst determine internal market strength.*

   The number of new highs and new lows gives a sense of the number of stocks participating in an advance or decline. When the market is rising, stocks should be reaching new highs. If stock prices are rising, but not many stocks are reaching new highs, market internals are weak, calling into question the strength and continuation of the uptrend.

5. *Assume that market indices are all trending upward. What type of market internals would you like to see to confirm these trends?*

   For confirmation, I would like to see a majority of stocks rising. In this way, I would know that the rally is not due to a few stocks having significant increases in value. I would like to see a positive advance/decline ratio. I would also like to see that these higher prices are occurring on high volume; a low Arms Index would indicate that the "up volume" is relatively high. A growing number of stocks hitting 52-week highs relative to stocks hitting 52-week lows would be favorable.

6. *The Web site http://finance.yahoo.com reports useful information about market internals every day. This information can be found under the heading Today's Markets by clicking on the Investing option. Look up the information for today's trading. What would you conclude about the internal market strength today? Explain what information leads you to your conclusion.*

   Answers vary depending on the particular day chosen:

   The data in the following chart gives some information about the market internals for the day. In all four markets, the number of shares advancing exceeds the number of shares declining, which suggests market strength. Also, all of the markets had significantly more stocks reaching new highs than stock falling to new lows. Another measure of market strength is up volume exceeding down volume. Therefore, all of the indicators suggest strong internals for all four markets.

Advances and Declines

	NYSE	AMEX	NASDAQ	OTC BB
Advancing Issues	1,992	637	1,680	787
Declining Issues	1,288	373	1,378	753
Unchanged Issues	142	85	133	460
Total Issues	**3,422**	**1,005**	**3,191**	**2,000**
New Highs	**252**	**131**	**203**	**195**
New Lows	**57**	**9**	**42**	**127**
Up Volume	1,584,360,520	339,776,290	1,388,464,351	1,228,190,061
Down Volume	817,006,440	47,591,323	638,329,592	1,122,989,556
Unchanged Volume	24,069,400	7,392,400	26,562,515	600,541,897
Total Volume	**2,425,436,360**	**394,760,013**	**2,053,356,458**	**2,951,721,514**

7. *Use the information you gathered for Question 6 to calculate the ARMS Index and the Modified ARMS Index for the day. What information does each of these indicators give you?*

For all four of the markets, the ARMS Index is less than one. This indicates a relatively large denominator in the ARMS calculation, pointing to high up volume. A high up volume indicates market strength. The Modified ARMS is positive, which indicates that the product of advancing shares and up volume exceeds the product of declining shares and down volume.

	NYSE	AMEX	NASDAQ	OTC BB
Advancing	1992	637	1680	787
Declining	1288	373	1378	753
Up Volume	1584360520	339776290	1388464351	1228190061
Down Volume	817006440	47591323	638329592	1122989556
ARMS Index	0.797526163	0.239202276	0.560493149	0.955630264
Modified ARMS Index	2,103,741,861,120	216,485,000,000	2,333,260,000,000	967,709,000,000

Self-Test

1. *Double divergence occurs when*

   a. Divergence occurs in both the NYSE and the NASDAQ stocks.

   b. There is divergence between the U.S. and Asian markets and between the U.S. and European markets.

   c. Two consecutive new highs occur in price action while the 90-day moving average is downward sloping.

   d. Two consecutive negative breadth divergences occur.

2. *The breadth line will rise on days when*

   a. The number of advancing stocks exceeds the number of declining stocks.

   b. The average price increase of advancing stocks exceeds the average price increase of declining stocks.

   c. The average daily range for advancing stocks exceeds the average daily range of declining stocks.

   d. More stocks are advancing than advanced the previous day.

3. *When more than 70% of stocks are trading above their 30-week moving average*

   a. The market is probably overbought and a correction is inevitable.

   b. A strong upward trend is confirmed and traders should expect a bull market.

   c. The majority of stocks are in a downtrend because a long-term moving average is being considered.

   d. There is positive market sentiment among informed players, but negative market sentiment among uninformed players.

4. *Which of the following points to weak market internals?*

   a. A high number of stocks advancing relative to the number declining

   b. A high advancing volume relative to declining volume

   c. A rise of the advance-decline line greater than its 32-week simple moving average

   d. A fall in the number of stocks reaching 52-week highs relative to stocks falling to 52-week lows

5. *Which of the following is a TRUE statement?*

   a. A problem with using breadth differences is that they are affected by the number of issues being traded, which is not stable over time.

   b. An increasing advance-decline line is an indication of weak market internals.

   c. When an oscillator's value equals zero, divergence has occurred.

   d. Divergence occurs when the stock market index is more than one standard deviation from its mean, and double divergence occurs when the stock market index is more than two standard deviations from its mean.

6. *Overbought and oversold levels are indicated*

   a. When an oscillator's value equals zero.

   b. When an oscillator's value moves from positive to negative.

   c. When an oscillator's value moves from negative to positive.

   d. By extreme levels in an oscillator.

7. *The Arms Index is based upon the idea that during a market advance,*

   a. Heavy volume in advancing stocks is healthy for the market.

   b. Low volume in advancing stocks is a sign of market strength.

   c. The percentage price change of advancing stocks is more important than the volume for advancing stocks.

   d. Knowing the number of stocks at 52-week extremes is more important than knowing the number of stocks higher than their 20-week moving average.

8. *A 90% downside day occurs when*

   a. 90% of stocks are trading below their 30-week price moving average.

   b. 90% of stocks are trading 90% below their 10-day moving average.

   c. Downside volume exceeds 90% of total upside and downside volume, and downside points exceed 90% of total upside and downside points.

   d. Declines equal 90% or more of the total of advance and declines, and the overall market average is below its 90-day moving average.

9. *Tick data*

   a. Is important to watch in the early moments of trading, as price is initially set for the day, but closing tick data is irrelevant because it is simply a summary of what has transpired during the day.

   b. Is used as a contrary indicator because it measures very short-term bursts or enthusiasm and fear.

   c. Is helpful in measuring the optimism of informed players, but is not useful in measuring the fear of uninformed players; therefore, it can only be used as a trend-following indicator.

   d. Is useful in measuring overall, long-term trends in the market, but is not useful in determining intraday movements because it oscillates throughout the day.

10. *You see that the S&P500 just made a new low, but the advance-decline line did not fall to a new low. This situation would be called*

   a. Positive divergence.

   b. Confirmation.

   c. Negative reversal.

   d. Breadth reversal.

CHAPTER 9
Temporal Patterns and Cycles

Chapter Objectives

By the end of this chapter, you should be familiar with

▶ The long (50–60-year) Kondratieff wave cycle

▶ The 34-year cycle

▶ The decennial cycle

▶ Four-year cycles, including the election year pattern

▶ Seasonal tendencies in stock performance

▶ The relationship between January stock market performance and the rest of the year

▶ The relationship between events and stock market performance

Chapter Summary

Periods Longer Than Four Years

Kondratieff waves, or K-waves, are associated with a long 50–60-year cycle studied by Nicolas Kondratieff in the 1920s. Aspects of K-Wave theory include the ideas that waves are attributes of the world economy led by a major national economy and that waves arise because of the bunching of innovations in products, services, technology, new sources of raw materials, and new production methods.

Historical data suggests that 34-year cycles, composed of a 17-year period of dormancy followed by a 17-year period of intensity, exist. The decennial pattern theory states that years ending in 3, 7, and 10 (and sometimes 6) are often down years, whereas years ending in 5, 8, and 9 are advancing years.

Periods of Four Years or Less

Mitchell originated the 40-month cycle theory, based upon the fact that between 1796 and 1923 the U.S. economy suffered a recession, on average, every 40 months. This time frame is closely tied to the election, or presidential cycle. On average, the market rises much more during the last two years of a president's term than the first two years of the term.

Seasonal patterns have been evident in agricultural prices for centuries. In addition to seasonality in commodity market, the U.S. Treasury bond market appears to have seasonal tendencies. "Sell in May and go away," refers to the tendency of the stock market to decline from May to September and rise from October to April.

January Signals

"As the Standard & Poor's goes in January, so goes the year," is an oft-heard phrase. The idea is if the stock market rises in January, the market will be up for the year. However, strong statistical evidence for this popular notion is lacking.

The January effect is the tendency for small-cap stock to have abnormal strength in the month of January. This effect has dissipated in recent years.

Event Trading

Patterns have been discerned around holidays. For example, stock market performance tends to be strong the five days prior to Independence Day and weaker the five days following Independence Day. The sixth day after Independence Day, however, tends to be associated with strong stock market performance. The two weeks before Thanksgiving tend to be strong weeks for the market. A popular rule of thumb has been to buy stocks on Monday and sell stocks on Friday, based on the idea that market performance is poor on Mondays and strong on Fridays. However, recent data does not support this notion.

Key Concepts and Vocabulary

A number of terms and concepts that might be new to you appear in this chapter. As you read through this chapter, pay close attention to the following terms and concepts. Write down a definition or explanation for each.

K-waves

Decennial pattern

Presidential cycle

January effect

End-of-Chapter Review Questions

1. *Consider K-wave cycle theory, 34-year cycle theory, and the relationship between birth rates and the stock market. Plot on a time line what each of these theories suggests stock market performance will be over the next 50 years. Do the predictions tend to agree and reinforce each other or do they tend to contradict each other?*

Three Cycles Next 40 Years

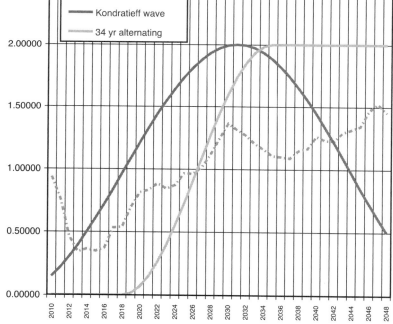

Projecting forward 40 years the current number of births, the approximate 51-year Kondratieff wave and the 34-year alternating cycle, the future looks relatively bright. A major low is expected during the 2012 through 2020 period, with the K-wave bolstering the market and keeping it from any major disaster. From 2020 to 2030, the market appears to have a strong underpinning from all cycles. Then a long decline in the Kondratieff wave and dormancy in the 34-year cycle and births suggest a long steady decline into 2050. It appears that the cycles shown coincide with each other with all three rising at the same time and then going dormant at the same time.

2. *Consider the four-year cycle. Plot out the pattern this theory would suggest for the stock market over the next 50 years. How well does your plot match what the decennial pattern theory would suggest would be positive years for stock returns?*

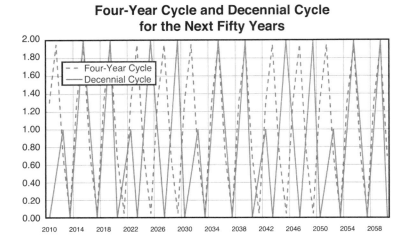

The previous chart illustrates the four-year cycle and the decennial cycle. The four-year cycle predicts that a low will occur approximately every four years. The last low occurred in 2009, which would suggest that the next low would occur in 2013, followed by a low in 2017, and so on. The decennial cycle considers a ten-year pattern in which years 3, 7, and 10 (and sometimes 6) are down years and thus presumably years of lows, and years 5, 8, and 9 are up years. The positive years under this theory would be those years in which both cycles are advancing. These are: 2014-2015, 2018-2019, 2022, 2025-2026, 2029, 2031, 2034-2035, 2038-2039, 2042, 2045-2046, 2049, 2051, 2054-2055, and 2058-2059. Major peaks, those years where both cycles peak, are 2019, 2035, 2039, 2055, and 2059. Notice that the time stretch between 2019-2035 and 2039-2055 is 16 years, approximating the 17-year cycle.

3. *Rosa said that over the past three years she has invested all of your money in an S&P500 index fund on October 1 and sold the fund 7 1/2 months later on May 15, remaining out of the market until the next October 1. Why do you think Rosa followed this strategy? How well has Rosa done following this strategy over the past three years?*

Rosa is following the "sell in May and go away" strategy. Historically, the stock market has had a tendency to decline from May to September and rise from October to April. The S&P500 was at 1029.85 on October 1, 2009; by May 14 it had risen by 12.39%. (May 15 was a Saturday in 2010.) The S&P500 increased by 16.71% from October 1, 2010 through May 13, 2011 and by 27.60% from October 3, 2011 through May 15, 2012. This has been a profitable strategy in that the S&P500 declined between mid-May and the beginning of October in 2010 and 2011. In other words, Rosa was able to lock in her gains she had earned through mid-May and then repurchase at a lower price at the beginning of October.

Date	S&P500	% Return
10/1/2009	1029.85	12.39%
5/14/2010	1157.44	
10/1/2010	1146.24	16.71%
5/13/2011	1337.77	
10/3/2011	1099.23	27.60%
5/15/2012	1402.6	

4. *Calculate the monthly rate of return in the S&P500 for the past two years. What about your results is in line with what you would have predicted given the information about seasonality in this chapter? What about your results seems to be contrary to the seasonality theory in this chapter?*

Answers may vary depending on the time period considered. The monthly returns for the S&P500 from January 2010 through May 2012 are shown in the following table:

2010	January	−3.697%
	February	2.851%
	March	5.880%
	April	1.476%
	May	−8.198%
	June	−5.388%
	July	6.878%
	August	−4.745%
	September	8.755%
	October	3.686%
	November	−0.229%
	December	6.530%
2011	January	2.265%
	February	3.196%
	March	−0.105%
	April	2.850%
	May	−1.350%
	June	−1.826%
	July	−2.147%
	August	−5.679%
	September	−7.176%
	October	10.772%
	November	−0.506%
	December	0.853%
2012	January	4.358%
	February	4.059%
	March	3.133%
	April	−0.750%
	May	−6.265%

Source: Yahoo! Finance

Historical results suggest that the market tends to decline from May to September and rise from October to April. In 2010, the market declined in May, June, and August. The autumn rise began earlier than what might have been predicted, with the market gaining almost 8.8% in September. The 2011 results appeared to follow closely the pattern which has existed over the past decade. The market declined from May through September. This decline was followed by a gain of almost 11% in October. The overall market trend was upward until April, despite a small decline of approximately 0.5% in November. The rule of thumb of buying at the beginning of October and selling in May would have proved profitable during this time period.

Self-Test

1. *The Kondratieff wave is a*

    a. 4-year cycle.

    b. 10-year cycle.

    c. 34-year cycle.

    d. 50–60-year cycle.

2. *Which of the following cycles arises from the bunching of innovations?*

    a. Decennial cycle

    b. Election year cycle

    c. Presidential cycle

    d. Kondratieff wave

3. *The 34-year cycle suggests that*

    a. The market experiences a 17-year period of dormancy followed by a 17-year period of intensity.

    b. Stock market activity is closely aligned with growth in GDP.

    c. Volatility rises during periods of intensity and falls during periods of dormancy.

    d. A buy-and-hold strategy works well during the period of dormancy, and technical analysis works well during the period of intensity.

4. *According to the decennial pattern, which of the following set of years would most likely be expected to be advancing years for the market?*

    a. Years ending in 5, 8, and 9

    b. Years ending in 3, 7, and 10

    c. Years ending in 1, 3, 5, 7, and 9

    d. Years ending in 2, 4, 6, 8, and 0

5. *The election year pattern suggests that*

    a. The market tends to rise more during the last two years of a president's term in office than in the first two years.

    b. The market tends to rise more in the first half of a president's term than in the second half of the term.

    c. The market tends to rise in the years a Democrat is in office and fall in the years a Republican is in office.

    d. The market tends to rise the year before the presidential election if it is expected that a Republican will win and fall if it is expected a Democrat will win.

6. *Which of the following is a common saying among traders?*

    a. "Buy in May, stay and play."

    b. "Spring forward and buy stocks, fall back and sell stocks."

    c. "Sell in May, and go away."

    d. "Bundle up in winter, lighten your load in summer."

7. *The January effect refers to the*

    a. Tendency for small-cap stocks to have abnormal strength in January.

    b. Tech stocks to underperform the broader market in January but outperform the remainder of the year.

    c. Largest stock declines of the last century occurring in January.

    d. The decline in stock prices that occurs as households liquidate their positions to pay off holiday debt.

8. *Which of the following is a TRUE statement?*

    a. Stock market performance tends to be extremely weak during the week leading up to U.S. Independence Day.

    b. January market behavior is a contrarian indicator in that when the market is down in January, the market tends to be strong the remainder of the year.

    c. November, especially the first two weeks of the month, tends to be a period of strength in the market.

    d. Small company stocks tend to underperform large company stocks in January as investors rebalance their portfolios at the beginning of the year.

9. *During the past 110 years,*

    a. More than half of the four-year cycle bottoms occurred in the month of September.

    b. More than half of the four-year cycle bottoms occurred in the month of January.

    c. About half of the four-year cycle bottoms occurred in May with the other half occurring in either June or July.

    d. Four-year cycle bottoms tended to occur in January, February, or March.

10. *Long-term interest rates*

    a. Tend to move in the same direction as long-term bond prices.

    b. Tend to decline in the summer and fall and rise in the winter and spring.

    c. Tend to fall in January, February, and October.

    d. Tend to move in the same direction as long-term bond prices in the winter, but in the opposite direction in the summer.

CHAPTER 10
Flow of Funds

Chapter Objectives

By the end of this chapter, you should

- ▶ Understand why knowledge of the flow of funds is important to determining stock market valuation

- ▶ Understand why liquidity plays an important role in potential stock market valuation

- ▶ Be familiar with measurements of market liquidity

- ▶ Understand the relationship between Federal Reserve policy and the cost of funds

Chapter Summary

Funds in the Marketplace

Money that is placed in money market mutual funds is money that can potentially flow into the stock market. Because households tend to sell stocks and place cash in money market mutual funds at market lows, the level of assets in these funds can be a contrarian indicator. **Margin debt** is the amount of funds that customers at brokerage houses borrow for commitments in stocks. When markets become speculative, households might take on more margin debt. An increase in **secondary offerings** is usually a bearish sign. First, increasing supply puts downward pressure on stock prices. Second, a secondary offering represents liquidation on the part of the sellers who are usually considered insiders, or informed market players.

Funds Outside the Security Market

The more liquid households are, the more able they are to invest in stocks. High **household liquidity** is favorable for the stock market. The higher the **money supply** is relative to the market value of stocks, the more money there is to go into the market. An increase in **loan activity** is a sign of increased business activity. Too rapid expansion of **bank loans**, however, is a sign that the economy is overheating, and a stock market decline is likely.

The Cost of Funds

The **interest rate** is the cost of borrowing funds. Higher short-term interest rates are generally viewed as negative for the stock market. First, households see interest-bearing securities as an alternative investment to stocks. The higher the interest rate on those securities, the more money households will put in the interest bearing securities rather than the stock market. Second, interest is a cost to businesses. As interest rates rise, the net incomes of companies fall, and confidence in the market falls. Bond prices and the stock market tend to be positively correlated, making bottoms at the same time. Bond yields and stock market prices tend to be inversely related; bond yields tend to be high at stock market bottoms. Higher rates of the **velocity of money** tend to be associated with higher rates of inflation and lower rates of growth in the stock market.

Stagflation occurs when high inflation is coupled with high unemployment. The Misery Index is calculated by summing the inflation rate and the unemployment rate. A high Misery Index is unfavorable for the stock market.

Fed Policy

When the Federal Reserve purchases securities, it adds money to the banking system. This drives up the demand for bonds, lowers interest rates, and increases the number of loans made by the banks. The Fed raising the **federal funds target rate**, margin requirements, or reserve requirements is not favorable for the stock market, especially when these increases occur three consecutive times.

The **yield curve** is a graphical relationship of the yield on bonds with various length of time to maturity. Normally, the yield curve will be upward sloping, with shorter-term interest rates lower than longer-term interest rates. At times, the yield curve becomes inverted, with shorter-term interest rates higher than longer-term interest rates. An inversion of the yield curve suggests that a recession will occur in two to six quarters.

Key Concepts and Vocabulary

A number of terms and concepts that might be new to you appear in this chapter. As you read through this chapter, pay close attention to the following terms and concepts. Write down a definition or explanation for each.

Liquidity

Money supply

Margin debt

Secondary offerings

Interest rate

Velocity of money

Stagflation

Misery Index

Federal Reserve System

Yield curve

Household liquidity

Loan activity

Federal funds target rate

End-of-Chapter Review Questions

1. *Explain how the amount of money in money market mutual funds can be a predictor of stock market performance. Calculate the ratio of money market mutual fund assets to the Wilshire 5000 index using the most recent statistics available. (Money market mutual fund asset statistics are included in the Federal Reserve Flow of Funds Report Z.1 in Chart L.122, available electronically at http://www.federalreserve.gov/releases/.) What does this ratio suggest about future stock market performance?*

   Answers will vary depending on period considered.

   When traders and investors are nervous about the stock market, they tend to place their funds in money market mutual funds. Because money market mutual funds are highly liquid investments, money in these funds is a potential source of funds for reinvestment in the stock market. When the money begins flowing back into the stock market, stock prices rise. As money leaves the money market mutual funds, the level of money market mutual fund assets falls. As money flows into the stock market and stock prices rise, the ratio of money market mutual fund assets to stock market value falls.

The following table shows that the ratio of money market mutual fund assets to the Wilshire 5000 was lower in 2011 than it had been in 2009 and 2010. However, money-market, mutual-fund assets representing about 20% of the stock market valuation are still a relatively high ratio. Households appear to be holding liquid assets that can be used to fund stock purchases in the future.

	2009	2010			
	Q4	Q1	Q2	Q3	Q4
Money Market Mutual Fund Assets	3258.3	2930.7	2760.4	2746.1	3755.3
Wilshire 5000 Index	11548.64	12222.3	10823.31	12020.91	13360.12
Ratio	0.2821	0.2398	0.2550	0.2284	0.2811

	2011			
	Q1	Q2	Q3	Q4
Money Market Mutual Fund Assets	2679.4	2637.8	2578.4	2642.5
Wilshire 5000 Index	14101.3	14023.08	11842.12	13189.98
Ratio	0.1900	0.1881	0.2177	0.2003

2. *Why would many public offerings occur at market tops (and few at market bottoms)?*

Companies making public offerings want to do so at the highest price possible because that generates more money for the corporation. Those inside the company who make the decision to make a public offering do so when they think that the price is at a relative high. When the companies think the market is at a bottom, they do not want to make public offerings because they would be selling interest in the company at what they consider to be a low price.

3. *Why might household liquidity be related to stock market performance?*

Households use cash to purchase securities. When households are illiquid, they have little cash to purchase securities. When households are holding cash and other highly liquid investments, they have a good deal of purchasing power to use to purchase stocks. They are not heavily invested in stocks at this point (because if they were, they could not be highly liquid). As people begin to think that the stock market is a favorable market in which to invest their money, they will start using their cash to purchase stocks. These purchases represent an increase in the demand for stocks and result in an increase in the price of stocks. The more liquid households are, the more potential there is for demand for stocks to increase and prices to rise.

4. *What has happened to the federal funds target rate over the past year? What does this suggest about stock market performance?*

Answers will vary depending on time period considered.

The following chart shows the fed funds rate, the market rate proxy for the target rate, for 2003 through 2008. During 2003 the rate was steady and low. At the same time the stock market rose. From July 2004 through July 2007 the rate rose, and the stock market slowed its advance, peaking in rates in July 2007. Rates then declined during the stock market decline, bottoming in early 2009, and remained low ever since, during which time the stock market advanced strongly.

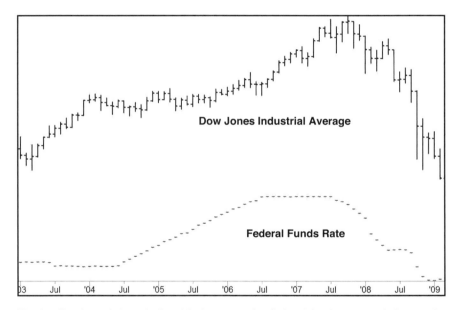

The implication of the relationship between the federal funds rate and the stock market is that the stock market prefers a low rate and its progress begins to deteriorate as the rate rises and remains at a high level. Conversely, when the rate reaches a low and remains low, the stock market does well.

5. *Determine the shape of the yield curve during the 2006–2007 time period. You can gather information to construct the yield curve from the Federal Reserve Web site. Alternatively, many Web sites, such as stockcharts.com (http://stockcharts.com/charts/YieldCurve.html), provide pictures of historical yield curves. Looking at this yield curve, do you think that the weak economic conditions and market downturn that began in the fall of 2008 were a surprise to an alert observer?*

Rates for constant maturity 1-month and 30-year Treasury securities in 2006 and 2007 are in the following table. You can see that the yield curve was inverted from the fall of 2006 through the spring of 2007. Because an inverted yield curve predicts a recession will occur in two to six quarters, an alert observer would not have been surprised to see the weak economic conditions beginning in the fall of 2008. Also, because stock market declines tend to be associated with inverted yield curves, the decline in stock prices would have been anticipated by someone watching the yield curve.

		1-Month Treasuries	30-Year Treasuries
February	2006	4.38	4.54
March	2006	4.55	4.73
April	2006	4.61	5.06
May	2006	4.7	5.2
June	2006	4.71	5.15
July	2006	4.9	5.13
August	2006	5.16	5
September	2006	4.77	4.85
October	2006	4.97	4.85
November	2006	5.21	4.69
December	2006	4.87	4.68
January	2007	4.94	4.85
February	2007	5.18	4.82
March	2007	5.21	4.72
April	2007	4.99	4.87
May	2007	4.82	4.9
June	2007	4.52	5.2
July	2007	4.82	5.11
August	2007	4.2	4.93
September	2007	3.78	4.79
October	2007	3.81	4.77
November	2007	3.68	4.52
December	2007	2.86	4.53

Source: http://www.federalreserve.gov/releases/h15/data.htm

6. *Gather data for the yield curve this week and for the yield curve one year ago. What changes do you notice? What impact do you think this will have on the stock market?*

Answers will vary depending on period considered.

The following chart shows the yield curve for June 1, 2011 and June 1, 2012. The yields on Treasury securities with one year or less to maturity are almost identical in the two years. These are extremely low rates by historical standards—all below 0.2%. Longer-term interest rates have fallen over the year. Although the level of interest rates in 2011 was low, the spread between the long-term interest rates and short-term interest rates was high, resulting in a relatively steep yield curve. As long-term interest rates fell, the yield curve became flatter. The June, 2012 yield curve would be considered more of a "normal" yield curve than the 2011 curve in that the spread between short-term rates and long-term rates as close to the 200 basis point historic average. If the yield curve were to become inverted, a recession and stock market decline would be predicted.

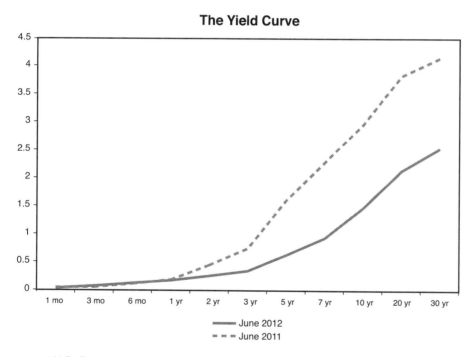

The Yield Curve

Data source: U.S. Treasury

Self-Test

1. *In which of the following situations would you be most likely to predict an increase in the stock market?*

    a. Margin debt has been substantially increasing.

    b. Money market mutual fund assets are high relative to the overall stock market value.

    c. Secondary offerings are relatively high.

    d. The Fed has increased the federal funds target rate three consecutive times.

2. *A high ratio of M2 relative to the overall value of the stock market*

    a. Means that M1 has been shrinking.

    b. Means that the velocity of money has been rising.

    c. Indicates that interest rates are relatively low and bond prices are relatively high.

    d. Is an indication that there is plenty of money around to go into the stock market.

3. *Which of the following tends to be associated with a high interest rate?*

    a. High stock market valuation

    b. Less borrowing

    c. The Federal Reserve purchasing a large amount of U.S. Treasury securities

    d. High corporate net income

4. _____ *is the measure of how fast money turns over in the economy.*

    a. M1

    b. M2

    c. Velocity

    d. Liquidity

5. *The Misery Index is calculated as the sum of*

    a. The bond market valuation and the stock market valuation.

    b. Bond prices and bond yields.

    c. M1 and M2.

    d. Inflation and the unemployment rate.

6. *When the Federal Reserve purchases securities*

    a. Bond prices fall and interest rates rise.

    b. Banks are left with less money in reserves.

    c. M1 and M2 fall.

    d. It adds money to the banking system.

7. *Whenever the yield curve is inverted*

    a. A recession is predicted within the next 6 to 18 months.

    b. A strong stock market is predicted.

    c. Short-term interest rates are lower than long-term interest rates.

    d. Bank profits are expected to rise.

8. *"Three steps and a stumble" refers to the tendency for*

    a. A substantial decline to occur in the stock market after the Federal Reserve raises the federal funds target rate, margin requirements, or reserve requirements three consecutive times.

    b. The yield curve to become inverted after three consecutive months of negative stock market returns.

    c. The market to stall when the Federal Reserve uses only one or two, rather than all three, of its main tools of raising the federal funds target rate, margin requirements, and reserve requirements.

    d. The fact that the economy goes into a recession and there is a poor outlook for the stock market when M1, M2, and money velocity do not move in the same direction.

9. *As the bond market makes a major bottom,*

    a. Interest rates and inflation tend to be very low.

    b. Interest rates and the Misery Index tend to be very low.

    c. The stock market tends to make a major top.

    d. The stock market also tends to make a major bottom.

10. *Which of the following would be most likely to predict a decline in the stock market?*

    a. High household liquidity

    b. An inverted yield curve

    c. A low number of secondary offerings

    d. The Federal Reserve buying U.S. Treasury securities

CHAPTER 11

History and Construction of Charts

Chapter Objectives

By the end of this chapter, you should be familiar with

▶ The advantages of presenting price information in a picture, or chart, format

▶ The construction of line charts

▶ The construction of bar charts

▶ The construction of candlestick charts

▶ The construction of point-and-figure charts

▶ The differences between arithmetic and logarithmic scales

Chapter Summary

History of Charting

Charts are merely graphical displays of data and are the traditional tool of the technical analyst. The invention of the ticker tape revolutionized charting in the late 1800s. More recently, computer technology has simplified the task of constructing charts.

What Types of Charts Do Analysts Use?

A **line chart** provides information about two variables, closing price and time. Simple line charts are useful when studying long-term trends and when plotting several different variables in the same graph. A **bar chart** shows at least three pieces of information: the high, the low, and the closing price for a given time period. Some bar charts also contain the opening price. **Candlestick charts**, which originated in Japan, are similar to bar charts in their construction. A box is used to represent the opening and closing prices. The box, known as the **real body**, is open, or white, if the price closes higher than it opened. If the closing price is lower than the opening price, the real body is closed, or black. The high and the low of the session are represented by thin vertical bars known as **shadows**.

What Type of Scale Should Be Used?

With an **arithmetic**, or linear, **scale**, a chart's vertical axis is marked with the same price unit at the same intervals. In other words, the vertical distance between $1 and $2 is the same as the vertical distance between $50 and $51. With a **logarithmic scale** the vertical distance on the chart's vertical axis represents the same percentage change in price. For example, the logarithmic scale would show the vertical difference between $1 and $2 (a 100% increase) the same as the vertical difference between $50 and $100 (also a 100% increase). Logarithmic scales are useful when observing long-term price movements.

Point-and-Figure Charts

Point-and-figure chart construction uses only one variable: price. It ignores time. Point-and-figure charts are plotted on a graph paper with squares that form a grid. Each square on the graph paper is called a **box**. The box size determines how much of a change in price must occur before a new plot is posted on the chart. For example, a box size of one point results in boxes being numbered in one dollar increments, such as 20, 21, 22, 23, 24, and so on. A plot is only made when price touches or passes through one of these amounts. All of the plots in one column represent movement in the same direction. Thus, a change in direction, a reversal, moves the plots to the next column. Larger box sizes result in less noise being plotted. The **reversal amount** refers to the amount by which price must reverse in order to move to the next column. Some analysts use logarithmic scales for the vertical axis and/or colors or numbers in each box to show either date or volume.

Key Concepts and Vocabulary

A number of terms and concepts that might be new to you appear in this chapter. As you read through this chapter, pay close attention to the following terms and concepts. Write down a definition or explanation for each.

Line chart

Bar chart

Candlestick chart

Real body

Shadows

Arithmetic scale

Logarithmic scale

Point-and-figure chart

Box

Reversal amount

Practice and Application

Charting stock data is an important skill for a technical analyst. Here is an exercise to help you practice this skill.

Stock NOP traded as follow this past week:

Day	Open	Close	High	Low
1	22	24	24	21
2	24	25	26	22
3	23	21	24	20
4	24	21	25	21
5	23	26	27	22

Sketch each of the following types of graphs for this data:

Line Chart of
Closing Price

Bar Chart

Candlestick
Chart

Your charts should look something like this:

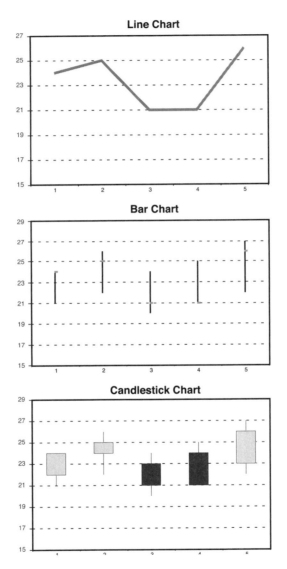

Line Chart

Bar Chart

Candlestick Chart

Point-and-figure charts provide an alternative way of plotting data. Suppose you have plotted the following data on a one-point, one-box reversal, point-and-figure chart: 35.2, 36.1, 36.9, 35.9, 37.2. Your chart would look like this:

41	
40	
39	
38	
37	X
36	X
35	
34	
33	
32	
31	

What would the next price have to be greater than in order to place another plot in the first column?

To place another "X" in the first column, price would have to reach or pass $38.

What would the next price have to be in order to place a mark in the second column?

In order to make a mark in the next column, the price would have to fall below $36. An "X" in the second column at the price of $36 would mean that price has passed through that level. So, if the next price were $35.99 an "X" would be placed in the second column at the $36 level.

End-of-Chapter Review Questions

1. *Melinda is analyzing Wal-Mart's stock over the past three months and notices that the price has ranged from $51 to $53 per share. Joshua is analyzing Merck's stock over the past five years and notices that the price has ranged from $25 to $90 a share over that period. Which analyst would be more likely to use an arithmetic scale, and which analyst would be more likely to use a logarithmic scale to analyze price information? Explain your reasoning.*

   Joshua would be more likely to use a logarithmic scale and Melinda would be more likely to use an arithmetic scale. For Melinda, the price of Wal-Mart has varied by $2 per share, or only about 4%. The percentage change in price from $51 to $52 is not much different from the percentage change when price moves from $52 to $53 a share.

   Joshua is looking at a much broader price range. When price is $90 per share, a $1 price change is only a little more than a 1% price change. When price is $25 a share, a $1 price change is a much more significant 4% price change. If Joshua were to use an algorithmic scale, a $1 move would appear the same whether it was occurring at the $25 price level or the $90 price level. However, we know that $1 price move is much more significant if it occurs at $25 than at $90. Using a logarithmic scale means that the $1 price move appears approximately four times as significant when it occurs at a $25 price level than at a $90 price level.

2. Gather open, high, low, and closing prices for Valero Energy Corp (VLO) for the period from September 2007 to September 2010. Gather this data for daily, weekly, and monthly quotes. Yahoo! Finance provides this information online at http://finance.yahoo.com; just put in the ticker symbol VLO and click the Historical Prices option. This data can be downloaded into a spreadsheet for easy manipulation.

   a. Graph a line chart using an arithmetic scale for VLO using the daily closing prices.

   b. Graph a line chart using an arithmetic scale for VLO using the weekly closing prices.

   c. Graph a line chart using an arithmetic scale for VLO using the monthly closing prices.

   d. What type of information can you gather about VLO stock by looking at these three graphs?

   e. What differences do you notice in the three charts that you created?

   a. A line chart using an arithmetic scale using daily prices looks like the following chart.

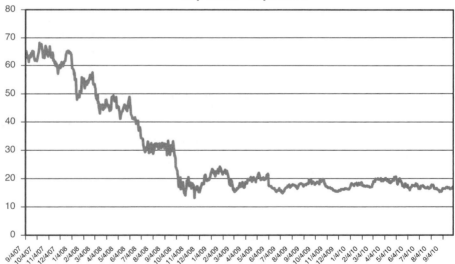

b. A line chart using an arithmetic scale using weekly prices looks like the following chart.

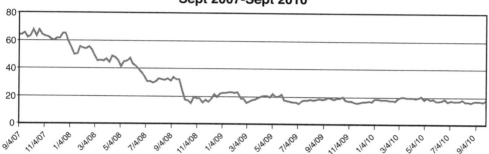

c. A line chart using an arithmetic scale using the monthly prices looks like the following chart.

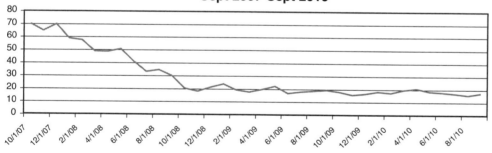

d. All three charts show that VLO was in a downtrend through October 2008. For much of 2009 and 2010, VLO was in a trading range around $20 per share.

e. Although all three charts clearly show a downtrend followed by a trading range, the daily chart shows much more detail. Looking at the daily chart, there are small pockets of time during the downtrend in which price moves upward. These smaller moves are eliminated when looking at the monthly chart.

3. *Repeat parts a, b, and c in Question 2 using a logarithmic scale. What differences do you notice between the graphs you have created in this question and the graphs you created in Question 2?*

   a. A line chart using a logarithmic scale using daily prices looks like the following chart.

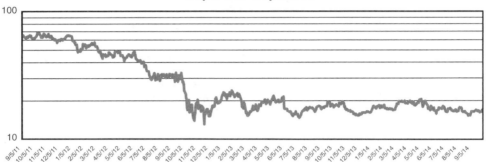

VLO Daily Line Chart
Logarithmic Scale
Sept 2007-Sept 2010

   b. A line chart using a logarithmic scale using weekly prices looks like the following chart.

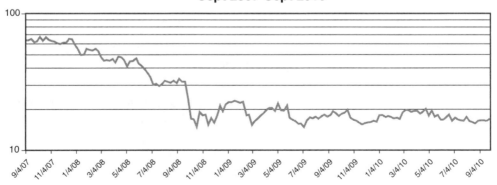

VLO Weekly Line Chart
Logarithmic Scale
Sept 2007-Sept 2010

c. A line chart using a logarithmic scale using monthly prices looks like the following chart.

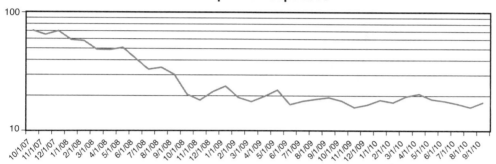

The horizontal lines in the three logarithmic charts mark $10 increments in price. The vertical distance between $10 and $20 is the same as the vertical distance between $20 and $40 and between $40 and $80; in other words, a doubling in price is always represented by the same vertical distance in the graphs.

VLO fell by approximately 50% (from about $60 a share down to about $30 a share) between December 2007 and August 2008. Then, it fell by another 50% (from about $30 a share to about $15 a share) in September and October 2008. The September through October 2008 fall was a much steeper fall because it occurred over a relatively short period of time. The logarithmic chart better highlights the steepness of this decline.

4. *Using the same data that you gathered in Question 2, create two candlestick charts for Valero using weekly data and monthly data. What type of information can you gather about VLO stock by looking at these two graphs?*

You can create candlestick charts with Excel. However, given the quantity of data in these charts, viewing whether an individual candle is a white or black candle can be difficult when the chart is printed rather than being viewed on a computer screen. Therefore, for demonstration purposes the following two charts have been generated using TradeStation.

The weekly candlestick chart looks like the following chart.

Chart created with TradeStation

The monthly candlestick chart looks like the following chart.

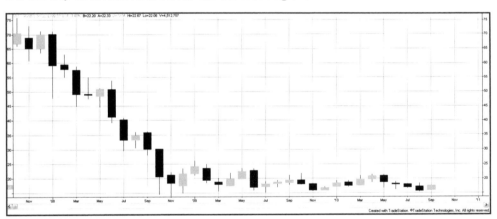

Chart created with TradeStation

With the candlestick charts, it is easy to tell the weekly and monthly directional movement of the stock price. For example, six consecutive black candles in mid-2008 on the weekly chart indicate that for six weeks in a row, VLO ended the week at a lower price than it began the week. Looking at the monthly chart, you can quickly see that for 9 of the 12 months in 2008, VLO closed at a lower price than it opened.

5. *Not having intraday, sequential trade data, instead, using the daily closing prices that you gathered for Question 2, create a one-point one-box reversal point-and-figure chart for VLO for September 2009–September 2010.*

One-Point, One-Box Reversal

25												
24												
23												
22												
21												
20						X	X					
19	X	X				X	X	X				
18	X	X	X	X	X		X	X			
17			X	X	X		X	X	X	X	
16			X				X		X		
15												

The daily closing data for VLO is provided in a chart at the end of this chapter. The prices that lead to a new mark in the one-point one-box reversal chart are bolded in the table.

6. *As in Question 5, using the daily closing prices that you gathered for Question 2, create a two-point one-box reversal point-and-figure chart for VLO for September 2009–September 2010.*

Two-Point, One-Box Reversal

22				
20		X		
18	X	X	X	X
16	X		X	X
14				

The daily closing data for VLO is provided in a chart at the end of this chapter. The prices that lead to a new mark in the two-point one-box reversal chart are in italic in the table.

7. As in Question 5, using the daily closing prices that you gathered for Question 2, create a one-point three-box reversal point-and-figure chart for VLO for September 2009–September 2010.

One-Point, Three-Box Reversal

21			
20		X	
19	O	X	O
18	O	X	O
17	O	X	O
16	O		O
15			

The daily closing data for VLO is provided in a chart at the end of this chapter. The prices that lead to a new mark in the one-point three-box reversal chart are shaded in the table.

Self-Test

1. Point-and-figure charts focus on charting

   a. Price.

   b. Price and time.

   c. Price and volume.

   d. Price, time, and volume.

2. Luke has created a stock chart. On the vertical axis $10 and $11 are an inch apart and $50 and $55 are an inch apart. Luke has used

   a. An arithmetic scale.

   b. A logarithmic scale.

   c. Candlestick scale.

   d. A box chart scale.

3. On Monday, WMT opened at $60 a share and closed at $61 a share. The high for the day was $61.20 and the low for the day was $59.60. A candlestick chart for that day would show

   a. An open real body.

   b. A closed real body.

   c. A black real body.

   d. No shadows.

4. *Candlestick charting*

    a. Was developed in the 1990s as a result of increased computer technology.

    b. Was developed by Thomas Edison in 1870 as a result of the invention of the ticker tape.

    c. Was used as early as the mid-1600s in Japan.

    d. Has become outdated because of the increased use of computer technology to create bar charts.

5. *A bar chart contains at least*

    a. Three pieces of information: opening, closing, and high prices.

    b. Three pieces of information: closing, high, and low prices.

    c. Three pieces of information: opening, closing, and low prices.

    d. Two pieces of information: opening and closing prices.

6. *A trader can quickly tell whether a stock closed at a higher price than it opened when looking at a candlestick chart by looking at the*

    a. Color of the real body.

    b. Length of the upper shadow.

    c. Length of the lower shadow.

    d. Height of the candle.

7. *An advantage of the point-and-figure chart is that it*

    a. Eliminates the plotting of noise data.

    b. Provides a visual representation of volume.

    c. Strikingly displays time.

    d. Quickly depicts small movements in price data, enabling a trader to spot periods of anxiousness and periods of congestion.

8. *In point-and-figure charting, as the box size used increases,*

    a. More columns are necessary to plot the data.

    b. Smaller changes in price data are more visible.

    c. The chart becomes squeezed to the left, and fewer columns are needed.

    d. A small change in trend is more quickly realized.

9. *A logarithmic scale would be most useful to which of the following analysts?*

   a. Jane, who is watching the intraday movement of UA

   b. Ken, who is analyzing how WMT has been in a trading range between $55 and $62 for the past two years

   c. Lucy, who is interested in analyzing the price movement the three days before and the three days after JNJ announced its dividends for the latest quarter

   d. Matt, who is analyzing the long run-return in the S&P500 over the past 50 years

10. *Which of the following is a method for recording time on a three-box reversal, point-and-figure chart?*

   a. Place a month number (1 for January, 2 for February, and so on) in the box rather than an X or O.

   b. Place a tick mark on the horizontal axis at the beginning of each month.

   c. Place a tick mark on the vertical axis at the beginning of each month.

   d. Place an "M" for month at the beginning of each month at the bottom of the column in which the first X is recorded for the month.

Daily Closing Prices for VLO

September 1, 2009–September 30, 2010

9/1/2009	17.44	12/8/2009	15.63	3/18/2010	19.88	6/24/2010	17.52
9/2/2009	17.16	12/9/2009	15.7	3/19/2010	19.65	**6/25/2010**	**18.2**
9/3/2009	17.33	12/10/2009	16.16	3/22/2010	19.63	6/28/2010	17.94
9/4/2009	17.56	12/11/2009	16.02	3/23/2010	19.64	6/29/2010	17.15
9/8/2009	17.93	12/14/2009	16.2	*3/24/2010*	*20.01*	6/30/2010	17.44
9/9/2009	17.61	12/15/2009	16.18	3/25/2010	19.22	**7/1/2010**	**16.74**
9/10/2009	17.93	12/16/2009	16.12	3/26/2010	19.08	7/2/2010	16.4
9/11/2009	*18.11*	12/17/2009	16.1	3/29/2010	19.24	7/6/2010	16.34
9/14/2009	18.24	12/18/2009	16.1	3/30/2010	19.19	7/7/2010	17.08
9/15/2009	18.06	12/21/2009	16.5	3/31/2010	19.06	7/8/2010	17.36
9/16/2009	18.39	12/22/2009	16.44	4/1/2010	19.37	7/9/2010	17.35
9/17/2009	**19.61**	12/23/2009	16.31	4/5/2010	19.96	7/12/2010	17.25
9/18/2009	19.34	12/24/2009	16.46	4/6/2010	20.06	7/13/2010	17.54
9/21/2009	19.26	12/28/2009	16.22	4/7/2010	19.45	7/14/2010	17.1
9/22/2009	19.46	12/29/2009	16.21	4/8/2010	19.37	7/15/2010	17.34
9/23/2009	18.96	12/30/2009	16.26	4/9/2010	19.36	7/16/2010	16.84
9/24/2009	18.11	12/31/2009	16.16	**4/12/2010**	**18.96**	7/19/2010	16.63
9/25/2009	18.61	**1/4/2010**	**17.26**	4/13/2010	19.03	7/20/2010	16.76

Series continues on the next page.

Daily Closing Prices for VLO

September 1, 2009–September 30, 2010

9/28/2009	18.85	1/5/2010	17.7	4/14/2010	19.7	7/21/2010	16.52
9/29/2009	18.61	*1/6/2010*	*18.15*	4/15/2010	19.22	7/22/2010	16.63
9/30/2009	18.55	1/7/2010	18.28	4/16/2010	18.52	7/23/2010	16.57
10/1/2009	18.16	1/8/2010	18.03	4/19/2010	18.39	7/26/2010	17.03
10/2/2009	**17.82**	1/11/2010	17.86	4/20/2010	18.94	7/27/2010	16.86
10/5/2009	18.4	1/12/2010	17.57	4/21/2010	18.6	7/28/2010	16.52
10/6/2009	18.33	1/13/2010	17.42	4/22/2010	18.82	7/29/2010	16.39
10/7/2009	18.47	1/14/2010	17.62	4/23/2010	19.23	7/30/2010	16.48
10/8/2009	18.75	1/15/2010	18.11	4/26/2010	19.46	8/2/2010	16.59
10/9/2009	18.54	1/19/2010	18.2	4/27/2010	19.25	8/3/2010	17.15
10/12/2009	18.35	1/20/2010	18.44	4/28/2010	19.76	8/4/2010	17.44
10/13/2009	18.35	1/21/2010	18.23	**4/29/2010**	**20.47**	8/5/2010	17.76
10/14/2009	17.99	1/22/2010	17.54	4/30/2010	20.11	8/6/2010	17.51
10/15/2009	**19.27**	1/25/2010	17.7	5/3/2010	20.67	8/9/2010	17.68
10/16/2009	18.88	1/26/2010	18.35	5/4/2010	19.8	8/10/2010	17.45
10/19/2009	18.8	1/27/2010	18.03	5/5/2010	19.7	8/11/2010	16.62
10/20/2009	19.24	1/28/2010	17.78	**5/6/2010**	**18.72**	8/12/2010	16.42
10/21/2009	19.26	1/29/2010	17.77	*5/7/2010*	*17.92*	8/13/2010	16.34
10/22/2009	19.24	2/1/2010	18.48	5/10/2010	19.09	8/16/2010	16.44
10/23/2009	19.77	2/2/2010	18.58	5/11/2010	18.93	8/17/2010	16.28
10/26/2009	19.39	2/3/2010	18.27	5/12/2010	19.89	8/18/2010	16.57
10/27/2009	18.55	2/4/2010	17.47	5/13/2010	19.96	8/19/2010	16.29
10/28/2009	**17.89**	2/5/2010	17.52	5/14/2010	19.47	8/20/2010	16.09
10/29/2009	18.12	2/8/2010	17.22	5/17/2010	18.87	*8/23/2010*	*15.92*
10/30/2009	17.31	2/9/2010	17.46	5/18/2010	18.46	8/24/2010	15.75
11/2/2009	**16.98**	2/10/2010	17.36	5/19/2010	18.25	8/25/2010	15.63
11/3/2009	17.18	2/11/2010	17.36	5/20/2010	17.34	8/26/2010	15.22
11/4/2009	16.93	2/12/2010	17.12	5/21/2010	17.59	8/27/2010	15.66
11/5/2009	16.95	2/16/2010	17.38	5/24/2010	17.17	8/30/2010	15.58
11/6/2009	16.68	2/17/2010	17.24	**5/25/2010**	**16.85**	8/31/2010	15.34
11/9/2009	16.72	2/18/2010	17.11	5/26/2010	17.06	9/1/2010	15.76
11/10/2009	16.67	2/19/2010	17.31	5/27/2010	18.23	9/2/2010	16.18
11/11/2009	16.83	2/22/2010	17.2	5/28/2010	18.12	9/3/2010	16.48
11/12/2009	16.41	**2/23/2010**	**16.91**	6/1/2010	17.03	9/7/2010	16.46
11/13/2009	16.46	2/24/2010	17.03	6/2/2010	17.29	9/8/2010	16.41

Series continues on the next page.

Daily Closing Prices for VLO

September 1, 2009–September 30, 2010

11/16/2009	16.47	2/25/2010	16.88	6/3/2010	17.65	9/9/2010	16.37
11/17/2009	16.28	2/26/2010	16.95	6/4/2010	16.75	9/10/2010	16.5
11/18/2009	16.23	3/1/2010	17.06	6/7/2010	16.59	9/13/2010	16.89
11/19/2009	*15.78*	3/2/2010	17.61	6/8/2010	16.35	9/14/2010	16.94
11/20/2009	15.89	*3/3/2010*	**18.01**	*6/9/2010*	*15.87*	9/15/2010	16.87
11/23/2009	15.66	3/4/2010	18.21	6/10/2010	16.75	9/16/2010	16.74
11/24/2009	15.44	3/5/2010	18.93	6/11/2010	16.73	9/17/2010	16.53
11/25/2009	15.77	3/8/2010	18.98	6/14/2010	17	9/20/2010	16.77
11/27/2009	15.43	3/9/2010	18.89	6/15/2010	17.65	9/21/2010	16.68
11/30/2009	15.33	3/10/2010	**19.85**	6/16/2010	17.61	9/22/2010	16.31
12/1/2009	15.51	3/11/2010	19.74	6/17/2010	17.4	9/23/2010	16.18
12/2/2009	15.44	3/12/2010	19.77	6/18/2010	17.45	9/24/2010	16.36
12/3/2009	15.41	3/15/2010	19.7	6/21/2010	17.59	9/27/2010	16.42
12/4/2009	15.83	3/16/2010	19.89	6/22/2010	17.26	9/28/2010	16.6
12/7/2009	15.78	3/17/2010	19.99	6/23/2010	17.61	9/29/2010	16.8
						9/30/2010	**17.03**

Source: Yahoo! Finance

CHAPTER 12

Trends—The Basics

Chapter Objectives

By the end of this chapter, you should

- ▶ Know why identifying trends is paramount to profits in securities

- ▶ Be able to recognize an uptrend, downtrend, and a trading range

- ▶ Understand the concept of support and resistance

- ▶ Be familiar with the major methods of determining trends

- ▶ Be familiar with the major signals that a trend is reversing

Chapter Summary

Trend—Key to Profits

Following these three steps is key to profiting in the securities market:

1. Determine, with minimum risk of error, when a trend has begun, at its earliest time and price.

2. Select and enter an appropriate position.

3. Close the position when the trend has ended.

Trends define a direction in prices. A sideways trend is known as a **trading range**. Trend-following techniques work poorly during trading ranges.

Basis of Trend Analysis—Dow Theory

Trends are **fractal** in that their behavior is the same regardless of the period. Trends tend to continue rather than reverse. Any particular trend is influenced by its next larger and next smaller trend.

How Does Investor Psychology Impact Trends?

Price is determined by the interaction of supply and demand. When prices are trending, they remain headed in one direction, indicating an imbalance of supply and demand. The power of buyers and sellers make a trend. If prices are rising, then buyers must have stronger positive expectations and money to continue buying stock. Contrarily, if prices are falling, sellers must have stronger negative expectations and positions to exit.

How Is the Trend Determined?

Trend is a direction rather than a straight line. In an uptrend, peaks are higher than earlier peaks, and troughs are higher than earlier troughs. A downward trend is characterized by lower and lower peaks and lower and lower troughs.

Determining a Trading Range

A trading range (or sideways trend) occurs when peaks and troughs appear roughly at the same levels. A trading range is also known as a **consolidation**, a **congestion area**, or a **rectangle formation**.

When prices have been rising and then reverse downward, the highest point in the rise is known as the **resistance point**. A **resistance zone** occurs when more than one resistance point occurs at roughly the same price level. A **support point** occurs when prices have been falling and then reverse upward. When more than one support point occurs at roughly the same price level, a **support zone** is formed.

The concept of support and resistance presumes that in the future prices will stop at these levels or zones. Some ways of determining important reversal points are the DeMark or Williams method, the percentage method, the Gann two-day swing method, and the high volume method. Support lines are drawn by drawing a horizontal line connecting price troughs. Resistance lines are drawn by connecting price peaks.

How Do Analysts Use Trading Ranges?

Trading within a range is difficult. Trading costs can be high, and execution levels can be difficult to determine. If the trading range is tipped at an angle, a **channel** is formed. One can trade channels in the direction of the trend.

Trading ranges represent a struggle between buyers and sellers. A breakout from a trading range is an indication of whether buyers or sellers have gained power. A breakout is a powerful signal.

Directional Trends (Up and Down)

Although you can use mathematical techniques, such as linear regression analysis, to spot trends, the oldest and easiest method is visual inspection of a stock chart. To draw an upward sloping trend line, you connect support reversal points with a straight line. You draw downward sloping trend lines by connecting resistance reversal points.

An accelerating trend line occurs when subsequent upward trend lines have steeper and steeper slopes. This indicates an increasingly steep rise in prices and is unsustainable. Decelerating trend lines, known as **fan lines**, occur when upward subsequent upward sloping trend lines become flatter and flatter. This indicates that prices are rising but at a slower and slower rate.

The longer a trend line exists, the more significant it is when the line is finally broken. Also, the more times a trend line has been touched by a reversal point, the more significant the break will be. Steeper trend lines seem to be broken sooner than flatter trend lines.

A **channel** exists when, in an uptrend, a line connecting the peak reversal points is parallel to the upward sloping trend line that connects the support reversal points, and during a downtrend, a channel exists when a line connecting the trough reversal points is parallel to the downward sloping trend line connecting the peak reversal points. Price movement is contained within the channel and bounces back and forth between the parallel lines. An **internal trend line** is a line drawn through trending price action such that a large number of minor reversals touch the line from above and below. A **retracement** refers to corrections to the principal trend. In an uptrend, retracements periodically interrupt the upward trend. When, after a downward breakout, price retraces quickly back up to the breakout zone a **pullback** occurs. A **throwback** occurs when, after an upward breakout, price quickly retraces back down to the breakout zone.

Other Types of Trend Lines

Trend lines may be drawn between successive lows or highs in point-and-figure charts. In the three-box reversal method, trend lines are drawn at 45-degree angles. **Bullish support lines** are drawn at a 45-degree angle from the lowest low, and **bearish resistance lines** are drawn at a 45-degree angle from the last peak.

Speed lines are created in an uptrend by taking the low point of the advance and the high point and creating a box whereby the low point is the lower-left corner and the high point is the upper-right corner. Horizontal lines are then drawn to divide the box into thirds and a horizontal line is drawn to divide the box in half. Then, three upward sloping lines are drawn, each connecting the lower-left corner of the box with the point where one of the horizontal lines intersects the right-hand side of the box. These lines are extended into the future and serve as natural levels of support.

Andrews pitchfork, in a downtrend, takes (1) the earliest high, (2) the next minor low, and (3) the first major retracement high. A line is drawn between (2) and (3). The halfway point on that line is marked. A trend line is then drawn from (1) through the halfway point mark and extended on into the future. Two lines, parallel to this trend line, are drawn, one from (2) and the other from (3).

Key Concepts and Vocabulary

A number of terms and concepts that might be new to you appear in this chapter. As you read through this chapter, pay close attention to the following terms and concepts. Write down a definition or explanation for each.

Trading range

Peak

Trough

DeMark or Williams method

Gann two-day swing method

Fractal

Support

Resistance

Channel

Fan lines

Internal trend line

Retracement

Pullback

Throwback

Bullish support line

Bearish support line

Speed lines

Andrews pitchfork

Reversal point

Practice and Application

This chapter contains a number of basic concepts integral to the practice of technical analysis. Visual recognition of some of these concepts on a stock chart is an important skill. Use the following space to draw a sketch of what these concepts might look like on a chart.

Concept	Sketch	Notes
Uptrend		
Downtrend		
Peak		

Concept	Sketch	Notes
Trough		
Trading Range (with support and resistance labeled)		
Upward Breakout from a Trading Range		

Concept	Sketch	Notes
Downward Breakout from a Trading Range		
Pullback		
Throwback		

End-of-Chapter Review Questions

1. *Explain what the term* trading range *means. Why is it hard for a trader to make money when the market is in a trading range?*

   A trading range occurs when price is in a sideways trend. Its bounds are horizontal. Consecutive peaks occur at approximately the same price level as do consecutive troughs. Price oscillates back and forth between these two price bounds. It is difficult to make money in a trading range for several reasons. First, it is difficult to recognize a trading range until it has been in existence for some time. Operating costs, such as commissions and slippage, are often too high to profit from range trading. Exact prices for order execution and the placement for a protective stop-loss order are difficult to determine.

2. *What does the term* support *mean? How is support generally drawn on a chart?*

   Support is a level at which price has reversed upward. This level is expected to halt future declines at the same level. Thus, support is like a floor that "supports" prices. Support is drawn with a horizontal line through a trough reversal point and extended into the future as well as the past. The past is to see how often price has halted at this price before and thus to determine the strength of the support. The future is to estimate where price can be expected to halt in the future.

3. *What does the term* resistance *mean? How is resistance generally drawn on a chart?*

   Resistance is a level at which price has reversed downward. This level is expected to halt future advances at the same level. Thus, support is like a ceiling that "resists" prices from advancing. Resistance is drawn with a horizontal line through a peak reversal point and extended into the future as well as the past. The past is to see how often price has halted at this price before and thus to determine the strength of the resistance. The future is to estimate where price can be expected to halt in the future.

4. *Explain the psychology behind support and resistance levels.*

   A support level is one in which buyers come in to stop any further price drop. A number of reasons could cause someone to want to buy a stock after it drops to a particular price. Players who sold short at a higher price might start buying to capture profits. Those who had previously thought about purchasing the stock but missed out as the price rose now see a chance to buy. Those who sold at the price before but then saw the price go higher see this as a chance to reenter their position and gain as the price again moves higher.

5. *Jonathon is watching the stock of his favorite company trade in a congestion area. He is watching closely for a breakout to jump into the market. He says he does not want to miss the breakout, but he is cautious not to assume a breakout prematurely.*

   a. *Why do you think Jonathon is sitting on the sidelines while the stock is trading in the congestion area?*

      Making money during a trading range is extremely difficult. Because support and resistance are often zones and not exact prices, determining an execution price can be difficult. Slippage and commission costs can be high, eating away potential profits.

b. *How might Jonathon recognize a breakout?*

Jonathon would be looking for a drop in price below the support zone or a rise in price above the resistance zone. Jonathon may want to make sure that the price closes below support or above resistance rather than just watching for an intraday break.

c. *Explain the trade-off Jonathon is facing about being cautious regarding prematurely assuming a breakout, but at the same time being careful not to miss the breakout.*

The trade-off Jonathon faces is between receiving an early, lower entry price with a higher risk of the breakout being false versus a later, and perhaps higher entry price, with more confidence that the breakout is valid.

6. *Below is a daily bar chart for MSFT for April 28, 1999–June 30, 1999. Much of this chart represents a trading range area.*

   a. *Make a photocopy of this chart and mark the peaks and troughs on the chart.[1]*

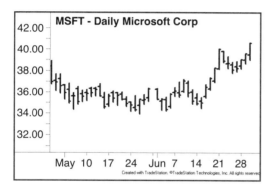

Peaks are marked with a down arrow and troughs are marked with up arrows.

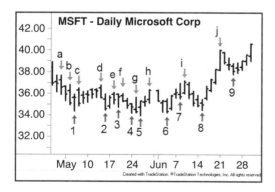

---

1. The prices in this chart are not identical to the prices presented in *Technical Analysis: The Complete Resource for Financial Market Technicians*. These differences are due to stock splits and dividends that have occurred since 1999. However, the same price pattern exists; thus, peaks and troughs occur on the same days.

b. *Which of the peaks and troughs that you marked fulfill the two-bar reversal point criterion?*

Two-bar reversal peaks occur at d, e, h, i, and j, where the two bars before and after the peak bar have lower highs.

Two-bar reversal troughs occur at 1, 2, 5, 6, 8, and 9, where the two bars before and after the trough bar have higher lows.

c. *Which of the peaks and troughs that you marked fulfill the Gann two-day swing criterion?*

Gann two-day swing peaks occur at a, b, d, h, i, and j where a peak bar is followed by two bars with lower lows than the peak bar.

Gann two-day swing troughs occur at 1, 4, 5, 6, 7, 8, and 9, where a trough bar is followed by two bars with higher highs than the trough bar.

d. *Draw support and resistance lines (or zones) on the graph.*

Using the two-day reversal bars as support and resistance levels and combining the outer levels into zone, they are plotted in the attached chart.

e. *When does a breakout from the trading range occur?*

A false upward breakout occurs at a point when the higher bound (at that time) of the resistance zone is penetrated with a bar close. This is quickly invalidated when the price declines back into the zone and produces a specialist breakout reversal by breaking below the breakout bar low. The upward breakout at point b turns out to be real with a series of closing prices above the upper bound of the resistance zone. Notice also the throwback several days after the breakout back to the upper bound of the earlier resistance zone.

7. Using the data that you gathered and the graphs that you created in Chapter 11, "History and Construction of Charts," for VLO (September, 2007–September, 2010), find the following items:

    a. Find a period of congestion on the graph. What were the levels of support and resistance during this trading range? In what direction did a breakout occur? What story does this breakout tell about the war between buyers and sellers?

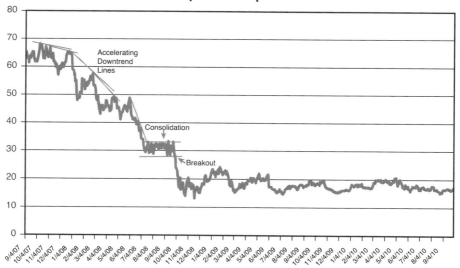

VLO Daily Line Chart
Arithmetic Scale
Sept 2007-Sept 2010

VLO experienced congestion, or trading range, during July and August of 2008. Price oscillated between about 29 and 32. VLO broke down through support at the end of September and began a downtrend. At this point, sellers became more powerful than buyers.

b. *Locate a period when an accelerating uptrend occurs on the graph. When does a reversal occur?*

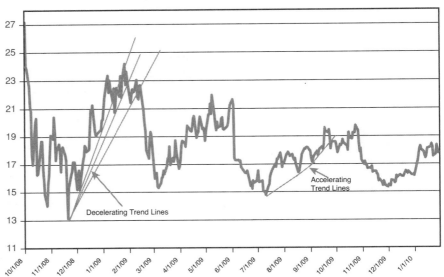

VLO Daily
October 2008-January 2010

The previous chart highlights the October 2008 through January 2010 period of the original chart so that the uptrends can be seen more easily. Accelerating trend lines occurred from July 2009 through September 2009. By the end of October, a downtrend began when the final upward trend line was penetrated.

c. *Locate a period when a decelerating uptrend occurs on the graph. When does a reversal occur?*

Decelerating trend lines, known as fan lines, occurred during the December 2008 through February 2009 time period. By mid-February a reversal had occurred, and price was trending downward when the third upward fan line was penetrated.

d. *Find a period on the graph when the major trend is upward, but a retracement occurs.*

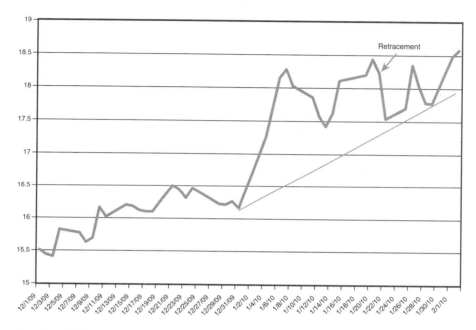

The chart highlights price movement from December 2009 through January 2010. Overall, price was in an uptrend. However, the price did not move up in a straight line. The price downturn of about $1 occurred around January 21 and 22.

Self-Test

1. *A downtrend is characterized by*

    a. Lower and lower peaks, and higher and higher troughs.

    b. Lower and lower peaks, and lower and lower troughs.

    c. Higher and higher peaks, and higher and higher troughs.

    d. Higher and higher peaks, and lower and lower troughs.

2. *Which of the following is TRUE regarding an uptrend?*

    a. An uptrend displays that buyers are more eager than sellers.

    b. An uptrend displays that sellers are more eager than buyers.

    c. An uptrend is characterized by higher peaks and lower troughs.

    d. An uptrend is characterized by lower peaks and higher troughs.

3. *When price oscillates between two parallel upward sloping lines, one connecting peaks and the other connecting troughs, _____ is formed.*

   a. An internal trend line

   b. A Gann line

   c. Pullback/throwback pattern

   d. Channel

4. *Between January and May, TGT had been in a trading range, oscillating back and forth between 50 and 53. In May, TGT broke out to the upside, hit 56, and then quickly returned to 53, before continuing an upward trend. TGT experienced a*

   a. Throwback.

   b. Pullback.

   c. Support bump.

   d. Internal resistance breakdown.

5. *An upward sloping 45-degree trend line on a three-box reversal point-and-figure chart is known as a*

   a. Bullish support line.

   b. Bullish resistance line.

   c. Speed line.

   d. Fan line.

6. *Which of the following is a TRUE statement regarding trend lines?*

   a. The longer a trend line is in play, the less significant is a break in the trend line.

   b. The more times a trend line has been touched by prices, the more significant is a break in the trend line.

   c. The flatter a trend line is, the sooner it will be broken.

   d. Using closing prices, rather than intraday prices, increases the chance of a false breakout from a trend line.

7. *Which of the following are synonyms for a sideways trend?*

   a. Consolidation, trading range, congestion area, rectangle formation

   b. Channel, fan range, trading range

   c. Accelerating range, rectangle formation, channel

   d. Non-trading range, congestion area, channel, rectangle formation

8. *A fan line is*

   a. An accelerating trend line.

   b. A decelerating trend line.

   c. The trend line that connects prices within a channel.

   d. An internal trend line that connects retracements.

9. *A smaller trend that runs counter to the principal trend is known as*

   a. A fan line.

   b. An internal trend line.

   c. A resistance line.

   d. A retracement.

10. *FOSL had been in a trading range over the past six months, oscillating back and forth between $120 and $140 a share. Today, the price fell to $90. Nathan had been sitting on the sidelines watching FOSL, but now jumps in and takes a short position in FOSL. Nathan is practicing*

    a. Breakout trading.

    b. Range trading.

    c. Channel trading.

    d. Gann trading.

CHAPTER 13

Breakouts, Stops, and Retracements

Chapter Objectives

By the end of this chapter, you should

- ▶ Understand what a breakout is
- ▶ Be familiar with the major methods of identifying a breakout
- ▶ Be familiar with the purpose of entry and exit stops
- ▶ Be familiar with the major methods of setting entry and exit stops

Chapter Summary

Breakouts

A **breakout** occurs when a price breaks through a support or resistance level or through a trend line. After the support level, resistance level, or trend line has been penetrated, the breakout must be confirmed to make sure a false breakout hasn't occurred. One way to confirm a breakout is to wait until the price closes beyond the penetration point. Another confirmation method is to establish a breakout zone either a certain number or fraction of points or percentage beyond the breakout level. Or, confirmation can occur if price remains beyond the breakout level for a certain period of time. A breakout that occurs on heavy volume is more likely to be a real breakout. Because some stocks are more volatile than others, a filter rule, based on the stock's volatility, also can be useful to confirm breakouts.

Stops

A **stop order** is an order to buy or sell a security when a specific price has been reached. A **buy stop** is an order to buy a security at a specified price higher than the current price. A **sell stop** is an order to sell a security at a specified price less than the current price when reached.

Stops can be used to enter a position. For example, you can use a buy stop to trigger a purchase if a breakout above resistance occurs. You can use a sell stop to trigger to sell short if a breakout through support occurs. You can also use a stop to exit a position. **Protective stops** protect capital from further loss. **Trailing stops** protect a profit from deteriorating into a loss.

Key Concepts and Vocabulary

A number of terms and concepts that might be new to you appear in this chapter. As you read through this chapter, pay close attention to the following terms and concepts. Write down a definition or explanation for each.

Breakout

Average true range

Pivot points

Buy stop

Sell stop

Protective stop

Trailing stop

Gap

Money stop

Time stop

Filter

Entry

Exit

Specialist breakout

End-of-Chapter Review Questions

1. *Explain what is meant by the term* whipsaw. *What could cause an investor to experience a lot of whipsaws?*

   A whipsaw occurs when an investor buys a security, the security price falls, and the investor sells the security at a loss. Then, the security price goes higher than the original price, as the investor had originally thought the price would. The investor's original opinion was correct and would have been profitable if the investor remained in the position; however, because of the initial price movement, the investor lost money. An investor can experience a lot of whipsaws by placing protective stops too close to a position's entry price. Stops placed too close to an entry price do not allow for enough price movement; a small, temporary move to the downside triggers the stop and removes the investor from the position at a loss.

2. The daily open, high, low, and close for two stocks, Biosite Inc. (BSTE) and Coca-Cola (KO), for April 15–May 13, 2005 are given in the following table.

   a. Calculate the five-day ATR for the two stocks for this time period.

   b. Compare the volatility of the two stocks given the ATR.

   c. How would these ATRs impact the filter you would want to use for a breakout for each of these stocks?

	KO				BSTE			
Date	Open	High	Low	Close	Open	High	Low	Close
15-Apr-05	42.08	42.13	41.15	41.29	58.65	60.26	58.18	58.35
18-Apr-05	41.12	41.33	40.74	40.97	58.33	58.81	57.52	58.42
19-Apr-05	42.7	42.92	42.06	42.4	58.33	59.92	58.14	59.82
20-Apr-05	42.52	42.55	41.63	41.88	60	60.85	58.97	59.3
21-Apr-05	42.3	42.3	41.74	41.98	59.4	60.89	59.29	60.8
22-Apr-05	41.95	42.56	41.89	42.13	58.03	62.5	58	58.89
25-Apr-05	42.43	42.73	42.11	42.68	59.51	60.2	59.09	59.77
26-Apr-05	42.68	43.31	42.6	42.96	59.35	59.69	58.15	58.4
27-Apr-05	42.89	42.95	42.48	42.82	58.55	58.55	57.15	57.75
28-Apr-05	42.63	42.92	42.62	42.69	58.04	58.04	55.99	55.99
29-Apr-05	42.71	43.5	42.6	43.44	56.46	57	55.45	57
2-May-05	43.49	43.62	43.24	43.57	56.61	56.85	55.76	56.64
3-May-05	43.57	44.02	43.52	43.76	56.78	57.06	56.01	56.26
4-May-05	43.98	44.24	43.69	43.93	56.56	57.82	56.55	57.61
5-May-05	43.78	44.24	43.76	44.15	57.59	57.96	56.81	57.42
6-May-05	44.22	44.53	44.1	44.19	57.87	57.99	56.11	56.76
9-May-05	44.2	44.6	44.1	44.57	56.65	57.7	56.27	57.47
10-May-05	44.12	44.41	44.02	44.23	57.18	57.65	57	57.21
11-May-05	44.13	44.32	43.79	44.27	57.01	57.37	55.9	56.73
12-May-05	44.17	44.75	43.75	44.17	56.7	57.87	56.51	57.65
13-May-05	44.47	44.47	43.87	44.11	57.52	58.26	56.91	57.58

a.

KO

Date	Open	High	Low	Close	Current Bar High – Current Bar Low	Abs Value of (Prior Bar Close – Current Bar High)	Abs Value of (Prior Bar Close – Current Bar Low)	True Range	5-Day ATR
15-Apr-05	42.08	42.13	41.15	41.29					
18-Apr-05	41.12	41.33	40.74	40.97	0.59	0.04	0.55	0.59	
19-Apr-05	42.7	42.92	42.06	42.4	0.86	1.95	1.09	1.95	
20-Apr-05	42.52	42.55	41.63	41.88	0.92	0.15	0.77	0.92	
21-Apr-05	42.3	42.3	41.74	41.98	0.56	0.42	0.14	0.56	
22-Apr-05	41.95	42.56	41.89	42.13	0.67	0.58	0.09	0.67	0.938
25-Apr-05	42.43	42.73	42.11	42.68	0.62	0.6	0.02	0.62	0.944
26-Apr-05	42.68	43.31	42.6	42.96	0.71	0.63	0.08	0.71	0.696
27-Apr-05	42.89	42.95	42.48	42.82	0.47	0.01	0.48	0.48	0.608
28-Apr-05	42.63	42.92	42.62	42.69	0.3	0.1	0.2	0.3	0.556
29-Apr-05	42.71	43.5	42.6	43.44	0.9	0.81	0.09	0.9	0.602
2-May-05	43.49	43.62	43.24	43.57	0.38	0.18	0.2	0.38	0.554
3-May-05	43.57	44.02	43.52	43.76	0.5	0.45	0.05	0.5	0.512
4-May-05	43.98	44.24	43.69	43.93	0.55	0.48	0.07	0.55	0.526
5-May-05	43.78	44.24	43.76	44.15	0.48	0.31	0.17	0.48	0.562
6-May-05	44.22	44.53	44.1	44.19	0.43	0.38	0.05	0.43	0.468
9-May-05	44.2	44.6	44.1	44.57	0.5	0.41	0.09	0.5	0.492
10-May-05	44.12	44.41	44.02	44.23	0.39	0.16	0.55	0.55	0.502
11-May-05	44.13	44.32	43.79	44.27	0.53	0.09	0.44	0.53	0.498
12-May-05	44.17	44.75	43.75	44.17	1	0.48	0.52	1	0.602
13-May-05	44.47	44.47	43.87	44.11	0.6	0.3	0.3	0.6	0.636

BSTE

Date	Open	High	Low	Close	Current Bar High – Current Bar Low	Abs Value of (Prior Bar Close – Current Bar High)	Abs Value of (Prior Bar Close – Current Bar Low)	True Range	5-Day ATR
15-Apr-05	58.65	60.26	58.18	58.35					
18-Apr-05	58.33	58.81	57.52	58.42	1.29	0.46	0.83	1.29	
19-Apr-05	58.33	59.92	58.14	59.82	1.78	1.5	0.28	1.78	
20-Apr-05	60	60.85	58.97	59.3	1.88	1.03	0.85	1.88	
21-Apr-05	59.4	60.89	59.29	60.8	1.6	1.59	0.01	1.6	
22-Apr-05	58.03	62.5	58	58.89	4.5	1.7	2.8	4.5	2.21
25-Apr-05	59.51	60.2	59.09	59.77	1.11	1.31	0.2	1.31	2.214
26-Apr-05	59.35	59.69	58.15	58.4	1.54	0.08	1.62	1.62	2.182
27-Apr-05	58.55	58.55	57.15	57.75	1.4	0.15	1.25	1.4	2.086
28-Apr-05	58.04	58.04	55.99	55.99	2.05	0.29	1.76	2.05	2.176
29-Apr-05	56.46	57	55.45	57	1.55	1.01	0.54	1.55	1.586
2-May-05	56.61	56.85	55.76	56.64	1.09	0.15	1.24	1.24	1.572
3-May-05	56.78	57.06	56.01	56.26	1.05	0.42	0.63	1.05	1.458
4-May-05	56.56	57.82	56.55	57.61	1.27	1.56	0.29	1.56	1.49
5-May-05	57.59	57.96	56.81	57.42	1.15	0.35	0.8	1.15	1.31
6-May-05	57.87	57.99	56.11	56.76	1.88	0.57	1.31	1.88	1.376
9-May-05	56.65	57.7	56.27	57.47	1.43	0.94	0.49	1.43	1.414
10-May-05	57.18	57.65	57	57.21	0.65	0.18	0.47	0.65	1.334
11-May-05	57.01	57.37	55.9	56.73	1.47	0.16	1.31	1.47	1.316
12-May-05	56.7	57.87	56.51	57.65	1.36	1.14	0.22	1.36	1.358
13-May-05	57.52	58.26	56.91	57.58	1.35	0.61	0.74	1.35	1.252

b. The ATR is a measure of the price volatility of a security. When comparing the ATR between stocks, you should use a percentage of the ATR to the current price to display the comparable figures. The raw ATR is specific only to the specific stock. BSTE has a higher ATR percent (2.17%) than KO (1.44%), meaning that BSTE typically has more variation in price than does KO.

c. Because BSTE has a larger ATR percent, a larger price move would be necessary to confirm a breakout for BSTE than for KO. With an ATR percent in the 1.4% range for KO, a 1.4% price move would be a normal move. A move in KO of 4.2% would be about three times the normal price move and would be a significant move. However, a price move of 4.2% in BSTE would be only twice the price move expected in a normal day. Also, you see a decline in the ATR for BSTE during the April through May period. Because of the higher ATR in April, a larger move in BSTE in April versus in May would be necessary for the move to be considered significant.

3. Using the same data that you used in Question 2, calculate the daily pivot points for the two stocks. Explain how these results can be used to determine points of resistance and support or breakouts.

KO

Date	Open	High	Low	Close	Pivot Point = (Previous High + Previous Low + Previous Close)/3	R1 = (2XP) − Previous Low	S1 = (2XP) − Previous High	R2 = (P + Previous High − Previous Low)	S2 = (P − Previous High + Previous Low)
15-Apr-05	42.08	42.13	41.15	41.29					
18-Apr-05	41.12	41.33	40.74	40.97	41.52	41.90	40.92	42.50	40.72
19-Apr-05	42.7	42.92	42.06	42.4	41.01	41.29	40.70	41.60	42.60
20-Apr-05	42.52	42.55	41.63	41.88	42.46	42.86	42.00	43.32	42.09
21-Apr-05	42.3	42.3	41.74	41.98	42.02	42.41	41.49	42.94	41.77
22-Apr-05	41.95	42.56	41.89	42.13	42.01	42.27	41.71	42.57	42.27
25-Apr-05	42.43	42.73	42.11	42.68	42.19	42.50	41.83	42.86	42.36
26-Apr-05	42.68	43.31	42.6	42.96	42.51	42.90	42.28	43.13	43.09
27-Apr-05	42.89	42.95	42.48	42.82	42.96	43.31	42.60	43.67	42.60
28-Apr-05	42.63	42.92	42.62	42.69	42.75	43.02	42.55	43.22	42.72
29-Apr-05	42.71	43.5	42.6	43.44	42.74	42.87	42.57	43.04	43.32
2-May-05	43.49	43.62	43.24	43.57	43.18	43.76	42.86	44.08	43.30
3-May-05	43.57	44.02	43.52	43.76	43.48	43.71	43.33	43.86	43.88
4-May-05	43.98	44.24	43.69	43.93	43.77	44.01	43.51	44.27	43.99
5-May-05	43.78	44.24	43.76	44.15	43.95	44.22	43.67	44.50	43.95
6-May-05	44.22	44.53	44.1	44.19	44.05	44.34	43.86	44.53	44.34
9-May-05	44.2	44.6	44.1	44.57	44.27	44.45	44.02	44.70	44.34
10-May-05	44.12	44.41	44.02	44.23	44.42	44.75	44.25	44.92	44.23
11-May-05	44.13	44.32	43.79	44.27	44.22	44.42	44.03	44.61	44.13
12-May-05	44.17	44.75	43.75	44.17	44.13	44.46	43.93	44.66	44.56
13-May-05	44.47	44.47	43.87	44.11	44.22	44.70	43.70	45.22	43.94

BSTE

Date	Open	High	Low	Close	Pivot Point = (Previous High + Previous Low + Previous Close)/3	R1 = (2XP) - Previous Low	S1 = (2XP) - Previous High	R2 = (P + Previous High - Previous Low)	S2 = (P - Previous High + Previous Low)
15-Apr-05	58.65	60.26	58.18	58.35					
18-Apr-05	58.33	58.81	57.52	58.42	58.93	59.68	57.60	61.01	57.48
19-Apr-05	58.33	59.92	58.14	59.82	58.25	58.98	57.69	59.54	59.36
20-Apr-05	60	60.85	58.97	59.3	59.29	60.45	58.67	61.07	60.22
21-Apr-05	59.4	60.89	59.29	60.8	59.71	60.44	58.56	61.59	59.75
22-Apr-05	58.03	62.5	58	58.89	60.33	61.36	59.76	61.93	61.94
25-Apr-05	59.51	60.2	59.09	59.77	59.80	61.59	57.09	64.30	57.50
26-Apr-05	59.35	59.69	58.15	58.4	59.69	60.28	59.17	60.80	59.18
27-Apr-05	58.55	58.55	57.15	57.75	58.75	59.34	57.80	60.29	57.61
28-Apr-05	58.04	58.04	55.99	55.99	57.82	58.48	57.08	59.22	57.31
29-Apr-05	56.46	57	55.45	57	56.67	57.36	55.31	58.72	55.63
2-May-05	56.61	56.85	55.76	56.64	56.48	57.52	55.97	58.03	56.33
3-May-05	56.78	57.06	56.01	56.26	56.42	57.07	55.98	57.51	56.63
4-May-05	56.56	57.82	56.55	57.61	56.44	56.88	55.83	57.49	57.20
5-May-05	57.59	57.96	56.81	57.42	57.33	58.10	56.83	58.60	57.47
6-May-05	57.87	57.99	56.11	56.76	57.40	57.98	56.83	58.55	57.43
9-May-05	56.65	57.7	56.27	57.47	56.95	57.80	55.92	58.83	56.66
10-May-05	57.18	57.65	57	57.21	57.15	58.02	56.59	58.58	57.10
11-May-05	57.01	57.37	55.9	56.73	57.29	57.57	56.92	57.94	57.01
12-May-05	56.7	57.87	56.51	57.65	56.67	57.43	55.96	58.14	57.17
13-May-05	57.52	58.26	56.91	57.58	57.34	58.18	56.82	58.70	57.73

The pivot point technique determines support and resistance levels based solely on the previous day's prices. The idea is that over time the effect of previous prices diminishes. April 29 is an example of resistance defined by the pivot point technique being broken. R1 for the day was 42.87 and R2 was 43.04. Price hit 43.5 intraday and closed at 43.44, higher than both R1 and R2. Thus, an upward break through resistance was confirmed by the pivot point technique.

4. *Explain why, during an uptrend, an investor would want to use trailing stops rather than setting one constant stop level.*

Trailing stops are used to help protect profits that have been accumulated. For example, suppose that you initially purchased a stock at $20, thinking that an uptrend had begun. At first, you would want a protective stop, in case you were incorrect about an uptrend beginning. As the trend continues, however, price has moved further and further from $20. If the price is now at $30, you have gained $10. You don't want to wait until price falls back to $20 or below to be stopped out of your position and lose all of your profits. You might set your stop at $27, locking in $7 of your profits but continuing your long position to ride the trend up more if it continues. If the trend does continue up, and price reaches $35, you would want to move your stop closer to $35 to lock in more of your profits.

5. *Explain the advantages and disadvantages of using time stops and money stops.*

Time stops are exit stops that you use to close a position after a predetermined period of time. The longer you look into the future, the less accurate your projections are. Whenever you have entered a position, the longer that time goes on without a profitable reaction to the position, the higher are the chances that the entered position will be unprofitable. Time stops are useful in that they provide for removal of capital from an investment after a predetermined amount of time, freeing up the capital for other investments. Their disadvantage is that they ignore price movements, the information the price movements provide, and can exit a position prematurely when the trend lasts a long time. Time stops are usually considered when one is testing a buy or sell strategy to measure similar outcomes not affected by the strategy itself or any other.

Money stops are based on the risk an investor is willing to take in terms of money. A money stop is based upon not only price movement but also the number of shares purchased. They are helpful in preventing a large loss of capital. However, using money stops can create a large number of whipsaws. If a large number of shares are purchased, a small change in price can lead to the triggering of a money stop.

Self-Test

1. *A protective stop is used to*

   a. Protect profits that have been earned from deteriorating.

   b. Protect capital from a large loss.

   c. Enter a long position when a breakout through resistance occurs.

   d. Enter a long position when a breakout through support occurs.

2. *A breakout through resistance is a sign that*

   a. Buyers have become more aggressive and are bidding up the price.

   b. Sellers have become more aggressive and are bidding up the price.

   c. Buyers have become more aggressive and are driving down the price.

   d. Sellers have become more aggressive and are driving down the price.

3. *When a breakout occurs, an analyst often waits until the close*

   a. Hoping to receive a better price than the breakout price.

   b. In order to avoid the high-volume trading and market confusion that often occurs on a breakout.

   c. In order to capture the large price moves that occur in after-hours trading as others realize a breakout has occurred.

   d. To confirm that the intraday price move was a real breakout.

4. *Howard has seen VZ in a trading range, oscillating between $37 and $41 a share over the past two months. Today he sees price break through the resistance level of $41 but waits until the price increases to $42.20, about 3% higher than the breakout level, before he enters a long position. Howard is using*

   a. A percentage filter rule to confirm the breakout.

   b. A protective stop to protect his capital.

   c. A trailing stop to confirm the breakout.

   d. The pivot point technique to confirm the breakout and protect his capital.

5. *Average True Range (ATR)*

   a. Is a measure of volatility based solely on the price of the security.

   b. Confirms a breakout by comparing the security's standard deviation to that of a market proxy.

   c. Determines support and resistance levels by comparing one day's range in price with that of a market proxy.

   d. Confirms a breakout by comparing the current price to an exponential moving average of price.

6. *The pivot point technique is used to confirm a breakout by considering*

   a. The average price of the security over the past 30 bars.

   b. The standard deviation of the security's price.

   c. The volatility of the security relative to the volatility of a market proxy.

   d. The high, low, and close for the security on the previous trading day.

7. *If a price is approaching a resistance level above which a new trend is expected to develop,*

   a. A buy stop order could be placed to be triggered if the resistance level is penetrated in a breakout.

   b. A sell stop order could be placed to be triggered if the resistance level is penetrated in a breakout.

   c. A trailing stop could be used to prevent a whipsaw effect.

   d. A sell stop order could be used in conjunction with a protective stop to protect the profits that have been accumulating during the trading range.

8. *Irene purchased CLX at $55 when she thought an uptrend was beginning. A trend was indeed beginning as CLX is now trading at $65. A trailing stop*

   a. Would move against the trend in this case.

   b. Would be lowered as time increases because Irene's trade has proved to be profitable.

   c. Would move up as the price trended upward, remaining close to the price action.

   d. Would not be adjusted as price changes occurred.

9. *Which of the following is an example of a "whipsaw"?*

   a. Thinking he sees a break through resistance, Jared purchases CROX at $20 and places a $19.50 protective stop. CROX quickly falls to $19.40, triggering Jared's stop. Later that day CROX is selling for $22.

   b. Karen purchases KKD at $6; the stock quickly rises to $7 and Karen sells. Then, Karen enters a short position at $7. The stock falls to $6.20 and Karen closes her short position.

   c. Omar purchases DAL at $10; the stock rises to $12 and Omar sells. DAL then falls to $9 and Omar purchases the stock again.

   d. Betty purchased XOM at $80. XOM fluctuated between $79 and $81 for a week, with no strong directional movement. Betty had a one-week stop. When the stop was triggered, XOM was selling for $80.01, so after commissions and transaction costs, Betty lost a little on the trade.

10. *Which of the following increases the chance of a trader experiencing a whipsaw?*

    a. Using a close filter to confirm a breakout

    b. Using a volume filter to confirm a breakout

    c. Placing a protective stop too close to the entry price upon a breakout

    d. Placing a protective stop too far away from the entry price upon a breakout

CHAPTER 14

Moving Averages

Chapter Objectives

By the end of this chapter, you should

▶ Be aware of how moving averages are used to identify trends

▶ Be able to calculate a simple moving average

▶ Be able to calculate an exponential moving average

▶ Be familiar with the concept of directional movement

▶ Be familiar with the construction of envelopes, bands, and price channels

Chapter Summary

What Is a Moving Average?

A **moving average** is a constant period average, usually of prices, that is calculated for each successive chart period interval. The result, when plotted, is a smooth line representing successive average prices. Moving averages are one of the oldest tools used by technical analysts and are used to smooth erratic data, making it easier to view the true underlying trend.

How Is a Simple Moving Average Calculated?

The **simple moving average** (SMA) is also known as an **arithmetic moving average**. The SMA is calculated by adding a set of data and then dividing by the number of observations.

A rising moving average indicates an upward trend and a falling moving average indicates a downward trend. A moving average is a lagging indicator because it helps us discern a trend after a trend has begun. A longer moving average is slower to pick up trend changes but less likely to falsely indicate a trend change due to a short-term blip in the data.

What Other Types of Moving Averages Are Used?

The **linearly weighted moving average** (LWMA) weights more recent data more heavily than earlier data. For example, in a 10-day LWMA, the most recent day's price is weighted 10 times more heavily than the first day's price 10 days previous.

Both the SMA and the LWMA suffer from the **drop-off effect**, the effect on the moving average when data from earlier observations is removed from the calculation. In order to avoid the complete ignoring of earlier observation, some analysts use an **exponential moving average**. Generally, in an exponential moving average, the most recent observation has twice the weight it would have in an SMA of equal length. You can calculate moving averages by other methods, such as the Wilder method, or in ways in which the weight of the most recent data is adjusted based on the volatility of the price data. You use geometric moving averages (GMA) most often in indexes. The triangular moving average is a doubly smoothed moving average, created by taking the moving average of a moving average.

Strategies for Using Moving Averages

You can use moving averages as a measure of trend by comparing the present price to the moving average. If a stock is higher than its moving average, the trend is considered upward; if a stock is lower than its moving average, the trend is considered downward.

The moving average also acts as support and resistance, often duplicating a trend line. In addition, deviations from the moving average are indicators of price extremes. Reversion to the average is common in stock prices; a price that is far away from the moving average will probably move back toward it. Some analysts use moving averages to give specific signals. Signals can occur when prices cross a moving average and when one moving average crosses another moving average.

What Is Directional Movement?

The concept of directional movement is based on comparing a stock's trading range for one day, or bar, with the trading range on the previous day to measure trend. **Positive directional movement (+DM)** occurs when the high for a day exceeds the high for the previous day. **Negative directional movement (–DM)** occurs when the low for the day is less than the low for the previous day. If one day's price movement is completely contained within the previous day's price movement, no directional movement occurs that day. If the previous day's range is completely within the current day's range, resulting in both the current day's high being higher than the previous day's and the current day's low being lower than the previous day's, then only the +DM or –DM that has the largest absolute value is recorded.

To calculate the Directional Movement Index +DI, we take the sum of the +DMs over 14 days, called the DM_{14}, and divide it by the 14-day sum of the True Ranges (TR), called the TR_{14}. After the first calculation, the next $+DM_{14}$ is calculated by taking the previous day's $+DM_{14}$, subtracting from it the previous day's quotient of $+DM_{14}$ divided by 14, and adding the current $+DM_1$. This process is also repeated with the TR to result in the day's TR_{14}. Each day the $+DM_{14}$ is divided by the $+TR_{14}$ to get the +DI for that day. The same process is used to calculate the –DI using the –DMs and TRs. When the +DI is greater than the –DI, the trend is upward. Crossovers often signal changes in trend direction, and high peaks signal turning points. The **DX** is the ratio of the difference between the +DI and –DI over the sum of the two DIs. The **ADX** is a moving average of the DX. As the difference increases, the ADX rises, thus indicating the intensity of the trend regardless of direction. A peak in the ADX often signals the end of a trend. Directional movement is applicable to monthly, weekly, and intraday bars..

What Are Envelopes, Channels, and Bands?

Price movement often fluctuates within a band or envelope around the moving average. **Percentage envelopes** are created by taking a percentage of the moving average and plotting it above and below the moving average. This plots two lines around the moving average, forming an envelope within which price can be expected to fluctuate. Movement outside the band becomes the trigger for signals.

Because envelopes are plotted a fixed-percentage away from the moving average, they do not account for the changing volatility of the underlying price. **Bands**, which are similar to envelopes, surround the moving average, but expand during times of increased volatility and contract during times of reduced volatility. Bollinger Bands are generally drawn as two-standard deviations above and two-standard deviations below a 20-bar moving average. When the outer edge of a band is broken, a trend is often beginning in the direction of the breakout. The greater the distance between the bands, the more volatile price is. Low volatility is generally associated with sideways trends, during which whipsaws are common.

Channels are two lines drawn parallel to a trend line to encompass price action. However, the definition can be relaxed so that the lines do not have to be parallel. The Donchian method, for example, creates a horizontal channel based on the highest price level and the lowest price level over the past four weeks.

---

1. In earlier editions of *Technical Analysis: The Complete Resource for Financial Market Technicians*, we used the notation DMI+ and DMI- to refer to +DI and –DI, respectively. Here, we have reverted to +DI and –DI to refer to the directional movement indicators to be consistent with Wilder's original work.

Key Concepts and Vocabulary

A number of terms and concepts that might be new to you appear in this chapter. As you read through this chapter, pay close attention to the following terms and concepts. Write down a definition or explanation for each.

Moving average

Simple moving average

Linearly weighted moving average

Exponential moving average

Drop-off effect

Geometric moving average

Triangular moving average

Exponential moving average

Simple moving average

Directional movement

ADX

+DM

−DM

Envelope

Band

Channel

Bandwidth indicator

End-of-Chapter Review Questions

1. *Explain why a rising moving average indicates an upward trend and a falling moving average indicates a downward trend in stock prices.*

   A moving average is a summary of price movement. The only way that an average can be brought up is for the latest observation to be higher than the average. Thus, a new, higher observation pulls a moving average up, suggesting an upward trend. Likewise lower observations drag a moving average down.

2. *Explain why there is a lag between the time a trend reverses and when the moving average signals this reversal. Why is this lag longer for a 200-day moving average than a 10-day moving average?*

   A moving average is an average of prices over a past period of time. A 10-day moving average is a summary of what happened over the past 10 days. Every 10 days, the average has a complete new set of prices. A 200-day moving average is a summary of what happened over the past 200 days. In 10 days, the 200-day average still has 190 old observations. If the market has changed direction, therefore, the 10-day reflects the change more quickly than the 200-day.

3. *What problems are associated with an SMA that an EMA calculation is designed to overcome?*

    The EMA calculation overcomes two shortcomings of the SMA. First, the SMA weights all observations over the period equally. The most recent observations might be most relevant to future price moves. The EMA puts heavier weight on more recent observations and less weight on earlier observations. Second, the SMA suffers from the **drop-off effect**. The drop-off effect is the impact the deletion of an earlier observation has in the calculation of an SMA. For example, in a 10-day moving average, the observation from 11 days ago is not included in the calculation. The elimination of the observation can cause a change in the SMA due to the omission of an earlier variable rather than to a significant change in the current price. The EMA addresses this issue by maintaining the older information in its calculation.

4. *Explain why a shorter-term moving average is considered to be a "faster" moving average and a longer-term moving average is considered to be a "slower" moving average.*

    A longer-term moving average is considered a slower moving average because it takes longer for it to signal a change in trend than a shorter-term moving average. Because the longer-term moving average weights the current observation less than does the shorter-term moving average, it more slowly reflects changes in the trend.

5. *Sophia says that she is watching a 10-day SMA and a 60-day SMA of her favorite stock, and she is planning to purchase the stock when the 10-day SMA crosses above the 60-day SMA. Explain the rationale for Sophia's strategy.*

    The 10-day SMA is a faster moving average than the 60-day SMA; thus, it spots a change in trend sooner. The 10-day SMA crossing above the 60-day SMA is an indication that prices are moving higher than where they have tended to be over the past 60-days, suggesting an uptrend in price. Just as a single price above a moving average suggests an uptrend, a shorter-period SMA above a longer-period SMA suggests an uptrend.

6. *Thomas warns Sophia that her strategy can easily lead to whipsaws. Explain what Thomas means by* whipsaws, *and describe the type of market in which whipsaws are most likely to occur.*

    Whipsaws occur when the market oscillates quickly over short distances that cause the trader or investor to buy and sell at the wrong time and price, resulting in a series of losses. A whipsaw occurs if Sophia enters a long position; price quickly moves down; she exits the position with a loss; and then price moves back up as she had expected. During a sideways trend, the shorter-term moving average repeatedly crosses above and below the longer-term moving average as price oscillates without any clear uptrend or downtrend. Trading with a moving average crossover system during a sideways trend can result in a number of whipsaw losses.

7. *If Sophia is concerned about whipsaws, how might she use envelopes or bands to minimize the likelihood of whipsaws?*

Whipsaws are common when prices are in a congestion area, bouncing between support and resistance. Sophia can minimize the likelihood of experiencing whipsaws by waiting for a clearer signal that a trend has begun by using envelopes, bands, or filters around a moving average. The envelope, band, or filter contains price movement within its normal oscillation. Waiting for price to break through the band prevents Sophia from trading on every little price change, common during a trading range. After the price breaks through the band or the envelope, Sophia can be more certain that the price movement is significant and a new trend is beginning.

8. *Why is choosing a stock that is trending upward or downward, rather than one that is moving sideways, an important key to trading profitability?*

Money is made by purchasing a stock at a low price and selling it at a high price. Some directional movement in price must occur to be able to purchase a stock at a lower price and sell it at a higher price. If the stock is trending upward, the trader buys the stock and then sells it at a higher price. If the stock is trending downward, the trader sells the stock short and then covers the position by buying the stock later at a lower price. Although it is theoretically possible to make some money during a sideways trend, doing so is very difficult. Transaction costs are high relative to any potential profit, and determining execution prices is problematic.

9. *Explain what Welles Wilder means by the term* directional movement *and how this concept is important to determining price trends.*

Directional movement determines whether a stock is experiencing higher highs or lower lows. If a stock has a higher high today than it did yesterday, then positive directional movement has occurred. Negative directional movement exists whenever today's low is lower than yesterday's low. During an uptrend, a stock's high should be moving higher. During a downtrend, the daily range should be showing lower lows.

10. *Why does a low value for ADX suggest a period of congestion?*

The ADX is a measure of the average difference between the absolute values of the +DI and the –DI. Each of these indicators reflects the direction and strength of a trend, up or down respectively. When the difference widens, one DI is overwhelming the other. The ADX, by measuring the difference, reflects the amount of that domination and thus measures the strength of the existing trend. A low value in the ADX therefore suggests that there is no dominant trend and that prices are directionless in a congestion or trading range.

11. *Gather the daily high, low, and closing prices for McDonald's stock (ticker symbol MCD) for January 2009 through July 2010 from Yahoo! Finance or another electronic source.*

   a. *Using a spreadsheet, calculate 10-day and 60-day SMAs. Plot these two curves with a bar chart of the stock prices.*

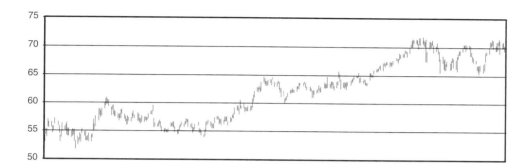

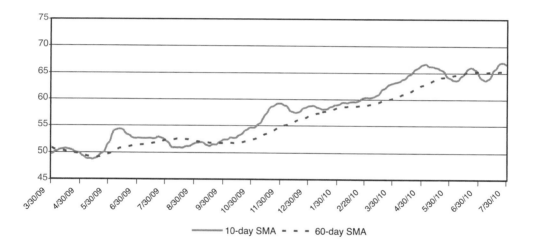

b. *Compare and contrast the 10-day and the 60-day SMA.*

The 10-day SMA is represented by the dotted line and the 60-day SMA is shown by the solid line. Although the two SMAs tend to move in the same direction, the 10-day SMA shows many more small moves. The 60-day SMA smooths out small variations in price.

c. *Explain the relationship between the market trend and the 60-day SMA during the following periods:*

i. *May 2009–October 2009*

During the May–October, 2009 time period, MCD was experiencing a sideways trading range, as indicated by the relatively flat 60-day SMA. The 10-day SMA shows pockets of upward trends and downward trends, but overall, the move in MCD is sideways.

ii. *October 2009–May 2010*

In October 2009, the 60-day SMA becomes upward sloping, indicating an upward trend in price. This uptrend continues until May 2010. During this time period, MCD experiences about a $13 increase in price, which is about a 25% increase.

iii. *May 2010–July 2010*

The uptrend that MCD was experiencing came to an end in May 2010, when the stock again entered a sideways trading range. This is shown by the flattening out of the 60-day SMA.

d. *Find a point in your graph where the faster moving average crosses the slower moving average. What type of signal would occur at this point? In hindsight, would trading on that signal have been profitable? Why or why not?*

In mid-September 2009, the faster, 10-day SMA crossed above the slower, 60-day SMA. This crossover signaled the beginning of an uptrend and would suggest that the trader should enter a long position. In hindsight, this would have been a profitable move. A trader purchasing the stock on the crossover would have been able to experience about a 25% gain over the next seven months.

The 10-day SMA crossed above the 60-day SMA four additional times in the graph, in April 2009, May 2009, June 2010, and July 2010. These crossovers occurred during a trading range and would not have been profitable trades. This is typical for a trader using a crossover trading system. Of the five trades signaled in the chart, the trader gets one profitable trade.

e. *Construct +DI and –DI for McDonald's for the period August 2009 through May 2010.*

First, it is necessary to calculate +DM and –DM for each day. If the day's high is higher than the previous day's high, the difference is +DM; if the day's low is lower than the previous day's low, the difference is –DM. If there is both +DM and –DM on a given day, only the larger of the two is recorded. Next, a 14-day sum +DM and a 14-day sum –DM is calculated using the Wilder method. The formula used is

Current DM_{14} = Previous DM_{14} – Previous $DM_{14}/14$ + Current DM.

The True Range for each day is calculated as the greatest of

▶ The difference between the day's high and low

▶ The absolute value of the difference between the prior day's close and the current day's high

▶ The absolute value of the difference between the prior day's close and the current day's low

A 14-day True Range sum (TR_{14}) is calculated in the same manner. The +DI is calculated as the $+DM_{14}/TR_{14}$, and the –DI is calculated as the $-DM_{14}/TR_{14}$. These calculations are shown below for a portion of the period.

A Date	B Open	C High	D Low	E Close	F TR(1)	G +DM(1)	H −DM(1)	I TR(14)
1/2/2009	62.38	64.13	62.20	63.75				
1/5/2009	63.26	63.84	62.89	63.56	0.95	0.00	0.00	
1/6/2009	63.99	64.46	61.83	62.14	2.63	0.00	1.06	
1/7/2009	61.93	62.57	60.84	61.24	1.73	0.00	0.99	
1/8/2009	60.83	60.83	59.70	60.52	1.54	0.00	1.14	
1/9/2009	60.71	60.95	59.85	60.07	1.10	0.12	0.00	
1/12/2009	60.10	61.23	59.75	60.16	1.48	0.28	0.00	
1/13/2009	60.31	60.80	58.82	59.32	1.98	0.00	0.93	
1/14/2009	58.51	58.62	56.41	57.33	2.91	0.00	2.41	
1/15/2009	57.20	58.59	56.55	57.98	2.04	0.00	0.00	
1/16/2009	58.74	59.98	58.54	59.67	2.00	1.39	0.00	
1/20/2009	59.59	59.80	56.91	57.07	2.89	0.00	1.63	
1/21/2009	57.98	58.94	57.16	58.70	1.87	0.00	0.00	
1/22/2009	58.07	59.47	57.69	58.72	1.78	0.53	0.00	
1/23/2009	57.24	58.72	56.75	58.02	1.97	0.00	0.94	26.87
1/26/2009	57.23	58.67	56.45	58.40	2.22	0.00	0.30	27.17
1/27/2009	58.80	59.22	58.30	58.52	0.92	0.55	0.00	26.15
1/28/2009	59.70	59.70	58.31	59.20	1.39	0.48	0.00	25.67
1/29/2009	58.78	59.06	58.02	58.14	1.18	0.00	0.29	25.02
1/30/2009	58.50	58.73	57.37	58.02	1.36	0.00	0.65	24.59
2/2/2009	57.62	58.44	57.45	57.90	0.99	0.00	0.00	23.82
2/3/2009	58.29	59.15	57.19	58.88	1.96	0.71	0.00	24.08
2/4/2009	59.17	59.77	57.50	57.86	2.27	0.62	0.00	24.63
2/5/2009	57.50	58.58	57.07	58.36	1.51	0.00	0.43	24.38
2/6/2009	58.12	59.33	58.12	58.46	1.21	0.75	0.00	23.85
2/9/2009	59.03	59.43	58.05	59.02	1.38	0.10	0.00	23.53
2/10/2009	59.00	59.02	56.88	57.28	2.14	0.00	1.17	23.99
2/11/2009	57.49	57.85	56.63	57.08	1.22	0.00	0.25	23.49
2/12/2009	56.79	57.05	55.63	56.96	1.45	0.00	1.00	23.27
2/13/2009	57.06	57.59	56.69	56.81	0.90	0.54	0.00	22.50
2/17/2009	55.90	56.41	55.26	55.68	1.55	0.00	1.43	22.45
2/18/2009	56.00	56.56	55.55	56.41	1.01	0.15	0.00	21.85
2/19/2009	55.92	57.11	55.31	55.31	1.80	0.55	0.00	22.09
2/20/2009	54.88	55.23	54.05	54.57	1.26	0.00	1.26	21.77
2/23/2009	54.75	55.39	53.69	53.87	1.70	0.00	0.36	21.92
2/24/2009	54.22	54.94	53.92	54.76	1.07	0.00	0.00	21.42
2/25/2009	54.40	55.15	53.92	54.29	1.23	0.21	0.00	21.12
2/26/2009	54.52	54.69	52.06	52.20	2.63	0.00	1.86	22.24
2/27/2009	51.57	52.92	51.50	52.25	1.42	0.00	0.56	22.08

A	J	K	L J/I	M K/I	N L–M	O L+M	P N/O	Q DX(14)
Date	+DM(14)	–DM(14)	+DI(14)	–DI(14)	DI DIFF	DI SUM	DX	ADX
1/2/2009								
1/5/2009								
1/6/2009								
1/7/2009								
1/8/2009								
1/9/2009								
1/12/2009								
1/13/2009								
1/14/2009								
1/15/2009								
1/16/2009								
1/20/2009								
1/21/2009								
1/22/2009								
1/23/2009	2.32	9.10	9	34	25	43	58	
1/26/2009	2.15	8.75	8	32	24	40	60	
1/27/2009	2.55	8.13	10	31	21	41	51	
1/28/2009	2.85	7.54	11	29	18	40	45	
1/29/2009	2.64	7.30	11	29	18	40	45	
1/30/2009	2.46	7.42	10	30	20	40	50	
2/2/2009	2.28	6.89	10	29	19	39	49	
2/3/2009	2.83	6.40	12	27	15	39	38	
2/4/2009	3.25	5.94	13	24	11	37	30	
2/5/2009	3.01	5.95	12	24	12	36	33	
2/6/2009	3.55	5.52	15	23	8	38	21	
2/9/2009	3.40	5.13	14	22	8	36	22	
2/10/2009	3.15	5.93	13	25	12	38	32	
2/11/2009	2.93	5.76	12	25	13	37	35	40.64
2/12/2009	2.72	6.35	12	27	15	39	38	40.45
2/13/2009	3.06	5.90	14	26	12	40	30	39.71
2/17/2009	2.85	6.90	13	31	18	44	41	39.80
2/18/2009	2.79	6.41	13	29	16	42	38	39.67
2/19/2009	3.14	5.95	14	27	13	41	32	39.12
2/20/2009	2.92	6.79	13	31	18	44	41	39.26
2/23/2009	2.71	6.66	12	30	18	42	43	39.52
2/24/2009	2.52	6.19	12	29	17	41	41	39.63
2/25/2009	2.55	5.75	12	27	15	39	38	39.51
2/26/2009	2.36	7.19	11	32	21	43	49	40.19
2/27/2009	2.20	7.24	10	33	23	43	53	41.11

Note: This chart is printed through February only but continues in the same format throughout the time period.

McDonalds (MCD)
Jan 1, 2009 - July 30, 2010

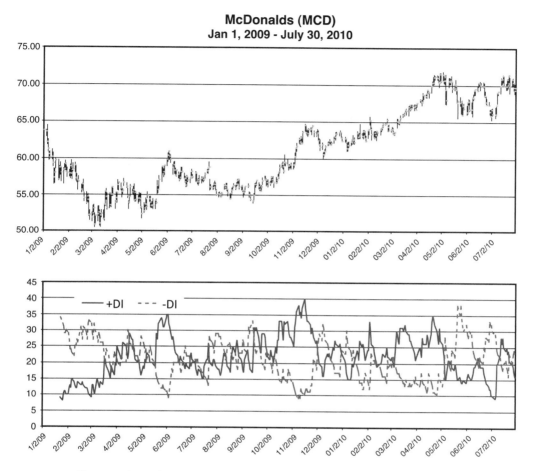

The top chart shows the price movement for MCD from August, 2009 through May, 2010. The solid line in the bottom portion of the chart represents +DI and the broken line represents –DI.

i. *Interpret +DI during this time.*

+DI rose in value, from 15 to 40 in June and November 2009. This indicated that the stock was consistently having higher daily highs and that the size of that positive movement was increasing. This is an indication of an uptrend, which is consistent with price movement over that period, and a peak above 35 indicated a price peak.

ii. *Interpret –DI during this time.*

The most significant increase in –DI occurs in May 2010, indicating that the stock was having lower daily lows. The peak above 35 indicated a price trough.

    iii. *Compare +DI and –DI with the price movement over this time. What type of relationships do you see?*

During periods in which +DI and –DI are fairly flat, experiencing frequent crossovers, MCD appears to be in a trading range. During periods in which +DI is heading up and –DI is declining, MCD appears to be in an uptrend. Whenever +DI approaches 35 or higher, it appears that it is reaching an extreme and that the trend will probably slow down and perhaps reverse.

Self-Test

1. *A 10-day SMA*

   a. Is subject to the drop-off effect unlike a 200-day SMA.

   b. Is not subject to the drop-off effect that a 200-day SMA is.

   c. Signals a change in trend sooner than does a 200-day SMA.

   d. Signals a change in trend later than does a 200-day SMA.

2. *Bollinger Bands*

   a. Are drawn as symmetrical lines around the SMA.

   b. Expand as price volatility increases.

   c. Contract as price volatility increases.

   d. Maintain a given percentage distance from the SMA.

3. *Yesterday, the low and high for JNJ were 62 and 64, respectively. The low and high for JNJ today were 63 and 67, respectively. For the day, there would be*

   a. Positive directional movement (+DI) of 2.

   b. Positive directional movement (+DI) of 3.

   c. Positive directional movement (+DI) of 4.

   d. No directional movement.

4. *A 20-day simple moving average is calculated by*

   a. Adding the prices over the previous 20 days and dividing by 20.

   b. Calculating the average true range (ATR) for the day and multiplying by 20.

   c. Adding the prices over the previous 19 days, dividing by 19, and then adding today's price.

   d. Adding the price from 20 days ago to today's price and dividing by 2.

5. *The exponential moving average*

    a. Suffers from the drop-off effect.

    b. Precedes, rather than lags, a change in trend.

    c. Weights today's price more heavily than the previous days' prices.

    d. Smoothes price variations by taking the average of an average.

6. *Which of the following would most likely be seen as a buy signal?*

    a. Price breaks below the lower Bollinger Band

    b. The 10-day moving average turns from upward sloping to downward sloping

    c. The 10-day moving average crosses above the 30-day moving average

    d. The 10-day moving average crosses below the 30-day moving average

7. *Using a shorter period for a moving average*

    a. Results in less lag in determining a trend but increases the number of false signals.

    b. Results in less lag in determining a trend and decreases the number of false signals.

    c. Results in more lag in determining a trend and increases the number of false signals.

    d. Results in more lag in determining a trend but decreases the number of false signals.

8. *Which of the following is a TRUE statement?*

    a. A moving average often duplicates the trend line.

    b. A 10-day moving average is said to be "faster" than a 30-day moving average.

    c. An upward sloping moving average is an indication of an uptrend in price.

    d. All of the above.

9. *The Positive Directional Movement Indicator (+DI) is the*

    a. Ratio of the sum of +DM and the average true range (ATR).

    b. Ratio of the sum of +DM to the moving average of –DM.

    c. Ratio of the difference between +DI and –DI and the sum of +DI and –DI.

    d. Ratio at the average true range (ATR) to the sum of +DI and –DI.

10. *In a 9-day exponential moving average, the last day's weight will be*

    a. 1/10 or 10%

    b. 2/10 or 20%

    c. 1/9 or 11%

    d. (9/2)×100 or 4.5%

CHAPTER 15
Bar Chart Patterns

Chapter Objectives

By the end of this chapter, you should be familiar with

- ▶ Controversy over whether patterns exist
- ▶ The influence that computer technology has had on the study of patterns
- ▶ The formation of classic bar chart patterns such as triangles, flags, pennants, double tops, and head-and-shoulders
- ▶ Historical performance measures of major bar chart patterns

Chapter Summary

What Is a Pattern?

A **pattern**, or formation, is a configuration of price action that is bounded, above and below, by a line or curve. All patterns have an **entry** that describes the trend preceding the formation and an **exit**, which is often a signal for action.

Do Patterns Exist?

Technical analysts believe that patterns exist. However, evidence of their existence and profitability is largely anecdotal. Humans have a tendency to want to see patterns even when they don't exist.

Computers and Pattern Recognition

Today, most price data is plotted by computer. Analysts can quickly calculate ratios and averages using a computer. Computer technology enables technicians to test strategies for accuracy and statistical significance. However, computers cannot recognize visual patterns as well as a human can.

Market Structure and Pattern Recognition

As knowledge of technical analysis is more widespread and patterns are more widely recognized, they are less effective. If large institutional players dominate the market, they might be able to "manipulate" a chart formation and cause **false breakouts.** Derivatives have influenced the price and volume action in individual securities for reasons other than the prospects for the underlying company.

How Profitable Are Patterns?

Because of the difficulty in defining a chart pattern on a computer, studies of chart performance and reliability are scarce. Early studies by Kirkpatrick, Levy, Merrill, and Lo and MacKinlay questioned the predictive ability of chart patterns. The most comprehensive study of patterns has been done by Bulkowski. Bulkowski's study suggests that pattern analysis outperforms the S&P500 on average.

Classic Bar Chart Patterns

A **double top** consists of three reversal points: two peaks separated by a trough. The pattern is completed when price falls below the trough reversal point price. The **double bottom** is a mirror image of the double top.

The **rectangle** is a simple pattern in which price oscillates between parallel support and resistance lines. A rectangle requires a minimum of four reversals. False breakouts are common, as are **throwbacks** and **pullbacks**. Increased volume on the breakout from a rectangle leads to more profitable trading.

The **triple top** is a rectangle in which the resistance line is touched three times. The **triple bottom** is a rectangle in which the resistance line is touched three times.

A **triangle** forms when price is bounded by nonparallel trend lines that cross each other when extended into the future. The point at which the lines cross is known as the **apex** or **cradle**. The distance between the first two reversal points in the triangle is known as the **base**.

With a **descending triangle**, the lower bound is a horizontal support zone and the upper bound is a downward sloping trend line. The **ascending triangle** has a rising lower trend line and a horizontal resistance zone for its upper bound. If the upper bound of a triangle is declining and the lower bound is rising, it is called a **symmetrical triangle**. A **wedge** pattern is a triangle pattern with both trend lines heading in the same direction. For a rising wedge, both lines head upward, with the lower bound rising more quickly than the upper bound. For a declining wedge, both lines head downward, with the upward falling more quickly than the lower. A rising wedge usually breaks downward, whereas most declining wedges break out upward. If the two boundary lines are diverging, regardless of their direction, a **broadening** pattern exists. Broadening patterns are relatively rare, are difficult to identify, and are difficult to profit from. A **diamond** pattern is a broadening pattern immediately followed by a triangle.

Rounding is more of a conceptual idea than a specific price behavior; rounding tops and bottoms are formed by price action that reverses slowly and gradually. Rounded bottoms and tops are rare and tend to be longer-term patterns, more easily identified in weekly or even monthly charts.

The **head-and-shoulders** pattern is a complex pattern that combines trend lines, support or resistance lines, and rounding. The head-and-shoulders top pattern has three well-defined peaks, with the second peak (known as the "head") higher than the first or third peak (known as the "shoulders"). The line connecting the two troughs is called the "neckline" and is the breakout level. The head-and-shoulders bottom is the mirror image.

A **flag** begins with a steep, sharp price trend and then forms a short channel sloping in the opposite direction from the trend. The **pennant** is the same, except a short triangle, rather than a channel, is formed after the steep price trend.

Key Concepts and Vocabulary

As you go through this chapter, pay close attention to the following vocabulary. Be sure that you can define each of the terms.

Pattern

Entry

Exit

Pullback

Throwback

Failure

Double top

Double bottom

Rectangle

Shortfall

Triple Top

Triple Bottom

Triangles

Apex

Base

Descending triangle

Ascending triangle

Symmetrical triangle

Wedge

Broadening pattern

Diamond pattern

Head-and-shoulders

Flag

Pennant

False breakout

Premature breakout

Cradle

Practice and Application

The following chart contains the names of the bar chart patterns contained in this chapter. Sketch each pattern; in your sketch label the entry and the breakout from the pattern as well as important characteristics (such as support or resistance) in your sketch. The third column provides space for you to make notes regarding characteristics of the pattern, such as frequency, failure rates, or profitability.

Pattern Name	Pattern Sketch	Notes
Double top		
Double bottom		
Rectangle (trading range or box)		
Triple top		

Pattern Name	**Pattern Sketch**	**Notes**
Triple bottom		
Descending triangle		
Ascending triangle		
Symmetrical triangle		
Broadening pattern (megaphone, funnel, reverse triangle, or inverted triangle)		

Pattern Name	Pattern Sketch	Notes
Diamond top		
Rising wedge		
Declining wedge		
Rounding top		
Rounding bottom (saucer, bowl, or cup)		

Pattern Name	Pattern Sketch	Notes
Cup-and-handle		
Head-and-shoulders top		
Head-and-shoulders bottom		
Flag		
Pennant		

Remember that patterns can occur on charts with bars of any length. The following chart is a three-minute bar chart for AAPL for May 17, 2012. Four patterns are marked on the chart. Can you name them?

Chart created with TradeStation

The first marked pattern is a symmetrical triangle. The second is an ascending triangle. The third is a declining wedge, and the fourth is a descending triangle.

End-of-Chapter Review Questions

1. *A pattern is a configuration of price movement bounded by lines and/or curves. Explain what is meant by this definition.*

   A pattern is price movement occurring between defined support/resistance or trend lines. Price remains within these lines until it breaks out of one, giving a directional signal. Lines can be straight or curved. Any combination of curves and straight lines can bound a pattern as long as the bounds are defined clearly enough to determine a breakout level.

2. *Define each of the following terms as they relate to the characteristics and formation of patterns:*

   a. *Pullback*

   A pullback occurs when price breaks out downward through the lower bound of a pattern and then returns or "pulls back" to that breakout level.

   b. *Throwback*

   A throwback occurs when price breaks out upward through the upper bound of a pattern and then returns or "throws back" to that breakout level.

   c. *Failure*

   A failure occurs when a breakout from a pattern does not result in the beginning of a new, distinct trend.

3. *Explain the differences among an ascending triangle, a descending triangle, and a symmetrical triangle.*

Triangles are formed when the upward boundary and lower boundaries of a pattern are not parallel and will cross when extended into the future. The upper boundary of an ascending triangle is a horizontal resistance line and the lower boundary is an upward sloping trend line. The price movement in a descending triangle is bounded on the top by a downward sloping trend line and bounded on the bottom by a horizontal support line. The symmetrical triangle is bounded at the top by a downward sloping trend line and bounded at the bottom by an upward sloping trend line.

4. *Describe both a rising wedge and a falling wedge. What trading strategy might you follow in each of these instances?*

A rising wedge occurs when price movement is bounded at the top by an upward sloping trend line and at the bottom by another upward sloping trend line. The bottom bound trend line is rising at a steeper slope than the top bound trend line, which means the two trend lines will eventually cross when extended into the future. A rising wedge's break is usually downward. Thus, a trader would want to take a short position on a break down through the lower bound.

A declining wedge is the opposite of a rising wedge in that both the top and bottom boundaries are sloping downward. The top boundary trend line falls more quickly than the lower boundary trend line, leading to narrower price movement as the pattern progresses. Because a high percentage of declining wedges break out to the upside, traders should wait for a break through the top boundary and immediately take a long position.

5. *Explain the difference between a flag and a pennant.*

Flags and pennants both are preceded by a steep, sharp price trend. For the flag, the upward movement is halted by a channel that slopes in the opposite direction from the trend. For the pennant, the upward price trend is halted by a short triangle. Both the flag and pennant are continuation patterns, with price usually breaking out in the direction of the preceding trend.

6. *Flags and pennants are often said to be "half-mast" formations. Explain what is meant by this and how you would use this information to set a price target.*

Flags and pennants are preceded by a strong price trend, and tend to break in the direction of that preceding trend. The channel of triangle often occurs halfway through the entire steep price trend. Thus, when the price trend has ended, the formation looks much like a flag flying at half-mast. Traders use this to set a price target by adding to the breakout price the distance from the beginning of the trend to the first reversal in the pattern. This method is known as the "measured rule."

7. *Explain the formation and characteristics of a head-and-shoulders top.*

   The head-and-shoulders top pattern is entered from below. Price rises to the first well-defined peak and then falls back to the neckline; this first peak is the left shoulder. Price then rises again to form a second peak that is higher than the first; this peak is called the "head." After price falls back to the neckline, it rises again to form a third peak. This third peak, known as the "right shoulder," must be lower than the middle peak, but it does not have to be the exact same height as the left shoulder. The left and right shoulders should be roughly symmetrical around the head. Breakout occurs when the price falls through the neckline, down from the right shoulder.

8. *Explain the formation and characteristics of a head-and-shoulders bottom.*

   The head-and-shoulders bottom is the reverse of the head-and-shoulders top. The pattern is entered from above. Three well-defined troughs are formed. The middle trough, the "head," is lower than the first trough, the "left shoulder," or the third trough, the "right shoulder." The first and third troughs are approximately symmetrical around the center trough. The tops that form between the troughs form a recognizable trend line called the "neckline." Breakout occurs when price rises above the neckline following the right shoulder.

9. *Select three companies, and look at the price charts for those companies over the past three months. Can you recognize any of the formations discussed in this chapter in those charts?*

   Your answer to this question will vary depending upon the stocks you choose and the time frame you consider. As you look at more charts, you will be able to recognize and identify patterns more quickly.

   The following figure shows the price action for BAC from February 15 through May 18, 2012. BAC was in a rectangle pattern for about a month and broke out to the upside on March 13. From mid-March through early April BAC formed a descending triangle, with a horizontal support level at about 9.30 and a descending upper bound trend line. On April 19 and 20, BAC experienced a steep decline in price. This decline was halted somewhat by the flag pattern that developed the last week of April. After price broke out of the flag, price continued its downward trend.

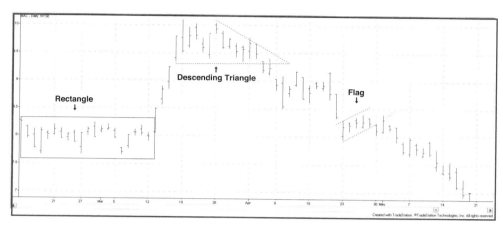

Chart created with TradeStation

The following figure shows the price action for MSFT from January 24 through May 18, 2012. During the month of March, a head-and-shoulders pattern developed. The pattern had a slightly upward sloping neckline, and breakout occurred at the beginning of April. Later that month, a descending triangle (with horizontal support and a downward sloping trend line for the upper boundary) formed. The triangle broke to the downside. The May 11 candle is an example of a pullback.

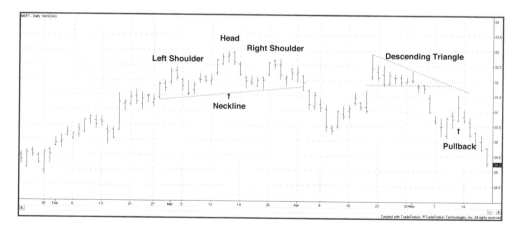

Chart created with TradeStation

Several patterns are shown in the following chart for UA from November 30, 2011 through May 18, 2012. UA ended 2011 with a double bottom at a price of about $70. Examples of symmetrical triangles are shown in mid-February and late April. An ascending triangle developed in May.

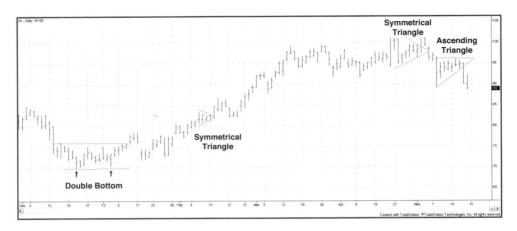

Chart created with TradeStation

Self-Test

1. *All patterns will have a combination of*

    a. A pullback and a throwback.

    b. A profit ratio and a probability ratio.

    c. A parallel boundary and a nonparallel boundary.

    d. An entry and an exit.

2. *Which of the following is usually a signal for action?*

    a. The entry into a pattern

    b. The midpoint of a pattern

    c. The second reversal point of a pattern

    d. The exit from a pattern

3. *Humans have a tendency to*

    a. Want to see patterns in data even when they do not exist.

    b. Be opposed to seeing patterns and ignore their existence.

    c. Ignore historical patterns and forego potential profits because they receive psychological rewards from trying new strategies.

    d. Ignore the most recent events and place too much emphasis on events that occurred in the distant past.

4. The _____ consists of three reversal points: two peaks separated by a trough.

   a. Double bottom

   b. Double top

   c. Rectangle

   d. Head-and-shoulders

5. A rectangle formation is also known as

   a. A trading range or a box.

   b. The multi-top pattern.

   c. An irregular triangle.

   d. A pullback/throwback pattern.

6. A _____ has nonparallel boundary lines that cross each other when extended into the future.

   a. Broadening pattern

   b. Triangle pattern

   c. Pullback pattern

   d. Throwback pattern

7. Which of the following is a list of synonyms for a broadening pattern?

   a. Megaphone, funnel, reverse triangle

   b. Wedge, flag, megaphone

   c. Funnel, diamond top, wedge

   d. Wedge, channel, cup

8. The price of XYZ appears to be bounded below by a support level of $20 and above by a downward sloping trend line. This pattern is known as a(n)

   a. Coil.

   b. Ascending triangle.

   c. Descending triangle.

   d. Triple top.

9. *Which of the following is the least-useful pattern?*

   a. Symmetrical triangle

   b. Ascending triangle

   c. Double top

   d. Broadening pattern

10. *Which of the following is most accurate regarding the diamond top pattern?*

    a. The diamond top is one of the most-frequent patterns.

    b. The diamond top is a combination of an ascending triangle and a descending triangle.

    c. The diamond pattern usually occurs at price bottoms and is one of the easiest patterns to spot.

    d. The diamond pattern consists of a broadening pattern followed by a symmetrical triangle.

11. *A rising wedge suggests that*

    a. Sellers are becoming more anxious and that a downward breakout is likely to occur.

    b. Sellers are becoming more anxious and that an upward breakout is likely to occur.

    c. Buyers are becoming fearful and that an upward breakout is likely to occur.

    d. Buyers are becoming more optimistic and that an upward breakout is likely to occur.

12. *A false breakout occurs*

    a. In the opposite direction of the final breakout.

    b. In the same direction as the final breakout.

    c. At a support level, whereas a premature breakout occurs at a resistance level.

    d. At a resistance level, whereas a premature breakout occurs at a support level.

13. *Which of the following patterns is preceded by a steep price trend?*

    a. Saucer

    b. Head-and-shoulders bottom

    c. Pennant

    d. Cup-and-saucer

14. The _____ of the head-and-shoulders pattern is the breakout level.

    a. Left shoulder

    b. Head

    c. Right shoulder

    d. Neckline

15. The _____ is a complex pattern, consisting of trend lines, support or resistance lines, and rounding.

    a. Wedge

    b. Inverted triangle

    c. Head-and-shoulders

    d. Pennant

16. The "measured rule" would be most likely applied to which of the following formations?

    a. Head-and-shoulders

    b. Coil

    c. Cup-and-saucer

    d. Flag

17. The first well-defined peak of a head-and-shoulders top is known as the

    a. Neckline.

    b. Left shoulder.

    c. Left ear.

    d. Head.

18. Which of the following is a TRUE statement regarding rounded bottoms?

    a. Rounded bottoms are one of the most frequently occurring patterns on daily stock charts.

    b. Rounded bottoms occur infrequently relative to rounded tops, but are easy to trade when they do occur because they are easily recognizable with a clearly defined breakout level.

    c. Rounded bottoms tend to be shorter-term patterns, occurring over a few days and are seldom seen on weekly or monthly charts.

    d. Although rounded bottoms are more common than rounded tops, they do not occur very often.

19. *Which of the following is true about flags and pennants?*

   a. Because throwbacks and pullbacks are so common with flags and pennants, a trader is wise to wait for these corrections to occur before trading either one of these patterns.

   b. Flags and pennants have low failure rates with few pullbacks or throwbacks, making them good trading patterns.

   c. Pullbacks tend to be associated with flags, whereas throwbacks tend to be associated with pennants, making it difficult to use either as a reliable trading pattern.

   d. Flags and pennants generally develop over a long period of time, weeks or even months, making them good for traders with a long time horizon, but they are not useful patterns for short-term traders.

20. *To calculate a price target for a head-and-shoulders pattern*

   a. Draw a vertical line from the peak of the head to where it intersects the neckline and measure the number of points between the two.

   b. Draw a vertical line from the peak of the left shoulder and another vertical line from the peak of the right shoulder. Add the number of points of these two vertical lines together.

   c. Measure horizontally from the peak of the left shoulder to the peak of the right shoulder. Add this distance vertically at the breakout price.

   d. Measure horizontally from the entry into the pattern to the exit from the pattern, and add this distance vertically at the breakout price.

CHAPTER 16
Point-and-Figure Chart Patterns

Chapter Objectives

After studying this chapter, you should be familiar with

- ▶ The difference between one-point reversal and three-point reversal point-and-figure charts
- ▶ How to construct trend lines, recognize areas of consolidation, and determine the count using one-point reversal point-and-figure charts
- ▶ How to construct trend lines, recognize patterns, and determine the count using three-point reversal point-and-figure charts

Chapter Summary

Point-and-Figure Method

Point-and-figure (PF) is a very old, unique method of plotting and analyzing prices. Concentration is on price and price change without regard to when (time) or how many (volume). In this it differs from bar, candlestick, and most other plotting methods. It includes a distinctive method of projecting prices, called the "count." Because it is time independent, it has an advantage over other methods in 24-hour markets that are not defined by open and closing prices. It requires, however, a steady and continuous flow of prices, tick by tick, to be plotted and cannot be estimated accurately from open, high, low, and close figures alone.

Construction

The chart plot is defined by a two-dimensional graph made of boxes. Each box represents a price on the vertical axis and each price reversal moves the plot to the right into the next column of boxes. The dimensions determining the plot are **price per box** and the **reversal amount**, which is the number of boxes required to reverse direction and move the plot to the next column. The plots are made with an X in each box in a column when the price for the box is touched or passed through. When a reversal occurs, based on the reversal amount necessary, the new set of plots begins in the next column.

One-Point-Reversal

The original PF chart was a **one-point, one-box reversal** chart. Each box was one point (23, 24, 25,...), and each reversal required only a reversal through one box (price sequence touching or crossing 23, 24, 25, 26, 25) as plotted here:

27		
26	X	
25	X	X
24	X	
23	X	

One-point (box) reversal charts can have any price for each box and can have any reversal amount. Descriptive nomenclature refers to the box size first, then the reversal amount such as 2-point, 4-box reversal or 1-point, 2-box reversal point-and-figure chart. The lower the price per box is, the more detail that will appear in the chart. Being time independent, the price flow depends on the number of price reversals rather than the amount of time in the market. One-box reversal charts have a number of specific patterns similar to those found on bar charts—triangles, rectangles, trend lines, head-and-shoulders, and so on. Action is signaled on breakouts, similar to other chart methods.

Three-Point (Box) Reversal

Three-point reversal charts (formally known as "one-point, three-box reversal point-and-figure charts") are a modern version of the old one-point charts. They arose from the laziness of analysts who didn't want to inspect every trade on the tape and in most cases can be plotted from the open, high, low, and close price in the newspaper. By not requiring a continuous trade flow, much shorter-term price action is lost. However, three-point reversal charts have fewer patterns and are more easily interpreted and quantified. The most basic patterns are the double top and double bottom.

						X	
		X			O	X	O
X		X			O	X	O
X	O	X			O		O
X	O	X					O
	O						

Double Top/Double Bottom

All eight patterns in three-point reversal charts derive from these basic two. Note that upward trends are plotted with an X and downward trends with an O. The nomenclature is a little backward from conventional nomenclature in that the double "top" pattern is actually a bottom formation and expected to breakout upward, and vice-versa for the double bottom pattern. Other common patterns are the rising bottom and declining top, the triple top and triple bottom. Triangles occur, and trend lines at 45 degrees are plotted from the lowest and highest filled box at a bottom and top respectively.

The Count

In one-point reversal charts the **count** is the amount by which price is expected to run after it breaks out. It is proportional to the "width" of the preceding PF pattern multiplied by the price per box and the reversal amount. As an example, a consolidation pattern in a 1-point, 2-box reversal chart that is 13 columns wide is expected to cause the price to rise 13×2 points. The count is usually taken from the row with the most filled boxes, and the projection is made from that row.

In three-point reversal charts the count can be either a horizontal count, as in the 1-point, 1-box reversal charts, or a vertical count taken as the number of boxes in the column in which an action signal has occurred, multiplying it by 3 (by 2 for downward projections). The count also must be adjusted to the scale. Scale in three-point reversal charts is a semi-logarithmic scale devised by Chartcraft Inc. Other scales using actual logarithms have been used as well.

Key Concepts and Vocabulary

A number of terms and concepts that might be new to you appear in this chapter. As you read through this chapter, pay close attention to the following terms and concepts. Write down a definition or explanation for each.

Point

Box

Reversal

Reversal amount

Figure

One-point versus three-point

Horizontal Count

Vertical Count

Wall

Fulcrum

Three-point top and bottom

Three-point bullish support and resistance line

Three-point bearish support and resistance line

End-of-Chapter Review Questions

1. *Time and volume are not pictured on a point-and-figure chart. Explain why point-and-figure analysts might consider these two factors irrelevant to their analysis.*

   Point-and-figure charts show the flow of prices. The flow depends on price changes (reversals) that are independent of time and volume. Price, not time or volume, is the single result of all information. An increase or decrease in volume is meaningless if the price remains the same.

2. *Why might one-point reversal point-and-figure charts be a useful tool for an analyst following currency trading?*

   Currency trading goes on throughout the world 24-hours per day. There is no open or close at arbitrary times of the day. Point-and-figure, by disregarding time, is unaffected by time intervals and is thus useful for analyzing continuous price flow.

3. *Explain the major difference between the one-point reversal method and the three-point reversal method, highlighting the advantages to each approach.*

   The one-point method requires a continuous flow of data because it accounts for every trade tick. It is thus more complete but also more complex. The plots are lengthy and sometimes difficult to interpret. The three-point method was designed to overcome the apparent shortcomings of one-point by being easily plotted without a continuous price flow, and its patterns are simple and direct. This method, of course, sacrifices the detail gained by the one-point method but is easier to learn and use.

4. *Explain each of the following terms as it relates to point-and-figure charting:*

   a. *Congestion area*

   A congestion area is a sideways movement in prices that interrupts or reverses a trend. Its importance in point-and-figure is that its width is proportional to the extent of the next directional move.

   b. *Trend line*

   In a one-point chart, a trend line can be drawn between reversal points just as is done in a bar or candlestick chart. In a three-point chart, a trend line is drawn at a 45-degree angle from the highest and lowest box.

   c. *Wall*

   In a congestion area, the sides of the area from which the number of boxes is counted for the target count are called walls. It is from wall to wall that the horizontal number boxes needed for the horizontal count are determined.

d. *Count*

In all point-and-figure charts, a price objective can be determined from what is called "the count." It is either the width of the congestion area adjusted for box size and reversal or, in three-point charts it can be the vertical distance of the column associated with the pattern breakout multiplied by the box size and the reversal amount. This figure, the count, is then projected in the direction of the trend to give the analyst a projected target objective price for the directional move.

5. *How is count used in one-point reversal charts to determine a price target?*

The count in a one-point chart is determined from a congestion area. It is the number of boxes in the row with the most filled boxes in one of the rows in the congestion area. The total number of boxes in that row, not the amount filled, is the count. It is adjusted for box size and reversal amount and added or subtracted to the price associated with the count row to produce a projected target for the breakout move from the consolidation area.

6. *Explain how the term top is used differently with three-point reversal charts than with bar charts and one-point reversal point-and-figure charts.*

In most charts—bar, candlestick, one-point reversal—top is used to designate a pattern that usually forms at a price top. It suggests that the next directional movement will be downward. In three-point reversal patterns, however, the term top is used to designate patterns that have several reversal tops (or peaks) that will likely be broken in a price breakout upward. They are thus really bottom patterns because the anticipated breakout is upward.

7. *How is horizontal count determined in a three-point reversal chart? How is vertical count determined in these charts? How would this count be used to determine a price target?*

In a three-point chart, the count is determined just as it is determined in a one-point chart. The width of the congestion area at the row where the most boxes are filled is the count. It is then adjusted for price reversal (usually 3) and the box size to arrive at a number that when added to the count row targets the price objective for a breakout. Vertical count is derived from taking the vertical distance of the column in which the initial breakout occurs, adjusting it for reversal amount (3) and box size. It is then multiplied by 3 to produce the count. This number is then added to the lowest box in the breakout column. In the case of a downward breakout, the vertical number is multiplied by 2 for the count and subtracted from the highest box in the breakout column.

8. *How do the trend lines that are drawn on three-point reversal point-and-figure charts differ from trend lines drawn on other types of charts? Describe each of the following types of trend lines on the three-point reversal chart:*

Trend lines in three-point reversal charts are drawn only at 45-degree angles from highs and lows unlike from reversal point to reversal point as in bar, candlestick, and one-point reversal charts.

As in all charts, a resistance line is drawn above prices at resistance points and represents resistance to an advance. Likewise a support line is drawn below prices at support points and represents support to a decline.

a. *Bullish support line*

The bullish support line is drawn at an upward sloping 45-degree angle below prices from a price low box (has an O).

b. *Bearish support line*

The bearish support line is drawn at a downward sloping 45-degree angle below prices from a price low box (has an O).

c. *Bullish resistance line*

The bullish resistance line is drawn at an upward sloping 45-degree angle above prices from a price high box (has an X).

d. *Bearish resistance line*

The bearish resistance line is drawn at a downward sloping 45-degree angle above prices from a price high box (has an X).

Self-Test

1. *The point-and-figure method concentrates on*

   a. Price and price change.

   b. Price change and volume.

   c. Price change and time.

   d. Price change, volume, and time.

2. *Which of the following is a TRUE statement?*

   a. Point-and-figure charting is a relatively new method that has developed due to increased computer power.

   b. Point-and-figure charting cannot easily be used in the currency markets because of the importance of the closing price in the plotting.

   c. One of the drawbacks of point-and-figure charting is that it does not provide a method of projecting prices.

   d. Point-and-figure charting has an advantage over bar charts in 24-hour markets because it is time independent.

3. *In point-and-figure charting, plotting moves to the next column of boxes*

   a. When a new trading period begins.

   b. When a price reversal occurs.

   c. When a volume criterion is met.

   d. When the count criterion has been met.

4. *The dimensions determining the plot of a point-and-figure chart are*

    a. Price per box and the volume per column.

    b. Volume per column and the reversal amount.

    c. Price per box and the reversal amount.

    d. Price per box and the count amount.

5. *A double top pattern on a three-point reversal chart*

    a. Is a bottom formation that is expected to break out upward.

    b. Is a top formation that is expected to break out downward.

    c. Is a consolidation pattern that is expected to break out downward.

    d. Is created when two columns of Xs lie between two columns of Os.

6. *The term "wall" refers to*

    a. The column in which a triangle formation begins.

    b. The trend line drawn at a 45-degree angle on a point-and-figure chart.

    c. Two consecutive columns of the same height on a point-and-figure chart.

    d. The sides of a congestion area from which the number of boxes is counted for the target.

7. *In a one-point reversal chart, count is calculated as*

    a. The number of filled boxes in a congestion area.

    b. The vertical height of a congestion area.

    c. The number of boxes between the two highest columns plus the number of boxes between the two lowest columns within a congestion area.

    d. The number of boxes in the row with the most filled boxes in a congestion area.

8. *A bearish support line on a three-point reversal point-and-figure chart is drawn*

    a. At a downward sloping 45-degree angle below prices from a price low box.

    b. At an upward sloping 45-degree angle below prices from a price low box.

    c. At an upward sloping 45-degree angle above prices from a price high box.

    d. At a downward sloping 45-degree angle above prices from a price high box.

9. *You are looking at a three-point reversal point-and-figure chart and see that the analyst has drawn a downward sloping, 45-degree angle line above prices from a box that has an X. This line is known as a*

    a. Bullish support line.

    b. Bearish support line.

    c. Bullish resistance line.

    d. Bearish resistance line.

10. *Which of the following is a TRUE statement?*

    a. Although the three-point reversal method ignores time and volume, the one-point reversal provides that information through more frequent plotting.

    b. Although continuous price data is necessary for the three-point reversal method, one-point reversal point-and-figure charts do not rely on continuous data.

    c. The one-point reversal method is more complete and more complex than the three-point reversal method, but the plots are lengthy and require a continuous flow of data.

    d. The one-point reversal method results in a more compact, but less precise, plot than the three-point reversal method.

CHAPTER 17
Short-Term Patterns

Chapter Objectives

After studying this chapter, you should be familiar with

- ▶ How short-term patterns can be used as a tool to identify reversals in longer-term trends
- ▶ The types of gaps that occur on bar charts and the significance of the various types
- ▶ Wide-range days and narrow-range days and their implications for volatility
- ▶ The formation and interpretation of the most common candlestick patterns

Chapter Summary

Short-term patterns are used to anticipate a sudden move, to take advantage of a period when prices have reached an emotional extreme, or to enter into a trend at an advantageous price as on a pullback or throwback. These methods usually have a **setup**. A setup occurs when certain known factors needed to establish the pattern have occurred, and the trader is waiting for the action to occur.

Traditional Short-Term Patterns

A **gap** occurs when either the low for the current bar is above the high for the previous bar or the high for the current bar is lower than the low of the previous bar. A **breakaway gap** occurs at the beginning of a trend. An **opening gap** occurs when the opening price for the day is outside the range of the previous day. A **runaway gap** occurs along a trend and is called a **measuring gap** because it often occurs at about the middle of a price run. An **exhaustion gap** occurs at the end of a price move; these gaps occur when a strong trend has reached a point where greed or fear has reached its apex and signal a potential trend reversal.

A **spike** is similar to a gap except the empty space associated with a gap is a solid line; a long bar, rather than discontinuity, is seen on the bar graph. Spikes can occur at the beginning of a trend, in the middle of a trend, or at the end of a trend. A **climax** is a spike that occurs as the last bar on an accelerated trend.

The **Dead Cat Bounce** is a failed rally that occurs after a sharp decline. The sharp decline that precedes the rally is often an **event decline** in that the sudden downward motion is often the result of an event such as an announcement of bad news about the company.

An **island reversal** occurs after a lengthy trend and requires two gaps at roughly the same price: the first in the direction of the trend (which is an exhaustion gap) and the second in the reverse direction (a breakaway gap). A **one-bar reversal** occurs during an uptrend when a bar's high is higher than the previous day's bar, but the close is below the previous bar's close. During a downtrend, the one-bar reversal occurs when a bar's low is lower than the previous day's bar, but the close is higher than the previous day's close. A **two-bar reversal**, also known as a **pipe formation**, is similar to the one-bar reversal pattern, but the reversal occurs over two bars; these two bars are above-average length, side-by-side bars that occur after a lengthy trend. If these two long, side-by-side bars are separated by a short bar, a **horn** pattern is formed.

An **inside bar** occurs when the range of the current bar is smaller than and completely contained within the previous bar. It reflects a pause in the trend. If two consecutive inside bars appear, a **shark** pattern is formed. An **outside bar** occurs when the high of the current bar is higher than that of the previous bar and the low of the current bar is lower than the previous bar's low.

Wide-range bars have a range that is considerably larger than that of the normal bar for the security and are a sign of increased volatility. **Narrow-range bars** indicate low volatility.

Candlestick Patterns

A **doji** is formed when the open and closing prices are identical, creating a candlestick with a real body that is simply a horizontal line. Gaps occurring on candlestick charts are known as **windows**. A **harami** pattern is a two-day pattern consisting of a large-bodied candle followed by a small-bodied candle, with the body of the second candle lying within the body of the first candle. The second, small-bodied candle is known as a **spinning top**. When the real body of a candle has a close higher than the previous candle's close and a low lower than the previous candle's close, an **engulfing** pattern occurs.

The **hammer** and the **hanging man** are both candlestick patterns in which the real body is located at the upper end of the trading range with the lower wick two to three times as long as the body. The hanging man has a closed body, while the hammer has an open body. The **shooting star** is the reverse of the hammer; it is a closed bodied candle with the body at the lower end of the trading range. The reverse of the hammer is simply known as an **inverted hammer**.

A **dark cloud cover** is a two-candle pattern at a top; the first body is large and open, and the second body is large and dark. The second open should lie above the upper shadow of the first candle, indicating an opening gap. The second candle's body should close within the body of the first candle, preferably below the 50% level. The **piercing line** pattern is opposite of the dark cloud cover, with a closed-bodied candle followed by an open-bodied candle, and appears at bottoms.

The **evening star** is a three-candle pattern that occurs at market tops. The middle candle, known as a **star**, has a small body that lies outside of the range of the body before it. The third candle of the evening star pattern has a large black body that closes well within the first candle's body. A **morning star** is the reverse of the evening star and occurs at market bottoms.

The **three black crows** pattern is a top-reversing formation in which three consecutive black bodies occur. Preferably, these bodies are long, closing near their lows, with openings within the previous candle's bodies. The opposite pattern, **three white soldiers**, is a bottom-reversing formation.

The **three inside up** pattern is a reversal pattern that occurs at the end of a downward trend. The first candle has a large, black body. The second candle is a white spinning top (or doji) that forms a harami pattern. The third bar is a large, white candle that breaks and closes above the large black body of the first bar. The **three inside down** is the reverse of this pattern and occurs at the end of an uptrend. The **three outside up** pattern occurs after a downtrend and consists of a small black-bodied candle, followed by a white-bodied engulfing candle, followed by another white-bodied candle with a higher close and a higher high. The **three outside down** pattern occurs at the end of an uptrend and is the reverse of the three outside up pattern.

Key Concepts and Vocabulary

A number of terms and concepts that might be new to you appear in this chapter. As you read through this chapter, pay close attention to the following terms and concepts. Write down a definition or explanation for each.

Gap

Breakaway gap

Opening gap

Runaway gap

Exhaustion gap

Spike

Dead Cat Bounce

Event decline

Island reversal

One-bar reversal

Two-bar reversal

Horn pattern

Inside bar

Outside bar

Wide-range bar

Narrow-range bar

Doji

Harami

Spinning top

Window

Hammer

Hanging man

Engulfing

Shooting star

Inverted hammer

Dark cloud cover

Piercing line

Morning star

Evening star

Three black crows

Three white soldiers

Three inside up

Three inside down

Practice and Application

This chapter introduces a large number of names for short-term patterns and formations. These patterns occur frequently but have a high rate of false signals. Watching for these patterns on a daily basis helps the analyst become skillful at using these patterns to distinguish profitable trading opportunities. You should be familiar with the basic formation of each of these patterns to know what to look for on a stock chart. Use the following to draw a sketch of what each of these patterns looks like and record notes regarding the characteristics of the patterns.

Pattern	Sketch	Notes
Gap		
Spike		
Dead Cat Bounce		
Island reversal		

Pattern	Sketch	Notes
One-bar reversal		
Two-bar reversal		
Horn pattern		
Inside bar		

Pattern	Sketch	Notes
Outside bar		
Shark		
Doji		
Harami		

Pattern	Sketch	Notes
Hammer or hanging man		
Shooting star or inverted hammer		
Engulfing pattern		
Dark cloud cover		

Pattern	**Sketch**	**Notes**
Piercing line		
Morning star		
Evening star		
Three black crows		

Pattern	Sketch	Notes
Three white soldiers		
Inside down		
Inside up		
Outside down		

Pattern	Sketch	Notes
Outside up		

End-of-Chapter Review Questions

1. *Why must investors know the underlying long-term trend before using short-term patterns?*

   Short-term patterns commonly occur as a combination of open, high, low, and close information for one or a few bars. Their significance depends upon the trend at the time they occur because by themselves they are unreliable. If the trend is rising, for example, and a short-term top pattern occurs, it is worth investigating. If under those same circumstances a bottom pattern occurred, it should be ignored.

2. *Explain what is meant by the term gap. How do breakout, runaway, and exhaustion gaps differ from each other? How would an analyst distinguish between these three types of gaps?*

   A gap occurs whenever the price range for one bar lies completely above or below the range for the previous bar. This leaves a hole or void in the price action on the chart. A breakout gap occurs at the beginning of a trend, while the runaway gap occurs during the middle of a trend. The exhaustion gap occurs at the end of a trend, somewhat like a last gasp of price movement. At the time a gap is occurring, it can be difficult to distinguish the type of gap it is. The runaway gap and the exhaustion gap share many characteristics. The primary way to distinguish an exhaustion gap from a runaway gap is that an exhaustion gap is usually filled within a few bars.

3. *What is a spike? How is it similar to a gap?*

   A spike is a wide-range bar. A spike represents a large movement in price, as does a gap, but it does not show the discontinuity in price on a chart as does a gap.

4. *In August, 2005, Merck (MRK) lost an initial Vioxx product liability lawsuit. Create a daily bar chart for MRK for August, 2005 through September, 2005. Use this chart to describe the Dead Cat Bounce. Did MRK follow the typical Dead Cat Bounce pattern?*

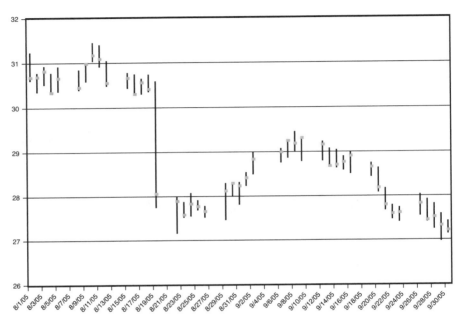

A Dead Cat Bounce (DCB) is a rally after a sharp—usually 20% or more—event-driven decline that fails to return to the breakdown price, and thus sets up a long-term short selling opportunity. On August 19, 2005 a large decline in MRK's price occurred, resulting in a spike, or wide-range bar. This sudden downward motion was an event decline as the company announced bad news. The drop in price was about 10%, about half of the typical 20% decline looked for in a Dead Cat Bounce. The price moved back up, regaining some of the loss seen on the spike day but never reached its breakdown level. This failure marks a DCB and implies that the price will decline again below the earlier event decline bottom at a slower rate. Recovery of the price should not be expected for at least six months.

5. *Define an inside day, outside day, narrow-range day, and wide-range day. Which of these days represents increasing volatility, and which represents contracting volatility? Explain your answer.*

An inside day occurs when the trading range for the day lies completely within the trading range of the previous day. In other words, the high for the day is lower than the previous day's high and the low for the day is higher than the previous day's low. A narrow range day refers to a day in which the difference in the high and low for the day is small compared to what is normal for that security. Both the narrow range day and the inside day represent declining volatility because they are both indications of a contraction in price movement.

The outside day and wide-range day both represent increasing volatility. On an outside day, the trading range completely covers the previous day's trading range. In other words, the high for the day exceeds the high for the previous day, and the low for the day falls below the low for the previous day. This is a sign that price has had more intraday movement than it did the previous day. A wide-range day is simply a day in which the difference between the high and low is large relative to what is normal for that security, indicating increased price variation or volatility.

6. *Schwager (1996) states that the one-day reversal pattern "successfully call(s) 100 out of every ten highs." What does he mean by this statement, and what is the implication for traders using these reversal patterns?*

Schwager's statement that one-day reversal patterns successfully call 100 out of every ten highs refers to the tendency for this reversal pattern to be very common. Although reversals are often accompanied by the one-day reversal pattern, the pattern can occur without a reversal happening. Therefore, a trader cannot rely simply upon seeing the pattern to call a reversal. The pattern serves as one piece of evidence that a reversal might be occurring. The analyst must look for corroborating evidence, including the evidence of a clear market trend leading up to the pattern.

7. *The candlestick chart in Figure 17.29 [in the Technical Analysis textbook and included here for reference] is of AmeriSourceBergen Corp. (ABC) for August 15, 2005–October 15, 2005. Find the following patterns in this chart. Does the price behave as you would expect after each of these patterns? Explain.*

   a. *Morning star*

   b. *Doji*

   c. *Hammer*

   d. *Inverted hammer*

   e. *Shooting star*

   f. *Harami*

   g. *Engulfing*

   h. *Hanging man*

Chart created with TradeStation

a. The morning star is a three-bar pattern: a black candle, a star, and a white candle. This pattern was seen August 22–24. It occurs at market bottoms, and price did indeed enter into an uptrend following this pattern.

b. A doji is a candle where the opening price and closing price are identical, or nearly identical. The real body appears as a horizontal line. Several dojis appear in the chart. A doji on September 27 is marked in the chart. A doji is a sign of market indecision. In this case, the doji occurs during a trading range.

c. A hammer is a candlestick with a body sitting within the top 1/3 of the bar's price range and occurs at a market bottom. The last candle in the chart might be a hammer. Price has been in a downtrend, so this candle might represent a bottom, but it is impossible to tell without knowing the future prices.

d. On October 2, it looked as if an inverted hammer might be forming. This pattern has a real body in the lower portion of the range, with a long upper wick. This occurs at a market bottom. However, an uptrend did not occur, so this ended up being an example of why knowing the trend is important in identifying the validity of short-term patterns.

e. On September 14, a candle with a small body located at the lower portion of the bar's range occurred. It looked as if this might be a top, but as price continued upward the next day, this was not a shooting star top.

f. The real body of the August 22 candle lies completely within the previous bar's real body, forming the harami pattern. The harami is a sign of decreased volatility and indecision. Often, watching the direction of the break of the harami signals the trend of future price movement. In this case, however, price broke to the downside, but quickly reversed, and an uptrend began.

g. Over October 4 and 5, an engulfing pattern formed. The first candle had a white body which was small relative to the next day's body. The second day's body was black and engulfed the first day's body. This is a bearish pattern when it occurs after an upward trend, and price did indeed begin to turn downward.

h. A hanging man occurs when a candle has a real body within the top 1/3 of the price range and the candle is a top. The October 7 candle had a real body that sat on a long lower shadow. Price moved lower over the next several days.

Self-Test

1. *You see that CAT has had a steep rise from 75 to 88 over the past few weeks. Yesterday, the stock gapped up and traded between 89 and 91. Today the stock gapped down and traded between 86 and 87. The pattern formed by this price behavior is*

   a. A Dead Cat Bounce.

   b. A hammer.

   c. An inverted hammer.

   d. An island reversal.

2. *FB opened today at 31.7, traded as high as 32.4 and as low as 31.1. The stock closed at 31.7. Today's trading formed a*

   a. Doji.

   b. Harami.

   c. Piercing line.

   d. Hammer.

3. *A spinning top refers to*

   a. A candle in which the real body lies within the top 25% of the candle.

   b. A candle in which the real body lies within the bottom 25% of the candle.

   c. A small, bodied candle that lies above the price action of the previous and subsequent candles.

   d. The second, small-bodied candle in the harami pattern.

4. *A hanging man is a candle with*

   a. A closed body lying at the top of a candle with a wick two to three times longer than the body.

   b. A closed body lying at the bottom of a candle with a wick two to three times longer than the body.

   c. An open body lying at the top of a candle with a wick two to three times longer than the body.

   d. An open body lying at the bottom of a candle with a wick two to three times longer than the body.

5. *On candlestick charts, gaps are known as*

   a. Jumps.

   b. Windows.

   c. Leaps.

   d. Dojis.

6. *Yesterday, UA traded at a high of 87 and a low of 84.5. Today, UA opened at 86, traded as high as 86.4 and as low as 85, and closed at 85.7. Today's bar represents*

   a. An inside day.

   b. An open body.

   c. Increased volatility.

   d. A window.

7. *One of the difficulties in profiting from the three black crows pattern is that*

   a. It is a top reversal pattern, and by the time the pattern is completed much of the downward price move might have already occurred.

   b. It is a bottom reversal pattern, and by the time the pattern is completed much of the upward price move might have already occurred.

   c. They often occur in the midst of a consolidation period and result in a large number of whipsaws.

   d. The pattern is so precisely defined, given the strict bar height and volume requirements, a trader can seldom find an instance to trade this pattern.

8. *A Dead Cat Bounce is most likely to occur*

   a. At the end of a long, steady downtrend.

   b. At the end of a long, steady uptrend.

   c. After a gap up in price.

   d. After an event decline.

9. *Yesterday's prices for a stock were O=52.5, L=51.9, H=53, C=52. Which of the following price combinations for today's trading in the stock would result in a gap?*

   a. O=54, L=52, H=55, C=54

   b. O=54, L =54, H =56, C=55

   c. O=50, L = 49, H =52, C =51

   d. O= 52, L=51, H=53, C=52

10. *T had been trading in a tight range, bouncing between support at 29 and resistance at 31 over the past two months. Today, the stock gapped up and closed at 32.5. This gap is most likely a*

   a. Runaway gap.

   b. Measuring gap.

   c. Exhaustion gap.

   d. Breakaway gap.

11. *Which of the following is most likely to be a top reversal pattern?*

   a. Three white soldiers

   b. Three black crows

   c. Morning star

   d. Inside up

12. *Which of the following patterns requires two gaps to occur?*

    a. Three black crows

    b. An island reversal

    c. Inside up

    d. Hanging man

13. *Which of the following is a TRUE statement regarding short-term patterns?*

    a. Short-term patterns can be used to help determine the beginning of a new trend, but they cannot be used as a tool to determine when a trend is ending.

    b. Short-term patterns can be used to help determine when a trend is ending, but they cannot be used as a tool to determine the beginning of a new trend.

    c. Short-term patterns rarely form, but when they do, they are extremely reliable.

    d. Short-term patterns are common but are often false patterns.

14. *The best way to distinguish an exhaustion gap from a runaway gap is*

    a. To see if the gap is filled within several bars; if it is, the gap is an exhaustion gap.

    b. To see if the gap is filled within several bars, if it is, the gap is a runaway gap.

    c. To look at previous price movement, because exhaustion gaps occur at the end of a congestion period.

    d. To look at previous price movement, because runaway gaps occur at the end of a congestion period.

15. *Which of the following is a TRUE statement?*

    a. The more complex a pattern, the less frequently it is going to occur.

    b. Short-term patterns occur infrequently but give highly accurate signals.

    c. Short-term patterns depend more upon the relationship between price trends and volume than between the open, high, low, and close prices of the security.

    d. Short-term patterns are useful for day traders, but they provide no valuable information to longer-term traders.

16. *A harami pattern is an indication of*

    a. Increasing market momentum.

    b. A market top if it occurs on high volume.

    c. The beginning of an uptrend.

    d. Market indecision.

17. *The pipe formation is*

    a. Comprised of one candle with a long body and a second candle of the same color with a small body at the upper end of the price range.

    b. Comprised of one candle with a long body and a second candle of the same color with a small body at the lower end of the price range.

    c. Common about half-way through a price trend and is known as a "measuring pattern."

    d. A two-bar reversal pattern.

18. *On Day 1, a stock has a price range of 13 to 16. On Day 2, the stock's price range is 13.5 to 15. On Day 3, the stock's price range is 14 to 14.5. What pattern has formed?*

    a. Horn formation

    b. Shark pattern

    c. Three dark crows pattern

    d. Three white soldiers pattern

19. *The dark cloud cover pattern has*

    a. A small, white candle surrounded by two large, black candles.

    b. Three consecutive black candles.

    c. A large, white-bodied candle followed by a large, black-bodied candle with the open on the second candle above the upper shadow of the first candle.

    d. Two consecutive black candles with the real bodies in the upper 1/3 of the price range.

20. *Which of the following patterns would most likely represent a market bottom?*

    a. Evening star

    b. Three black crows

    c. Three white soldiers

    d. Harami

CHAPTER 18
Confirmation

Chapter Objectives

By the end of this chapter, you should be familiar with

- ▶ The methods of plotting volume information on charts

- ▶ Traditional general rules for interpreting volume statistics

- ▶ The major indexes and oscillators that are designed to use volume information as confirmation

- ▶ The concept of open interest and how it might be used for confirmation

- ▶ The concept of momentum

- ▶ The major indexes and oscillators that use price data

Chapter Summary

Analysis Methods

Indexes are cumulative sums of data, usually some variation of volume and price that continuously measure supply and demand over time rather than over a specific period. They do not have an upper or lower bound and the level of the index is irrelevant. What is important is the trend of the index relative to the price trend. Indexes are used to spot a divergence to signal a change in trend. A **negative divergence** occurs when price makes a new high, but the index does not. A **positive divergence** occurs when price reaches a new low, but the index does not reach a new low. A **negative reversal** occurs when an index reaches a new high, but the price does not. A **positive reversal** occurs when an index reaches a new low, but the price does not.

Oscillators are often bounded and limited to a specified past period. **Bounded** means that the oscillator swings back and forth within certain bounds or limits. The upper zone represents an **overbought** situation; the lower zone suggests that an **oversold** level has been reached. In a trading range, the overbought and oversold levels are indications of potential reversal levels.

A **negative failure swing** occurs when the oscillator breaks down out of an overbought zone, creates a reversal point, pulls back but fails to reenter the zone, and then breaks back down below the earlier reversal point. A **positive failure swing** is the opposite at an oversold zone.

Volume Confirmation

Volume is the number of shares or contracts traded over a specified period. Volume is most commonly portrayed in a vertical bar at the bottom of the price chart. In an **Equivolume chart**, the price bar is widened in proportion to the volume associated with that bar.

Price change on high volume tends to occur in the direction of the trend; price change on low volume tends to occur on corrective price moves. Higher volume is important in an advance because it demonstrates active and aggressive interest in owning the stock. Higher volume in a decline is not as important because price declines can occur because of a lack of interest and potential buyers.

On-Balance-Volume is calculated by adding daily volume to the previous day's index level on days when price advances and subtracting the volume on days when price declines. The **price-volume trend** accounts for the importance of the price move by multiplying the percentage price change times the total volume for the day. **Williams Variable Accumulation Distribution (WVAD)** calculates the difference between the close and open as a ratio to the price range for the day. This percentage is then multiplied by the daily volume to estimate the amount of the volume traded between the open and close. The **Accumulation Distribution (AD) index** uses the following formula:

Volume X ([close – low] – [high – close])/(high – low)

Thus, if the close occurs higher than its midpoint for the day, the result is a positive number, called accumulation. If the close occurs lower than its midpoint, the result is a negative number, called distribution. The **Williams Accumulation Distribution (WAD)** uses the concept of True Range. In this index, **accumulation** occurs on days in which the close is greater than the previous day's close; the price move is calculated as the difference between the current day close and the True Range low. **Distribution** occurs on a day when the close is less than the previous day's close; the price move on these days is the difference between the current day close and the True Range high. The price move is multiplied by the volume for the day, and the resulting figures are cumulated to form the index.

The **volume oscillator** is simply the ratio between two moving averages of volume and is used to determine whether volume is expanding or contracting. The **Chaikin Money Flow** is an oscillator calculated by summing the ADs over the past 21 days and dividing the sum by the total volume over the past 21 days. Other volume-related oscillators include the Twiggs Money Flow, the Chaikin Oscillator, the Money Flow Index, the Elder Force Index (EFI), the Ease of Movement (EMV), and the Volume Rate of Change.

Volume spikes are most common at the beginning and the end of trends. Sharp declines in volume generally indicate a decline in interest in the security and are usually not meaningful.

Open Interest

Open interest is the number of futures contracts outstanding at any one time in each delivery month. Because futures contracts are created as interest develops in the specific futures market, expanding open interest is usually interpreted as confirmation of the existing trend. The **Herrick Payoff Index** is a commonly used oscillator based upon price, volume, and open interest.

Price Confirmation

Momentum deals with the rate at which prices are changing. Momentum is the second derivative of price action. **Moving Average Convergence-Divergence (MACD)** is calculated using the difference between two exponential moving averages, often the difference between the 12-period EMA and the 26-period EMA. A signal line is also calculated as an exponential moving average of the MACD, often a 9-period EMA. When the MACD is higher than the zero line, it signals that the faster moving average is higher than the slower moving average, an indication of an uptrend. During this uptrend, buy signals occur when the MACD crosses from below to above the signal line.

The **rate of change (ROC)** oscillator is a measure of the amount a stock's price has changed over a given number of past periods. The formula for calculating ROC is

$$\text{ROC} = [(P_{today} - P_{N \text{ periods ago}})/P_{N \text{ periods ago}}] \times 100$$

where P is the closing price.

The ROC is extremely easy to calculate but suffers from many problems, including the drop-off effect.

The **Relative Strength Index (RSI)** measures the strength of an issue against its history of price change by comparing "up" days to "down" days. It is based on the notion that overbought levels generally occur after the market has advanced for a disproportionate number of days, and that oversold levels generally follow a significant number of declining days.

The **stochastic** oscillator looks at the most recent close price as a percentage of the price range over a specified past window of time. Three formulas are used in calculating the stochastic:

$$\%K = [(\text{Close} - \text{Low})/(\text{High} - \text{Low})] \times 100$$

fast %D = 3-bar SMA of %K

slow %D = 3-bar SMA of fast %D

The stochastic indicates whether a stock is at a relatively low point in its trading range; a similar oscillator, the Williams %R, tells whether a stock is at a relatively high point in its trading range.

Key Concepts and Vocabulary

A number of terms and concepts that might be new to you appear in this chapter. As you read through this chapter, pay close attention to the following terms and concepts. Write down a definition or explanation for each.

Index

Oscillator

Negative divergence

Positive divergence

Negative reversal

Positive reversal

Bounded

Negative failure swing

Positive failure swing

Volume

On-Balance-Volume

Price-volume trend

Open interest

Volume spike

Momentum

MACD

RSI

Stochastic

Williams R

Accumulation

Distribution

End-of-Chapter Review Questions

1. *General rules for interpreting volume data date back to the mid-1930s. According to these general rules, how should volume statistics be used?*

   Price change on high volume tends to occur in the direction of the trend; price change on low volume tends to occur on corrective price moves. Higher volume is usually necessary in an advance because it demonstrates active and aggressive interest in owning the stock. High volume is not necessary, however, in a decline; prices can decline because of a lack of interest and potential buyers for the stock, resulting in relatively light volume.

2. *In terms of oscillators, describe what each of the following terms means:*

   a. *Overbought*

   b. *Oversold*

   c. *Negative divergence*

   d. *Positive divergence*

   e. *Failure swing*

   f. *Negative reversal*

   g. *Positive reversal*

   a. Oscillators swing back and forth within bounds; the upper zone to which the oscillator swings is known as the **overbought** zone. When a stock reaches an overbought level, a downward reversal (and price decrease) is likely.

   b. The **oversold** zone is the lower zone to which an oscillator swings. When a stock reaches an oversold level, an upward reversal (and price increase) is likely.

   c. **Negative divergence** occurs at a series of price highs when the price reaches a new high but the oscillator does not reach a new high.

   d. **Positive divergence** occurs at a series of price lows when the price reaches a new low but the oscillator does not reach a new low.

   e. A **failure swing** occurs when an oscillator breaks out from an overbought or oversold zone, returns to the zone, but fails to reenter the zone.

   f. A **negative reversal** occurs when price and an oscillator have been making new highs, and the oscillator makes a new high but price does not.

   g. A **positive reversal** occurs when price and an oscillator have been making new lows, and the oscillator makes a new low but price does not.

3. *What is meant by the term momentum? Looking at the prices for a hypothetical stock, XYZ, explain what is happening as far as the price trend and momentum over time. Sketch a graph of this stock's price and comment on how the curve's shape is impacted by momentum.*

Day	Price of XYZ
1	28
2	28
3	29
4	30
5	32
6	35
7	39
8	43

Day	Price of XYZ
9	47
10	51
11	54
12	57
13	59
14	60
15	61
16	61
17	60
18	55
19	50
20	45
21	42
22	40
23	39
24	40
25	41
26	43

Momentum deals with the rate at which prices are changing. Consider the following price chart for XYZ. For the first portion of the chart (up to Day 16), the stock is in an uptrend. The uptrend indicates that price is rising. Momentum refers to how quickly price is rising. The direction of the curve indicates the trend; the steepness of the curve indicates momentum. Notice, for example, that between Days 2 and 4 price is increasing by $1 a day. Between Days 6 and 10, price is increasing by $4 a day. During this entire period the curve is upward sloping, but it is steeper between Days 6 and 10 than between Days 2 and 4. Between Days 13 and 15, the slope is again $1 per day. Price is still rising, but momentum has slowed.

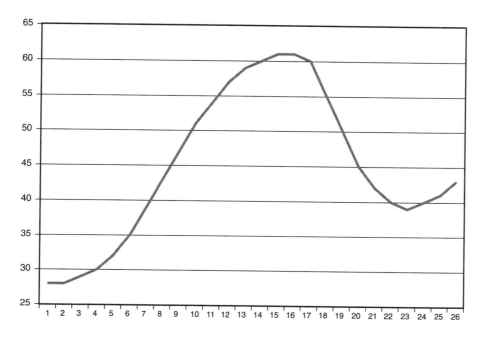

4. Gather trading information for Valero (VLO) from August 1 to October 31, 2005.

   a. Using this information, calculate the following:

   i. On-Balance-Volume

   ii. Price-volume trend

   iii. Williams Variable Accumulation Distribution

   iv. Accumulation Distribution

   v. Chaikin Money Flow

   vi. Money Flow Index (using a seven-day period)

Date	Open	High	Low	Close	Volume	OBV	Price Volume Trend	WVAD	Accumulation Distribution	Chaikin Money Flow	MFI
8/1/2005	83.4	83.8	82.95	83.25	7979600			-1408165	-2346941		
8/2/2005	83.5	85.07	83.15	84.8	9868400	9868400	183736	5273564	4745971		
8/3/2005	85.5	87.82	85	86.46	17089000	26957400	518261	11091096	5351964		
8/4/2005	87.19	90.32	86.61	89.24	14366200	41323600	980186	19029293	11354015		
8/5/2005	89.5	89.98	86.68	88.32	13695600	27628000	838994	14132079	11271012		
8/8/2005	89.3	89.97	88.13	88.32	9758800	27628000	838994	8934457	3527616		
8/9/2005	88.32	89.36	87.5	89.16	6994800	34622800	905521	12093399	9018158		
8/10/2005	89.71	91	89.22	90.77	12714800	47337600	1135118	19665134	18447111		75.36755
8/11/2005	91.65	92.71	90.9	92.71	15966800	63304400	1476371	29015856	34413911		77.31666
8/12/2005	93.6	94.2	92.25	93.8	9858600	73163000	1592280	30026995	40227957		75.63764
8/15/2005	93.67	93.99	92.6	93.85	9082000	82245000	1597121	31203081	47480489		74.17421
8/16/2005	93.5	93.75	90.68	90.73	11689200	70555800	1208519	20656148	36172045		75.64265
8/17/2005	90.5	92.25	85.56	86.52	23798600	46757200	104230	6497938	19203537		53.66722
8/18/2005	85.62	86.88	83.85	85.83	21443400	25313800	-66782	7984114	25785174		46.7326
8/19/2005	86.97	88.23	86.32	87.89	11268200	36582000	203666	13411729	33041659		45.79306
8/22/2005	88.97	89.55	86.75	88.12	10555000	47137000	231287	10207532	32815480		42.42212
8/23/2005	88.69	89.08	86.8	88.3	8906200	56043200	249480	8684103	35627965		32.33142
8/24/2005	88.4	90.89	88.1	90.49	13505400	69548600	584438	18801052	45260849		35.09512
8/25/2005	90.1	90.24	89.08	89.47	8764600	60784000	485644	14040967	42389686		36.26173
8/26/2005	89.52	90.13	88.56	89.36	9148800	51635200	474396	13108605	42564504		42.57393
8/29/2005	91.4	91.88	89.5	91.88	13722200	65357400	861369	15876108	56286704		64.72122
8/30/2005	92.08	97.19	91.98	96.79	26487600	91845000	2276847	39821712	78707110	0.2715	71.25883
8/31/2005	97.24	108.75	96.82	106.5	72333000	164178000	9533314	95966186	123756079	0.2717	83.97895
9/1/2005	110	113.25	106.75	109.5	52484000	216662000	11011736	91928955	115681617	0.2700	91.93776
9/2/2005	107.17	110.25	105.45	108.43	37974200	178687800	10640664	101897183	124858715	0.2740	74.94155
9/6/2005	108.92	109.92	105.61	109.41	28583600	207271400	10899005	105146826	146677751	0.2783	80.38141

Date	Open	High	Low	Close	Volume	OBV	Price Volume Trend	WVAD	Accumulation Distribution	Chaikin Money Flow	MFI
9/7/2005	110.86	112.3	109.55	111.03	33628600	240900000	11396934	107225685	149245753	0.2803	85.34368
9/8/2005	111.74	112.7	109.97	111.47	21135600	262035600	11480692	105135351	151336087	0.2815	85.89984
9/9/2005	113.2	115.12	112.7	114.97	26250000	288285600	12304905	124334732	174331955	0.2829	86.12614
9/12/2005	114.3	114.8	110.4	110.85	23224600	265061000	11472641	106124534	155857842	0.2834	72.8014
9/13/2005	111.14	112.35	110.04	111.1	17446600	282507600	11511988	105822428	154422840	0.2828	58.49251
9/14/2005	112	112.48	110.25	111	19867800	262639800	11494105	96913101	147919031	0.2823	76.01439
9/15/2005	111.7	111.7	107.69	108.69	24697000	237942800	10980141	78374954	135539737	0.2825	60.93293
9/16/2005	108.93	109.5	107.3	108.05	18308800	219634000	10872333	71051434	129714209	0.2839	45.05388
9/19/2005	110.1	112.79	109.84	111.27	25842600	245476600	11642469	81300872	128925791	0.2821	46.71145
9/20/2005	110.96	110.96	108.05	109.2	17987400	227489200	11307842	70421894	125155236	0.2811	31.24601
9/21/2005	111.73	113.3	110.81	113.14	24478400	251967600	12191037	84283157	146487818	0.2806	47.70988
9/22/2005	114.77	116.88	109.53	112.8	32928400	219039200	12092083	75457450	142858974	0.2809	63.48001
9/23/2005	112.3	112.34	109.7	110.77	16783200	202256000	11790045	65730822	139680337	0.2823	52.34578
9/26/2005	109	113.21	108.5	113.04	19180600	221436600	12183111	82182972	157476351	0.2836	66.41032
9/27/2005	112.65	113.74	111.37	112.58	12584800	208851800	12131899	81811269	157741853	0.2850	77.1192
9/28/2005	113.5	116.53	111.44	116.12	23991200	232843000	12886286	94160374	177868066	0.2860	76.94764
9/29/2005	116.97	117.25	114.4	114.99	15838600	217004400	12732156	83156715	168587202	0.2875	88.69914
9/30/2005	114.3	114.59	112.75	113.06	11840000	205164400	12533432	75177585	160736767	0.2910	78.72647
10/3/2005	113.99	116.29	113.64	116.06	12192000	217356400	12856942	84701147	170812420	0.2959	74.86036
10/4/2005	115.1	115.26	112.12	112.52	12410200	204946200	12478413	74504231	161564054	0.2990	77.63572
10/5/2005	112.73	113.6	105.2	105.77	33141200	171805000	10490294	47044379	132920589	0.3006	53.89179
10/6/2005	102	104.8	99.5	103.04	41269400	130535600	9425101	55142526	146780878	0.3050	36.17879
10/7/2005	105	107.97	103.39	107.7	23854800	154390400	10503938	69205399	167823103	0.3104	35.34012
10/10/2005	107.2	107.25	104.24	105.04	15463600	138926800	10122014	58108597	160579357	0.3165	24.43436
10/11/2005	106.25	108.25	106	107.6	13893000	152819800	10460610	66444397	166445290	0.3224	33.36641
10/12/2005	107.5	107.6	102.91	104.01	16508800	136311000	9909805	54159597	157680490	0.3293	24.24846
10/13/2005	102.55	102.94	97.7	100.29	26920200	109390800	8946983	42548976	157372244	0.3371	22.49549

Date	Open	High	Low	Close	Volume	OBV	Price Volume Trend	WVAD	Accumulation Distribution	Chaikin Money Flow	MFI
10/14/2005	98.5	102.09	95.75	101.27	28735800	138126600	9227780	55103892	178674808	0.3445	23.43873
10/17/2005	104.5	105	102.46	103.49	14341200	152467800	9542162	49401289	175964660	0.3512	38.18088
10/18/2005	103	104.35	99.5	99.87	17508000	134959800	8929745	38102311	161127984	0.3597	21.76576
10/19/2005	99.87	100.25	93.8	98.98	31940600	103019200	8645104	33695004	180490425	0.3695	19.62975
10/20/2005	97.1	98.2	91.71	92.95	28488000	74531200	6909575	15478486	162888440	0.3810	9.085381
10/21/2005	93	96.45	92.23	94.65	21789400	96320600	7308090	23998038	166089727	0.3909	21.2386
10/24/2005	94.5	98.27	92.9	97.75	18980800	115301400	7929754	35485487	181394543	0.3992	33.96805
10/25/2005	98.25	102.27	97.9	101.05	18807800	134109200	8564698	47536251	189700963	0.4074	48.92964
10/26/2005	100.69	105.36	99.51	100.94	23705400	110403800	8538893	48549302	177584869	0.4148	51.94151
10/27/2005	102.2	103.1	97.75	97.82	18545400	91858400	7965665	33366339	159524770	0.4242	51.69953
10/28/2005	98.4	99.77	94.6	99.5	22165600	114024000	8346345	38082425	179375201	0.4326	54.99214
10/31/2005	103.65	106.64	103.55	105.24	31381200	145405200	10156678	54230032	182320362	0.4375	74.09317

b. *Looking at the calculations you have made, what observations can you make about Valero over the three-month period observed?*

Following are a price chart for VLO and a chart containing OBV, WVAD, and Accumulation Distribution. Price was rising through the first week in September; OBV, WVAD, and AD all showed strength during that period. As price exceeded 115 in early October, the higher price was not confirmed by OBV, WVAD, or Accumulation, which signals a potential reversal in trend. Indeed, price did reverse.

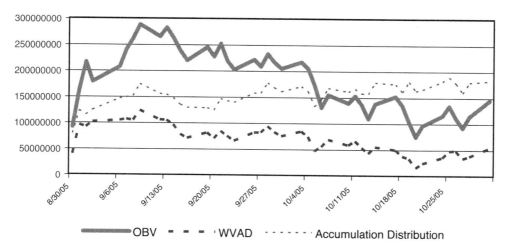

5. *Look at the volume data for Valero in Question 3. Do you see any spikes or dips in volume? If so, how might these volume patterns enter into your analysis of the stock?*

A volume spike occurred at the end of August. The volume for August 30 was 199% higher than the 10-day moving average of volume, and almost twice the previous day's volume. August 31 volume was 490% of the 10-day moving average of volume, and more than two-and-a-half times the previous day's volume. This volume spike was associated with a price increase. VLO closed at 91.88 on August 29 and at 109.5 on September 1.

A dip in volume occurred from September 24 through October 4. This dip was followed by a volume spike on October 5 (182% of 10-day average) and on October 6 (216% of 10-day average). This volume spike was associated with a price decline.

   a. *Use the data you collect in Question 3 to calculate the following:*

      i. *MACD (using 12- and 26-day EMA)*

      ii. *14-day rate of change (ROC)*

      iii. *14-day relative strength index (RSI)*

      iv. *14-3-3 stochastic*

      v. *Williams %R*

i.–iii.

Date	Close	MACD Calculation 12-Day EMA	26-Day EMA	MACD	Signal Line (9-Day EMA of MACD)	14-Day ROC	14-Day RSI Calculation Gain	Loss	UPS	Downs	RS	RSI
8/1/2005	83.25											
8/2/2005	84.8						1.55	0				
8/3/2005	86.46						1.66	0				
8/4/2005	89.24						2.78	0				
8/5/2005	88.32						0	0.92				
8/8/2005	88.32						0	0				
8/9/2005	89.16						0.84	0				
8/10/2005	90.77						1.61	0				
8/11/2005	92.71						1.94	0				
8/12/2005	93.8						1.09	0				
8/15/2005	93.85						0.05	0				
8/16/2005	90.73						0	3.12				
8/17/2005	86.52						0	4.21				
8/18/2005	85.83					3.1	0	0.69				
8/19/2005	87.89					3.64	2.06	0	0.97	0.64	1.52	60.3
8/22/2005	88.12					1.92	0.23	0	0.92	0.59	1.55	60.73
8/23/2005	88.3					-1.05	0.18	0	0.86	0.55	1.57	61.09
8/24/2005	90.49					2.46	2.19	0	0.96	0.51	1.88	65.23
8/25/2005	89.47					1.3	0	1.02	0.89	0.55	1.63	61.93
8/26/2005	89.36					0.22	0	0.11	0.83	0.52	1.6	61.56
8/29/2005	91.88					1.22	2.52	0	0.95	0.48	1.98	66.41

Date	Close	MACD Calculation				14-Day ROC	14-Day RSI Calculation					
		12-Day EMA	26-Day EMA	MACD	Signal Line (9-Day EMA of MACD)		Gain	Loss	UPS	Downs	RS	RSI
8/30/2005	96.79					4.4	4.91	0	1.23	0.45	2.76	73.44
8/31/2005	106.5					13.54	9.71	0	1.84	0.41	4.44	81.63
9/1/2005	109.5					16.68	3	0	1.92	0.38	5	83.34
9/2/2005	108.43					19.51	0	1.07	1.78	0.43	4.12	80.46
9/6/2005	109.41	96.35	92.3	4.04		26.46	0.98	0	1.73	0.4	4.29	81.1
9/7/2005	111.03	98.6	93.69	4.91		29.36	1.62	0	1.72	0.37	4.6	82.15
9/8/2005	111.47	100.58	95.01	5.58		26.83	0.44	0	1.63	0.35	4.69	82.43
9/9/2005	114.97	102.8	96.49	6.31		30.47	3.5	0	1.76	0.32	5.47	84.54
9/12/2005	110.85	104.04	97.55	6.49		25.54	0	4.12	1.63	0.59	2.76	73.37
9/13/2005	111.1	105.12	98.55	6.57		22.78	0.25	0	1.54	0.55	2.79	73.6
9/14/2005	111	106.03	99.48	6.55		24.06	0	0.1	1.43	0.52	2.75	73.33
9/15/2005	108.69	106.44	100.16	6.28		21.63	0	2.31	1.32	0.65	2.05	67.19
9/16/2005	108.05	106.68	100.74	5.94	5.85	17.6	0	0.64	1.23	0.65	1.9	65.55
9/19/2005	111.27	107.39	101.52	5.87	5.85	14.96	3.22	0	1.37	0.6	2.29	69.57
9/20/2005	109.2	107.67	102.09	5.58	5.8	2.54	0	2.07	1.27	0.7	1.81	64.37
9/21/2005	113.14	108.51	102.91	5.6	5.76	3.32	3.94	0	1.46	0.65	2.24	69.11
9/22/2005	112.8	109.17	103.64	5.53	5.71	4.03	0	0.34	1.36	0.63	2.15	68.26
9/23/2005	110.77	109.42	104.17	5.25	5.62	1.24	0	2.03	1.26	0.73	1.72	63.3
9/26/2005	113.04	109.97	104.83	5.15	5.52	1.81	2.27	0	1.33	0.68	1.96	66.25
9/27/2005	112.58	110.37	105.4	4.97	5.41	1	0	0.46	1.24	0.66	1.87	65.11
9/28/2005	116.12	111.26	106.2	5.06	5.34	1	3.54	0	1.4	0.62	2.28	69.48
9/29/2005	114.99	111.83	106.85	4.99	5.27	3.73	0	1.13	1.3	0.65	2	66.61
9/30/2005	113.06	112.02	107.31	4.71	5.16	1.76	0	1.93	1.21	0.74	1.63	61.91
10/3/2005	116.06	112.64	107.96	4.69	5.07	4.56	3	0	1.34	0.69	1.94	65.94
10/4/2005	112.52	112.62	108.29	4.33	4.92	3.52	0	3.54	1.24	0.89	1.39	58.13

Date	Close	MACD Calculation 12-Day EMA	26-Day EMA	MACD	Signal Line (9-Day EMA of MACD)	14-Day ROC	14-Day RSI Calculation Gain	Loss	UPS	Downs	RS	RSI
10/5/2005	105.77	111.57	108.11	3.46	4.63	-2.11	0	6.75	1.15	1.31	0.88	46.77
10/6/2005	103.04	110.26	107.73	2.53	4.21	-7.4	0	2.73	1.07	1.41	0.76	43.1
10/7/2005	107.7	109.86	107.73	2.13	3.79	-1.37	4.66	0	1.33	1.31	1.01	50.27
10/10/2005	105.04	109.12	107.53	1.59	3.35	-7.16	0	2.66	1.23	1.41	0.87	46.66
10/11/2005	107.6	108.89	107.54	1.35	2.95	-4.61	2.56	0	1.33	1.31	1.01	50.36
10/12/2005	104.01	108.14	107.27	0.86	2.53	-6.1	0	3.59	1.23	1.47	0.84	45.58
10/13/2005	100.29	106.93	106.76	0.17	2.06	-11.28	0	3.72	1.14	1.63	0.7	41.22
10/14/2005	101.27	106.06	106.35	-0.29	1.59	-10.05	0.98	0	1.13	1.52	0.75	42.77
10/17/2005	103.49	105.66	106.14	-0.47	1.18	-10.88	2.22	0	1.21	1.41	0.86	46.24
10/18/2005	99.87	104.77	105.67	-0.9	0.76	-13.15	0	3.62	1.12	1.57	0.72	41.8
10/19/2005	98.98	103.88	105.18	-1.3	0.35	-12.45	0	0.89	1.04	1.52	0.69	40.76
10/20/2005	92.95	102.2	104.27	-2.07	-0.13	-19.91	0	6.03	0.97	1.84	0.53	34.51
10/21/2005	94.65	101.04	103.56	-2.52	-0.61	-15.88	1.7	0	1.02	1.71	0.6	37.42
10/24/2005	97.75	100.53	103.13	-2.6	-1.01	-7.58	3.1	0	1.17	1.59	0.74	42.45
10/25/2005	101.05	100.61	102.98	-2.36	-1.28	-1.93	3.3	0	1.32	1.47	0.9	47.3
10/26/2005	100.94	100.66	102.82	-2.16	-1.46	-6.28	0	0.11	1.23	1.38	0.89	47.16
10/27/2005	97.82	100.23	102.45	-2.23	-1.61	-6.87	0	3.12	1.14	1.5	0.76	43.18
10/28/2005	99.5	100.11	102.24	-2.12	-1.71	-7.53	1.68	0	1.18	1.39	0.85	45.83
10/31/2005	105.24	100.9	102.46	-1.56	-1.68	1.18	5.74	0	1.5	1.29	1.16	53.77

iv.–v.

Stochastic Calculation

Date	High	Low	Close	H	L	%K	Fast %D	Slow %D	Williams %R
8/1/2005	83.8	82.95	83.25						
8/2/2005	85.07	83.15	84.8						
8/3/2005	87.82	85	86.46						
8/4/2005	90.32	86.61	89.24						
8/5/2005	89.98	86.68	88.32						
8/8/2005	89.97	88.13	88.32						
8/9/2005	89.36	87.5	89.16						
8/10/2005	91	89.22	90.77						
8/11/2005	92.71	90.9	92.71						
8/12/2005	94.2	92.25	93.8						
8/15/2005	93.99	92.6	93.85						
8/16/2005	93.75	90.68	90.73						
8/17/2005	92.25	85.56	86.52						
8/18/2005	86.88	83.85	85.83	94.2	82.95	25.6			74.4
8/19/2005	88.23	86.32	87.89	94.2	83.15	42.9			57.1
8/22/2005	89.55	86.75	88.12	94.2	83.85	41.26	36.58		58.74
8/23/2005	89.08	86.8	88.3	94.2	83.85	43	42.38		57
8/24/2005	90.89	88.1	90.49	94.2	83.85	64.15	49.47	42.81	35.85
8/25/2005	90.24	89.08	89.47	94.2	83.85	54.3	53.82	48.56	45.7
8/26/2005	90.13	88.56	89.36	94.2	83.85	53.24	57.23	53.51	46.76
8/29/2005	91.88	89.5	91.88	94.2	83.85	77.58	61.71	57.58	22.42
8/30/2005	97.19	91.98	96.79	97.19	83.85	97	75.94	64.96	3
8/31/2005	108.75	96.82	106.5	108.75	83.85	90.96	88.52	75.39	9.04
9/1/2005	113.25	106.75	109.5	113.25	83.85	87.24	91.74	85.4	12.76
9/2/2005	110.25	105.45	108.43	113.25	83.85	83.61	87.27	89.17	16.39

Stochastic Calculation

Date	High	Low	Close	H	L	%K	Fast %D	Slow %D	Williams %R
9/6/2005	109.92	105.61	109.41	113.25	83.85	86.94	85.93	88.31	13.06
9/7/2005	112.3	109.55	111.03	113.25	83.85	92.45	87.66	86.96	7.55
9/8/2005	112.7	109.97	111.47	113.25	86.32	93.39	90.93	88.17	6.61
9/9/2005	115.12	112.7	114.97	115.12	86.75	99.47	95.1	91.23	0.53
9/12/2005	114.8	110.4	110.85	115.12	86.8	84.92	92.59	92.87	15.08
9/13/2005	112.35	110.04	111.1	115.12	88.1	85.12	89.84	92.51	14.88
9/14/2005	112.48	110.25	111	115.12	88.56	84.49	84.84	89.09	15.51
9/15/2005	111.7	107.69	108.69	115.12	88.56	75.79	81.8	85.49	24.21
9/16/2005	109.5	107.3	108.05	115.12	89.5	72.4	77.56	81.4	27.6
9/19/2005	112.79	109.84	111.27	115.12	91.98	83.36	77.19	78.85	16.64
9/20/2005	110.96	108.05	109.2	115.12	96.82	67.65	74.47	76.41	32.35
9/21/2005	113.3	110.81	113.14	115.12	105.45	79.52	76.85	76.17	20.48
9/22/2005	116.88	109.53	112.8	116.88	105.45	64.3	70.49	73.94	35.7
9/23/2005	112.34	109.7	110.77	116.88	105.61	45.79	63.2	70.18	54.21
9/26/2005	113.21	108.5	113.04	116.88	107.3	59.92	56.67	63.46	40.08
9/27/2005	113.74	111.37	112.58	116.88	107.3	55.11	53.61	57.83	44.89
9/28/2005	116.53	111.44	116.12	116.88	107.3	92.07	69.03	59.77	7.93
9/29/2005	117.25	114.4	114.99	117.25	107.3	77.29	74.82	65.82	22.71
9/30/2005	114.59	112.75	113.06	117.25	107.3	57.89	75.75	73.2	42.11
10/3/2005	116.29	113.64	116.06	117.25	107.3	88.04	74.41	74.99	11.96
10/4/2005	115.26	112.12	112.52	117.25	107.3	52.46	66.13	72.09	47.54
10/5/2005	113.6	105.2	105.77	117.25	105.2	4.73	48.41	62.98	95.27
10/6/2005	104.8	99.5	103.04	117.25	99.5	19.94	25.71	46.75	80.06
10/7/2005	107.97	103.39	107.7	117.25	99.5	46.2	23.62	32.58	53.8
10/10/2005	107.25	104.24	105.04	117.25	99.5	31.21	32.45	27.26	68.79
10/11/2005	108.25	106	107.6	117.25	99.5	45.63	41.01	32.36	54.37
10/12/2005	107.6	102.91	104.01	117.25	99.5	25.41	34.08	35.85	74.59
10/13/2005	102.94	97.7	100.29	117.25	97.7	13.25	28.1	34.4	86.75

Stochastic Calculation

Date	High	Low	Close	H	L	%K	Fast %D	Slow %D	Williams %R
10/14/2005	102.09	95.75	101.27	117.25	95.75	25.67	21.44	27.87	74.33
10/17/2005	105	102.46	103.49	117.25	95.75	36	24.97	24.84	64
10/18/2005	104.35	99.5	99.87	117.25	95.75	19.16	26.95	24.45	80.84
10/19/2005	100.25	93.8	98.98	116.29	93.8	23.03	26.07	25.99	76.97
10/20/2005	98.2	91.71	92.95	116.29	91.71	5.04	15.75	22.92	94.96
10/21/2005	96.45	92.23	94.65	115.26	91.71	12.48	13.52	18.44	87.52
10/24/2005	98.27	92.9	97.75	113.6	91.71	27.59	15.04	14.77	72.41
10/25/2005	102.27	97.9	101.05	108.25	91.71	56.47	32.18	20.25	43.53
10/26/2005	105.36	99.51	100.94	108.25	91.71	55.8	46.62	31.28	44.2
10/27/2005	103.1	97.75	97.82	108.25	91.71	36.94	49.74	42.85	63.06
10/28/2005	99.77	94.6	99.5	108.25	91.71	47.1	46.61	47.66	52.9
10/31/2005	106.64	103.55	105.24	107.6	91.71	85.15	56.4	50.92	14.85

b. *What information do you gain about Valero from these calculations? Do you see many similarities among the results of the five different calculations?*

The various oscillators indicate that VLO is in an uptrend during the first part of the time period. MACD is positive until October 14, and ROC is positive until October 4. The RSI is higher than 50, indicating an uptrend until October 4. The RSI is higher than 70 from August 30 through September 14, suggesting VLO is overbought. The stochastic is also suggesting the stock is overbought from September 1 through September 16.

6. *Most analysts will choose one oscillator to use in their analysis. Explain why using one oscillator is preferable to using the information from multiple oscillators.*

The various oscillators tend to provide similar information and tell the same story. Thus, using several oscillators is redundant and nonproductive. By focusing on one oscillator, the analyst is able to learn the complexity and intricacies of that particular oscillator well.

7. *Explain how moving averages and oscillators can be used in conjunction with each other for trading in trending and trading markets.*

Moving averages tend to be profitable during trending markets; oscillators are more profitable in trading markets. Using Wilder's ADX can help a trader distinguish whether a market is trending or is in a trading range. When markets are trending, use moving averages; when markets are in a consolidation period, use oscillators.

8. *Explain what is meant by the term confirmation. What are some general concepts the analyst should consider when looking for confirmation?*

Confirmation refers to using an indicator to increase the odds that a technical price signal is correct. The primary confirmation indicator is volume; high volume can help confirm a breakout. Momentum, or rate of price change, can also provide confirmation. Strong momentum suggests a trending market, and weak momentum suggests a consolidating market. Oscillators are helpful tools during a trending market.

Self-Test

1. *When price makes a new high, but an oscillator does not a*

   a. Negative divergence occurs.

   b. Positive divergence occurs.

   c. Negative reversal occurs.

   d. Positive reversal occurs.

2. *Which of the following is a TRUE statement regarding volume?*

   a. Volume indicators are such an important indicator of investors' emotions, they can be used without considering the underlying price movement for signals.

   b. Because it is a measure of liquidity in a security, volume by itself, rather than an indicator based on a change in volume, is most often used for confirmation.

   c. Higher volume during an uptrend demonstrates active and aggressive interest in owning the stock.

   d. A decline in price should only be trusted if it occurs on rising volume.

3. *The beginning of a trend often*

   a. Arises out of a pattern with a breakout on high volume.

   b. Occurs at the beginning of a pattern on low volume.

   c. Occurs at the beginning of a pattern on high volume.

   d. Occurs on volume dips.

4. *Open interest refers to*

   a. The number of shares of a stock traded during a given time period.

   b. The number of unique purchasers of a stock during a given time period.

   c. The number of unfilled orders at a given price.

   d. The number of futures contracts outstanding at any one time in each delivery month.

5. *Open interest and volume declining during an uptrend*

   a. Is an indication that the price trend may soon reverse.

   b. Is an indication that the uptrend is strong.

   c. Warns that the stock is experiencing a correction.

   d. Lead to positive confirmation.

6. *Momentum deals with*

   a. The degree to which volume is confirming price movement.

   b. The amount of convergence that is occurring between price and an oscillator.

   c. The price movement of one security relative to that of another security.

   d. The rate at which prices are changing.

7. *Strong momentum suggests*

   a. A trending market, whereas weak momentum suggests a consolidating market.

   b. A consolidating market, whereas weak momentum suggests a trending market.

   c. An uptrend, whereas weak momentum suggests a downtrend.

   d. A market peak, whereas weak momentum suggests a market bottom.

8. *The relative strength index (RSI) measures*

   a. The strength of an issue against its history of price change by comparing "up" days to "down" days.

   b. The strength of an issue by comparing its current volume with its historical average volume.

   c. The returns of an issue relative to the returns of the market index.

   d. The strength of an issue relative to the strength of other companies in the same industry index.

9. *Which of the following is a TRUE statement?*

   a. The rate of change (ROC) is not widely used because it is complex to calculate.

   b. Calculating the relative strength index (RSI) is complex and depends on knowing the day's volume that traded at a higher price relative to the previous day's close.

   c. The Money Flow index is a momentum indicator simply based on price, whereas the relative strength index (RSI) is an oscillator based on an issue's performance relative to the broader market.

   d. The rate of change (ROC) is a simple indicator, but suffers from the drop-off effect.

10. *Volume spikes*

    a. Are most common at the beginning of a trend and at the end of a trend.

    b. Are usually not meaningful, but sharp declines in volume often indicate a trend reversal.

    c. Are usually not meaningful, but sharp declines in volume often indicate a breakout.

    d. Often occur at the end of a trend, but seldom occur at the beginning of a trend.

CHAPTER 19
Cycles

Chapter Objectives

By the end of this chapter, you should be familiar with

▶ The controversy about whether cycles exist in financial market data

▶ How cycles are defined by their amplitude, period, and phase

▶ Detrending data and plotting centered moving averages

▶ The major methods of determining cycles in market data

▶ The major methods of using cycles to project future price highs and lows

Chapter Summary

Cycle analysts look at prices as a form of complex harmonics or waves. Some oppose this concept because financial market data does not easily fit into mathematical formulas that give precise predictions similar to what we know about ocean tides and sunrises. Others oppose the concept because of a lack of ability to identify causes of specific cycles that seem to exist in stock prices.

Some have suggested a moon cycle exists for the stock market. A well-defined annual cycle exists in agricultural commodity prices, and we see a seasonal cycle in the stock market. Although the business cycle affects market prices, it is not truly a market cycle because it does not have a periodic element.

Market cycles are not truly harmonics; they tend to be periodic events or extremes that can be measured in time but not necessarily in amplitude. However, they tend to demonstrate **harmonic** action in that cycles tend to be fractions of larger and multiples of smaller cycles. **Proportionality** refers to the tendency for longer cycles to have larger amplitudes.

What Are Cycles?

The **amplitude** of a cycle is the distance from the horizontal axis to the extreme peak or trough. **Period** is the distance between consecutive highs or consecutive lows. Cycles in financial markets are not precise; therefore, cycle periods are indefinite and have error. **Inversions** can occur, causing a cycle low to occur where a peak is expected or causing a cycle high to occur where a trough is expected. **Translation** occurs when a peak occurs before or after the halfway point in a cycle.

How Can Cycles Be Found in Market Data?

Fourier analysis and Maximum Entropy Spectral Analysis (MESA) provide methods for determining cycles but depend upon complex mathematics. Detrending, envelopes, and centered moving averages are simpler tools for identifying cycles. A **centered moving average** plots a moving average at the center of the time span of the average; thus a 21-day moving average would be plotted at Day 11. Detrending is done by dividing the current prices by a centered moving average of those prices. The resulting plot oscillates above and below a zero line, with the lows corresponding to the lows of the cycle being analyzed.

Projections

Three facts are needed to project the time for the next low in a cycle: The period length of the cycle of interest, the standard error of that cycle, and the ideal starting point from which to measure it into the future. Prediction of amplitude is difficult because amplitudes can vary enormously. The concept of **commonality** suggests that issues of the same nature tend to have the same cycles, but with different amplitudes.

Key Concepts and Vocabulary

A number of terms and concepts that might be new to you appear in this chapter. As you read through this chapter, pay close attention to the following terms and concepts. Write down a definition or explanation for each.

Amplitude

Period

Phase

Summation

Inversion

Harmonic

Translation

Detrending

Centered moving average

Commonality

Focal point

Future line of demarcation (FLD)

Forward line

Principle of variation

Nesting

Cosine function

Radians

End-of-Chapter Review Questions

1. *A great deal of controversy surrounds cycles. What are the reasons why some oppose cycle theory? How do the supporters of cycle theory respond to these criticisms?*

   There are two main reasons why some oppose cycle theory. First, mathematical formulas cannot be used to precisely describe cycles in the financial markets as can be done with ocean tides or celestial objects. This faction claims that the lack of mathematically definable cycles is evidence that cycles do not exist. Second, no logical reasons for what would cause cycles in financial data exist. Correlations between events such as the Super Bowl or amounts of rainfall are merely curious correlations; because there is no logical theory of why these events would affect financial data, the relationships cannot be causal or explanatory.

   Supporters of cycle theory admit that the cycles in financial markets are not mathematically equivalent to the harmonics found in nature. Mathematics is not developed enough to describe the patterns with varying amplitude. However, we do observe cycles, and cycles of these types are acknowledged in other disciplines. For example, psychologists have documented changes in emotional behavior that are tied to lunar phases. These supporters also point to ways in which seasonal cycles and agricultural cycles can relate to markets as well as human behavior. Economists readily admit to non-harmonic business cycles.

2. *Explain what each of the following terms means as it refers to cycles:*

   a. *Amplitude*

   b. *Period*

   c. *Phase*

   d. *Summation*

   e. *Inversion*

   f. *Harmonics*

   a. Amplitude can be thought of as the height of the cycle. It is the distance between the horizontal axis and the peak or trough of the cycle.

   b. Period is the distance between consecutive highs or consecutive lows. In other words, it is the length of time from one trough to the next trough or from one peak to the next peak.

   c. Phase determines how far from the Y-axis the cycle begins. It is a measure of what part of the cycle occurs at a particular point in time. It is used to determine how off-set two cycles are from each other.

   d. Summation is the adding together of multiple cycles. In financial markets many cycles exist; the plot of prices observed is the result of these multiple cycles being summed together.

   e. Inversion occurs when a cycle high (low) is expected but instead a low (high) is observed.

   f. Harmonic refers to the tendency of one cycle to be a fraction of a longer cycle and a multiple of a shorter cycle. A particular cycle is usually a part of a cycle that is either two or three times longer. For example, a 20-day cycle is usually part of a cycle that is either 40 or 60 days long. Also, the 20-day cycle is composed of two 10-day or three 7-day cycles.

3. *What do* left translation *and* right translation *mean? When would you expect to see each of these occurring in a cycle?*

   In markets, cycles are measured from trough to trough. Peaks rarely occur at the halfway period of a cycle. For example, in a 20-day cycle from trough to trough, the peak rarely occurs 10 days from the cycle low. If the peak occurs before the tenth day, left translation exists; if the peak occurs after the tenth day, right translation exists. During an uptrend, right translation usually occurs. If during an uptrend a cycle peaks at the halfway point, rather than the common right translation, the analyst should be suspicious that the uptrend is ending.

4. *What is the argument for plotting a centered moving average centered over the time period in the calculation rather than plotting it at the end of the time period?*

   A moving average represents the average price over the period the average is being calculated. For example, a 21-day moving average gives information about the data from days 1 through 21. Traditionally, this moving average is plotted at day 21. This means each plot represents data from the previous 21 days. Plotting this moving average at day 11 centers the information over the period the information is summarizing and represents the average time of the cycle. This better represents the time for which that moving average is being calculated because it denotes the average price and time about that point.

5. *Download daily data for the S&P500 for the period July 1, 2009 through July 1, 2010. (This historical data is available at http://finance.yahoo.com.)*

   a. *Plot this data in a chart. Are any cycles apparent in your chart?*

   b. *Detrend the data by creating an oscillator that is constructed using a ratio of the current close to the 11-day SMA.*

   c. *Does the plot of this oscillator reveal any cycle in your data?*

   a. The following chart plots the S&P500 from July 1, 2009 through July 1, 2010. Although the overall trend is upward, there appears to be cyclical behavior, especially in the first few months of the chart and at major intervals of three months.

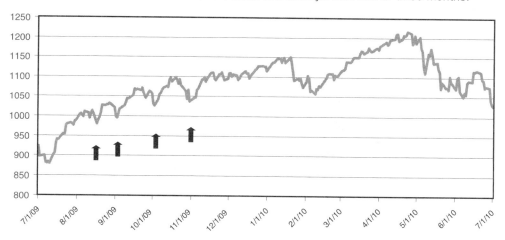

b.-c. The following graph shows the same S&P500 data along with an oscillator created by taking the ratio of the S&P500 and the 11-day SMA of the S&P500. The oscillator is reaching lows at some of the same times that the price data appeared to be making lows in the previous chart at roughly three months apart.

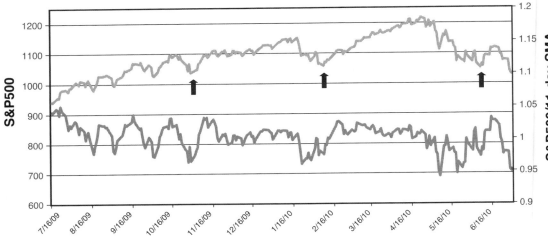

6. *Using the S&P500 data you collected in Question 5, plot a 41-day centered SMA and a 21-day centered SMA. Explain ways in which this information might be used to determine and project cycles.*

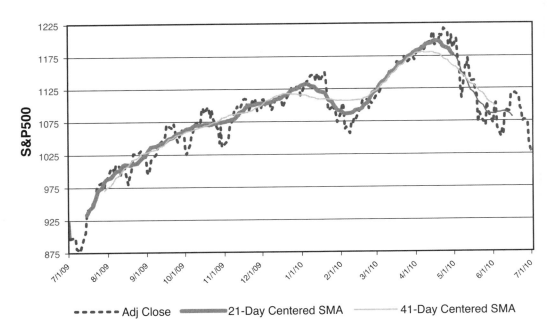

A centered moving average better reflects the price action than the conventional moving average plot. The analyst can determine when the large price deviations below and above the moving average occur to determine the cyclical nature of the price movement.

7. *What is a focal point? How is it used to project cycles?*

A focal point occurs when three or more half-cycle, centered, moving averages cross at roughly the same location. Focal points occur at roughly the halfway point of cycle advances or declines; the time from the cycle high to the focal point is roughly the same as the time from the focal point to the cycle low. A trend line drawn between two successive focal points estimates the direction of the next higher-order cycle and the extent to which the next directional move will travel.

Self-Test

1. *Harmonics refers to*

    a. The tendency of a cycle to be a fraction of a longer cycle and a multiple of a shorter cycle.

    b. The tendency for cycles to be similar, but not identical, over time.

    c. The tendency for cycles for stocks within a particular industry to have similar amplitudes and periods.

    d. The tendency for left translation in inverted cycles.

2. *You have determined a 40-day cycle for a particular security. You find that the peak occurs 22 days after the trough. This is referred to as*

    a. A harmonic.

    b. An amplified cycle.

    c. An extended period cycle.

    d. Right translation.

3. *The concept of commonality suggests that*

    a. Stocks within the same industry tend to have cycles with the same amplitude.

    b. Left translation is common in an uptrend and right translation is common in a downtrend.

    c. Individual stocks generally have the same cycles as the stock market averages.

    d. Cycles of different lengths tend to share common troughs and common amplitudes.

4. *You have calculated a 13-day moving average for a stock. The centered moving average would be*

   a. Plotted at day 7.

   b. Calculated by computing a 7-day moving average of the 13-day moving average.

   c. Calculated by computing a 26-day moving average of the 13-day moving average.

   d. Calculated by weighting the price on day 7 twice as heavily as the price on day 1 or day 13.

5. *Detrending is done by*

   a. Dividing current prices by a moving average of those prices.

   b. Dividing the current price by the price at the beginning of the cycle.

   c. Dividing the current price by the price at the trough of the previous cycle.

   d. Dividing the current price by the number of days in the cycle.

6. *Emma thinks that a security has an 18-day cycle. She has divided daily prices for the security by the 6-day price moving average. A plot of this calculation will*

   a. Oscillate around the price action of the security and bound price movement.

   b. Oscillate above and below a zero line and the lows of the plot correspond to the lows in the cycle.

   c. Estimate the amplitude of the cycle.

   d. Create an envelope around the price action.

7. *In order to project the time for the next low in a cycle, you need to know*

   a. The period length of the cycle of interest.

   b. The standard error of the cycle.

   c. The ideal starting point from which to measure the cycle into the future.

   d. All of the above.

8. *Which of the following is a TRUE statement?*

   a. Just as with radio waves, the cycles of financial markets can be precisely described by mathematical methods.

   b. Most standard technical analysis patterns can be broken down into cycle layers.

   c. The business cycle is an example of a truly harmonic cycle with a predictable magnitude.

   d. One complicating factor for cycle analysis is that cycles of differing lengths tend to be unrelated, with troughs occurring at different time periods.

9. *You are watching a 20-day cycle of a stock. You are expecting to see a cycle low, but instead, a peak occurs. This is known as*

   a. An inversion.

   b. A translation.

   c. A detrended harmonic.

   d. A trend projection error.

10. *A centered moving average*

    a. Is used to identify cycles but is not a signaling method because it leads price movements.

    b. Is used to identify cycles but is not a signaling method because it lags behind prices.

    c. Weights prices in the middle of the time period being analyzed more heavily than prices at the beginning or the end of the time period.

    d. Is used to signal changes in trend and cycle amplitude, but is not useful in identifying cycles themselves.

CHAPTER 20
Elliott, Fibonacci, and Gann

Chapter Objectives

After reading this chapter, you should be familiar with

▶ The basic tenets of and vocabulary used with the Elliott Wave Theory

▶ The rules and guidelines of the Elliott Wave Theory

▶ The construction of the Fibonacci sequence

▶ The derivation and characteristics of the golden ratio

▶ The reasons why Elliott Wave Theory can be difficult for the average analyst to apply

Chapter Summary

Elliott Wave Theory (EWT) is based upon the notion that the market behaves in an irregular cyclic manner. Proponents of EWT believe that this cyclic structure is classifiable and predictable.

A **wave** is a sustained price move in one direction as determined by the reversal points that initiated and terminated the move. A **wave cycle** is composed of two waves: The **impulse wave** is in the direction of the current trend, and the **corrective wave** moves against the trend's direction. During a bull market, the overall trend is called a **motive impulse wave**.

The impulse wave is always made up of five subwaves, traditionally labeled with numbers. Waves 1, 3, and 5 are smaller waves that contribute to the larger wave's upward trend. Waves 2 and 4 are corrective subwaves. The corrective wave is broken into three subwaves, labeled by letters.

The six inviolate rules for impulse waves are the following:

1. Impulse waves move in the same direction as the trend of the next higher degree wave.

2. Impulse waves divide into five subwaves.

3. Within an impulse wave, subwaves 1, 3, and 5 are themselves impulse waves of a lesser degree, and subwaves 2 and 4 are corrective waves.

4. Within an impulse wave, subwaves 1 and 5 might be either an impulse or diagonal pattern.

5. Within an impulse wave, subwave 3 is always an impulse pattern.

6. In cash markets, within an impulse pattern, subwave 4 never overlaps any portion of subwave 1. This is not always true for futures markets.

A **diagonal** is the same as the classic wedge pattern and can appear in wave 1 or wave 5, but never in wave 3. A diagonal appearing in wave 1 is called a **leading diagonal**, and one appearing in wave 5 is called an **ending diagonal**. A **truncation** occurs when the fifth wave fails to exceed the third wave.

Price movement during a corrective wave can either be sideways or sharply opposite to the prevailing trend of the impulse wave. Corrective waves can appear in many different configurations and pattern combinations but are generalized into three categories: zigzags, flats, and triangles. **Alternation** refers to the tendency for the corrective wave 2 to be a different type than corrective wave 4.

Two of the three impulse subwaves in a five-wave sequence tend to be of equal length. This is known as **equality**. Price often oscillates between a line drawn between the end of wave 1 and wave 3 and a parallel line through the end of wave 2. This is known as **channeling**.

The Fibonacci Sequence

Fibonacci numbers are a sequence in which the last number is added to the previous number to arrive at the next number. The Fibonacci sequence includes the numbers 1, 2, 3, 5, 8, 13, and 21. The ratio of a number in the Fibonacci sequence to the next lower number is 1.618; the ratio of a number in the sequence to the next highest number is 0.618. Elliott Wave enthusiasts use Fibonacci ratios to predict retracements, price targets, and the timing of the next series of waves.

Key Concepts and Vocabulary

A number of terms and concepts that might be new to you appear in this chapter. As you read through this chapter, pay close attention to the following terms and concepts. Write down a definition or explanation for each.

Elliott Wave Theory

Wave

Wave cycle

Impulse wave

Corrective wave

Motive impulse wave

Diagonal

Leading diagonal

Ending diagonal

Throw-over

Truncation

Zigzag

Flat

Triangle

Alteration

Equality

Channeling

Fibonacci sequence

Golden ratio

End-of-Chapter Review Questions

1. *Explain the following Elliott Wave Theory terms:*

   a. *Motive wave*

   During a bull market the overall trend (upward price movement) is a motive impulse wave. The motive wave continues until a major change in market direction (a downward motive impulse wave) begins.

   b. *Corrective wave*

   A corrective wave is a move against the direction of the trend.

   c. *Impulse wave*

   An impulse wave is a move in the direction of the market trend.

   d. *Subwave*

   Impulse waves and corrective waves are composed of smaller subwaves. For example, an impulse wave can be broken down into five subwaves (with 1, 3, and 5 moving in the direction of the underlying trend of the impulse wave and 2 and 4 breaking up the movement of the trend with a correction).

e. *Truncation*

Generally, the fifth subwave of an upward impulse wave ends at a higher price than the third subwave does. When the fifth subwave does not end at a higher price than the third (that is, the fifth subwave does not regain the entire price decline that occurred during the correction of the fourth subwave) truncation is said to occur.

f. *Equality*

Equality refers to the fact that often two of the three impulse subwaves in a five wave sequence are the same length.

g. *Alternation*

Alternation refers to the fact that the correction that occurs in wave 4 is often a different type than the correction that occurred in wave 2.

h. *Rule*

In EWT a rule is inviolate. These rules cannot be broken. If the analyst ignores a rule, EWT is not correctly applied and the analyst's conclusions and projections are likely to be incorrect.

2. *The EWT pattern is often said to be like "three steps forward and two steps back." Explain this phrase as it relates to EWT.*

Assume that the underlying market trend is upward. A security price does not continuously increase during a market trend. Instead the security price moves in waves. EWT states that the advance will take the form of five waves. An initial upward movement in price occurs, which is like a step forward. Then a corrective wave occurs in which prices retrace some of their gain (or step back). A third wave of upward price movement occurs as a second step forward. This is followed by a fourth wave which is a corrective wave, or a step back. Finally, a fifth wave is a step forward with upward price movement.

3. *Explain what a Fibonacci number is.*

The Fibonacci numbers are derived from a sequence in which the two previous numbers of the sequence are added together to determine the next number. For example, the sequence begins with the number 1. One plus one equals two. Then, $1 + 2 = 3$. Then, 2 and 3 are added together to derive the next number in the sequence, 5. Next, 3 plus 5 produces 8. Fibonacci numbers continue to be derived by adding the two previous numbers of the series. The ratio between the last number and the one prior in the series approaches 1.618, called the Golden Ratio or *phi*.

4. *Explain the difference between a zigzag and a flat in EWT.*

Zigzags and flats are corrections to the general trend movement. In a zigzag, wave A moves in the opposite direction of the prevailing impulse wave. For example, if the prevailing impulse wave is up, then wave A of the zigzag correction is down. Wave B then moves up but does not regain the entire decline that wave A brought. Then wave C moves in the same direction as wave A, falling lower than the low of wave A. This results in something that looks like the following diagram.

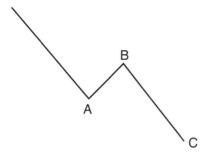

A flat is a sideways pattern. Flats are similar to zigzags, but move in a sideways direction. Their subwaves generally overlap, resulting in something that looks like the following diagram.

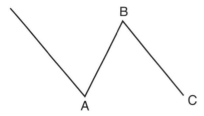

5. *Choose any two numbers and go through the method shown in Box 20.1 [in the* Technical Analysis *textbook] to demonstrate how you will arrive at the Golden Ratio.*

   Numbers will vary depending on numbers chosen.

   Two numbers chosen 54 and 1999

   1. 54 + 1999 = 2053
   2. 1999 + 2053 = 4052   4052/2053 = 1.974
   3. 2053 + 4052 = 6105   6105/4052 = 1.507
   4. 4052 + 6105 = 10,157   10,157/6105 = 1.664
   5. 6105 + 10,157 = 16,262   16,262/10,157 = 1.601
   6. 10,157 + 16,262 = 26,419   26,419/16,262 = 1.625
   7. 16,262 + 26,419 = 42,681   42,681/26,419 = 1.616
   8. 26,419 + 42,681 = 69,100   69,100/42,681 = 1.619
   9. 42,681 + 69,100 = 111,781   111,781/69,100 = 1.618

6. *Explain why using EWT can be difficult for the average analyst.*

The EWT is complex with unclear standard rules, and its interpretation is subject to later revision. Thus, using EWT to make a profit can be difficult. The rules in EWT have many exceptions. This often leads to confusion for the student trying to learn and apply EWT. The waves that occur in the market can often be determined after the fact, which is of no use to the analyst trying to make money in the market. Because the theory is so complex, it is not easily computerized. The EWT student must carefully study the theory and use it to understand the position of the market rather than as a mechanical trading system.

Self-Test

1. *The number 1.618 is known as*

   a. The Golden Ratio.

   b. The pyramid sequence ratio.

   c. Pi.

   d. Beta.

2. *Which of the following is a list of numbers in the Fibonacci sequence?*

   a. 1, 2, 4, 16, 25, 36, 49, 64, 81

   b. 1, 2, 3, 6, 18, 108

   c. 2, 4, 16, 36, 64, 100

   d. 1, 1, 2, 3, 5, 8, 13, 21, 34, 55

3. *In Elliott Wave Theory, impulse waves are generally labeled _____ and corrective waves are generally labeled _____.*

   a. 1, 2, 3, 4, and 5; A, B, and C

   b. 1, 2, 3, 4, and 5; I, II, and III

   c. A, B, C, D, and E; 1, 2, and 3

   d. A, B, C, D, and E; a, b, and c

4. *_____ and _____ are corrections to the general price movement.*

   a. Motive waves; retracements

   b. Zigzags; flats

   c. Motive waves; zigzags

   d. Flats; impulse waves

5. *In EWT,*

  a. Rules are inviolate.

  b. Motive waves follow rules, but corrective waves do not.

  c. Rules are defined as being correct more than 75% of the time.

  d. All waves are subject to interpretation; thus, there are no precise rules.

6. *The tendency for the type of correction occurring in wave 4 to differ from the type of correction that occurred in wave 2 is known as*

  a. Channeling.

  b. Zigzagging.

  c. Alternation.

  d. Truncation.

7. *Truncation refers to*

  a. The third wave being shorter than the first wave and the fifth wave being shorter than the third wave.

  b. Situations in which a corrective wave fully reverses the gains made in an impulse wave.

  c. The tendency for a leading diagonal to be followed by an ending diagonal.

  d. Situations of the fifth wave failing to exceed the end of the third wave.

8. *Equality refers to*

  a. The tendency for two of the three impulse subwaves in a five-wave sequence to be equal in length.

  b. The tendency for all three impulse subwaves in a five-wave sequence to be equal in length.

  c. The situation in which the impulse and corrective waves in a five-wave sequence are equal in length.

  d. The tendency for wave 2 and wave 4 corrective waves in a five-wave sequence to be identical.

9. *Channeling refers to*

   a. The tendency for price to oscillate within a channel formed by drawing a line between the end of wave 1 and wave 3 and drawing a parallel line through the end of wave 2.

   b. The tendency for price to oscillate between the high of wave 1 and the low of wave 2 during waves 3, 4, and 5.

   c. Situations in which the corrective waves are characterized by zigzags within the price range of the motive waves.

   d. The price move of each subsequent wave in a five-wave sequence to be smaller than that of the previous wave.

10. *The ratio of any number in the Fibonacci sequence to the next highest number in the sequence*

    a. Approaches 0.618.

    b. Is 1.618 times higher than the previous ratio of the two adjacent numbers.

    c. Is a square number.

    d. Asymptotically approaches zero.

CHAPTER 21

Selection of Markets and Issues: Trading and Investing

Chapter Objectives

By the end of this chapter, you should be familiar with

- ▶ The major factors to consider when choosing a security to trade

- ▶ The major factors to consider when choosing an investment security

- ▶ The relationship between hard asset and soft asset markets

- ▶ The basics of intermarket analysis

- ▶ The concept of relative strength among different investment vehicles and its implications for investors

- ▶ The basic methods of determining an individual stock's relative strength

Chapter Summary

Which Issues Should I Select for Trading?

It is wise to trade more than one issue. First, when one issue begins trading in a small trading range, other issues can take its place. Second, following more than one issue increases the odds that you will not miss a profitable trend. Third, diversification reduces the risk of capital loss.

You must consider trading costs. In addition to commissions, you must consider equipment costs, data feed, and slippage. Traders must consider their tolerance for risk and the effect of leverage on the risk they take.

Scalping is trading that takes very small profits between the bid and ask prices of a stock. **Day trading** is trading an issue and closing all positions by the end of the day. **Swing trading** is the holding of positions over several days or weeks, attempting to catch the small trends accompanying or counter to a longer trend.

Which Issues Should I Select for Investing?

Top-down analysis begins with a study of the major markets such as interest rates, currencies, and stock market to determine which market has the highest possibility of profit in the future. After you select the market, you select groupings of issues in that market, and then you choose individual issues within those groupings. **Ratio analysis** compares different markets with each other to determine which is performing most favorably.

Hard assets are commodities, and **soft assets** are financial assets. Generally, when hard assets rise in value, interest rates rise, and soft assets decline.

Bottom-up analysis begins with a screening of stocks from the entire stock market for anticipated trend changes. **Relative strength** analysis is based on evidence demonstrating that individual stock price strength will continue into the future, just as a trend will also continue. The **ratio method**, calculating the ratio between two investments, is the most common way to determine relative strength, but for screening of a large number of stocks you use various methods measuring stock price breakouts, chart pattern, and momentum.

Key Concepts and Vocabulary

A number of terms and concepts that might be new to you appear in this chapter. As you read through this chapter, pay close attention to the following terms and concepts. Write down a definition or explanation for each.

Scalping

Day trading

Swing trading

Top-down analysis

Hard assets

Soft assets

Ratio analysis

Relative strength

Ratio method

Intermarket analysis

Law of percentages

Alpha

Bottom-up analysis

End-of-Chapter Review Questions

1. *Explain the differences between scalping, day trading, and swing trading.*

   Scalping is taking very small profits between the bid and ask prices of a security. A scalper must have fast-feed charting equipment and excellent execution. Because the scalper is competing against the market makers, specialists, floor traders, and desk traders, profitable scalping is very difficult and is not for the amateur trader.

   Day trading is trading an issue and closing all positions by the end of the day. Because the day trader does not hold any overnight positions, the day trader has the advantage of no overnight risk.

   Swing trading is the holding of positions over several days or weeks. The swing trader is attempting to catch the small trends (or countertrends) that accompany a longer trend. Swing trading is the most practical type of trading for amateurs. Unlike scalping and day trading, watching the market throughout the trading day is often not necessary for the swing trader. The swing trader is able to determine entry and exit prices during non-trading hours and can judiciously place orders for the next trading day to enter or exit positions.

2. *A trader should consider a particular instrument's volatility, liquidity, and volume when choosing instruments to trade. Explain why each of these three characteristics is an important component of the trader's decision.*

   Much of the profit that can be derived from trading occurs when a security breaks out from low volatility to high volatility. In fact, it is difficult to profit from trading a security that has low volatility. With low volatility there is little price change, making it difficult for the trader to buy at a relatively low price and profit from selling at a relatively high price.

   Liquidity refers to the ability to transact a meaningful number of shares or contracts easily and without bringing about a large price change. When a trader is ready to sell a position, he or she wants to be able to find a buyer easily. The trader is also concerned that liquidating the position does not result in a fall in the price of the security, making the trade less profitable.

   Volume is also important to the trader. If a security is thinly traded, an individual trader's execution might adversely affect the market price of the security.

3. *Explain the difference between a hard asset market and a soft asset market.*

   Hard assets are commodities: gold and silver are examples of hard assets. They are things you can touch and feel and are often called "tangibles." These hard assets are considered a hedge against inflation. Financial assets, called "paper assets," are soft assets. They exist on paper or computers and are often called "intangibles." Both stocks and bonds are soft assets.

4. *Explain the basic premise of secular analysis and its importance to the investor.*

Secular analysis is the alternating emphasis between soft asset and hard asset markets over long secular periods. (These long secular periods are longer than the business cycle.) Generally, when hard assets rise in value, soft assets decline in value. Periods of higher hard asset prices and inflation are generally associated with periods of higher interest rates. When interest rates rise, the value of paper assets declines. Therefore, when the investor thinks that the economy is entering into a long-term inflationary period, the investor wants to invest in hard assets. When the investor expects inflationary pressure to cease, hard asset prices to fall, and interest rates to fall, he or she wants to emphasize the soft assets that are expected to increase in value.

5. *Explain the basic principle behind cyclical analysis and its importance to the investor.*

The business cycle refers to the tendency of the economy to experience a cycle of contraction and expansion every four to five years. The leadership in trading markets often switches within the business cycle. A period of U.S. dollar appreciation generally precedes a period of inflation. During periods of inflation and rising interest rates, investors want to purchase industrial raw materials, such as gold and energy. As inflationary pressures in the economy ease, investors want to switch to bonds. This is because the lower inflation rates will be associated with lower interest rates and as interest rates fall, bond prices will rise. After investors have taken advantage of rising bond prices, they should switch their emphasis to the stock market. The low interest and inflation rates at this point in the business cycle favor stocks.

6. *Lauren inherited $10,000 and immediately invested the money in the stock market. Unfortunately she lost 30% of her investment. Explain why she will have to have a return greater than 30% to get back to her initial capital level of $10,000.*

If Lauren originally invested $10,000 and lost 30% of that investment, she is left with $7,000 of capital. A 30% return on a $7,000 investment is $2,100. Therefore, Lauren will only have $9,100 after a 30% gain. In fact, in order to return to the $10,000 capital level, Lauren must earn $3,000 on a $7,000 investment. Lauren needs to earn a 42.86% return on $7,000 to bring her back to her initial $10,000 wealth level. This principle is called the "law of percentages."

7. *Explain what is meant by the term relative strength in this chapter and the implications of a stock's relative strength for the investor.*

In this context, *relative strength* refers to how a particular investment is performing compared to other investment possibilities. For example, if the value of a particular stock is increasing more rapidly than the S&P500, that stock is outperforming the market average. Many studies show that this strength generally continues. By recognizing the strongest investments, an edge can be obtained by investing in them until their strength abates.

8. *Andrew has been following the performance of the stock of his favorite company, Back Country Driving Equipment (BCDE). He has plotted the ratio of BCDE to the S&P500 for the past year, and has found a strongly upward sloping line. He thought that this meant that BCDE was a relatively strong stock; however, he noticed that investors in BCDE have lost money over the past year. He is confused as to how investing in a relatively strong stock could result in a loss. Explain how this could happen.*

The strong upward sloping line that Andrew found indicates that BCDE is outperforming the S&P500. However, outperforming the S&P500 does not guarantee profits. The S&P500, for example, might have declined by 15% over the past year. If BCDE declined by 6% over the same period, Andrew would find that BCDE performed relatively better than the S&P500; investors in BCDE lost only 6% whereas investors in the S&P500 lost 15%.

Self-Test

1. _____ is the making of small profits between the bid and ask prices of a security.

   a. Day trading

   b. Swing trading

   c. Options trading

   d. Scalping

2. *Hard assets*

   a. Include stocks and bonds.

   b. Are used as a hedge against inflation.

   c. Include financial assets.

   d. Both a and b.

3. *Generally, when hard assets increase in value*

   a. Interest rates and soft assets also rise in value.

   b. Interest rates fall, and soft assets rise in value.

   c. Interest rates rise, and soft assets decline in value.

   d. Interest rates and soft assets both fall in value.

4. *Intermarket analysis is based upon the notion that*

   a. Market movements are random and unpredictable.

   b. Markets are interrelated and follow certain patterns.

   c. Soft assets are affected by inflation, but hard assets are not.

   d. Hard assets are affected by inflation, but soft assets are not.

5. *The notion of relative strength suggests that*

   a. The strongest stocks remain strong.

   b. The strongest stocks in one period will, on average, be the weakest in the next time period.

   c. Stock price movement is random, and markets are efficient.

   d. Momentum indicators are not useful because of reversion to the mean.

6. *A trader wants to trade a security*

   a. With low volatility so that price movements do not occur so quickly that the trader cannot enter at the expected price.

   b. With low volume to minimize the number of transactions that need to be analyzed.

   c. With enough liquidity to allow the trader to transact a meaningful number of shares without bringing about a large price change.

   d. That has a large bid-ask spread to ensure low slippage costs.

7. *Top-down analysis*

   a. Begins with a study of the major markets to determine which market has the highest probability of profit in the future.

   b. Refers to projecting the time frame in which a market will peak and trough.

   c. Is performed by calculating a ratio of price movement to average volume for each security within a sector.

   d. Begins with a fundamental analysis of the individual securities of interest to the trader.

8. *Nick is interested in investing in ABT. As part of his analysis he has plotted the ratio of ABT to the S&P500 for the past year. This formed a line that was steeply downward sloping. This is an indication that*

   a. Investors who owned ABT over the past year have lost money and a portion of their capital.

   b. The performance of ABT is negatively correlated with that of the S&P500.

   c. ABT has been stronger than the market average over the past year.

   d. ABT has been weaker than the market average over the past year.

9. *Much of the profit that can be made from a security occurs*

   a. When the security moves from a period of low volatility to a period of high volatility.

   b. When the security has low liquidity.

   c. Between the security's bid price and ask price.

   d. When the volume for the security is low.

10. *Swing trading*

    a. Requires reliable intraday data feed and access to high-speed order execution to be profitable.

    b. Is the attempt to ride small trends in price and does not require constant watch of price behavior.

    c. Is the attempt to profit by moving from one market to another during the business cycle.

    d. Is the movement back and forth between hard assets and soft assets as the value of the dollar changes.

CHAPTER 22

System Design and Testing

Chapter Objectives

By the end of this chapter, you should be familiar with

▶ The importance of using a system for trading or investing

▶ The difference between a discretionary and a nondiscretionary system

▶ The mindset and discipline required to develop and trade with a system

▶ The basic procedures for designing a system

▶ The role that risk management plays in system design

▶ How to test a system

▶ Standard measures of system profitability and risk

Chapter Summary

Why Are Systems Necessary?

A system aids the investor in using well-controlled entries and exits, especially those that limit the amount of loss that can occur and that will react to changing conditions in the market. A **discretionary system** is one in which entries and exits are based on the trader's intuition. In a **nondiscretionary** (or algorithmic) **system**, entries and exits are determined by a computer program. Using a nondiscretionary system avoids emotions and reduces other trading problems, such as overtrading, premature action, no action, and constant decision making. Properly designed systems prevent large losses and risk of ruin. It can be difficult, however, to know when a system needs to be updated due to a changing marketplace.

How Do I Design a System?

Designing a workable, profitable trading system begins with some basic personal attitudes. Although the underlying objective is to make a profit, the system designer needs to remember to consider risk. The amount of money potentially lost with a trading system is called **drawdown**. Drawdown is the amount by which the equity in an account declines from a peak. **Maximum drawdown** is the largest drawdown of equity in the account, usually expressed as a percentage, and is used as a measure of potential capital risk.

The trader must decide on a trading philosophy and premises. In addition, the trader must choose on which markets to focus. A time horizon for a system must be established. The trader must have a risk control plan. The traders should also establish a time routine to update the system, plan new trades, and update exit points for existing trades.

There are four main categories of technical systems; trend following, pattern recognition, countertrend, and exogenous signal systems.

How Do I Test a System?

Data provided by the same source that will be used when a system is running in real time should be used to test the system. Data that covers periods where the market traveled up, down, and sideways should be used.

Parameters of a system should be tested to ensure that small changes in the parameter do not lead to significantly different results. After the parameters have been determined to be valid, the system can be optimized. Optimizing is useful in determining which parameters achieve the best results. Optimizing is also useful in determining whether certain types of stops are useful. However, the system designer must be careful to avoid curve-fitting when optimizing the system. An optimization method used to test systems with data not used in the original optimization is called Out-of-Sample (OSS) optimization. These reduce the chances of curve-fitting because the successful systems must also profit in data not used during the initial tests.

Robustness refers to the ability of a system to adjust to changing circumstances. At least 30 trades are needed to make sure the test results are significant.

Key Concepts and Vocabulary

A number of terms and concepts that might be new to you appear in this chapter. As you read through this chapter, pay close attention to the following terms and concepts. Write down a definition or explanation for each.

    Discretionary system

    Nondiscretionary system

    Drawdown

    Perpetual contracts

    Optimizing

    Curve-fitting

Robustness

Profit factor

Outlier-adjusted profit

Percentage winning trades

Annualized rate of return

Payoff ratio

Length of the average winning trade

Efficiency factor

Net profit to maximum drawdown ratio

Maximum consecutive losses

Longest flat time

Time to recovery

Maximum favorable and adverse excursions

Sharpe ratio

Equity curve

Underwater curve

Parameter

End-of-Chapter Review Questions

1. *Explain the difference between a discretionary and nondiscretionary system.*

   In a discretionary system, the investor exercises discretion in making trades. The investor's intuition plays a role in determining entries and exits. In a nondiscretionary system, entries and exits are determined by a computer program. After a nondiscretionary system is designed it runs on autopilot.

2. *What are the advantages and disadvantages of a nondiscretionary system?*

   An investor using a nondiscretionary system avoids emotion. Because traders often lose money due to emotional decisions, this is an advantage of a nondiscretionary system. Other trading pitfalls, such as overtrading, premature action, no action, and constant decision-making, are avoided. The non-discretionary system can be tested and adjusted. The investor knows in advance the risks associated with the system.

   However, there are some disadvantages of nondiscretionary systems. Results in the future will never be exactly the same as in the test period because history doesn't repeat itself precisely. During periods of poor performance, the investor cannot easily determine if there has been a change in the market that requires a new system or if the system will soon be profitable. Even with a nondiscretionary system, the investor must decide when to continue with the system and when to abandon or alter the system.

3. *How would you describe the discipline and mindset necessary to develop and follow a trading or investing system?*

   In addition to having knowledge about the financial markets, to be a successful trader or investor you have to have a plan. It is important to be realistic about what you can do and what a system can do. You must realize that you will not profit constantly or consistently; you know that losses will occur. Instead of becoming upset about these losses, you should be prepared for them and work to keep them small and infrequent. You must be realistic about the time that you can commit to your trading and your investment horizon. You need to be organized and disciplined. You can't just wing it; you must develop a plan and spend the time and effort to test it properly.

4. *Your brother is a physician who does not have the time to manage his own money. Knowing that you have an interest in investments and have taken a class in technical analysis, he asks you to develop a trading system for him. Before you agree to take on this job, you want to make sure that he understands the concept of risk. How would you explain risk to him, especially as it is related to using a system for investing?*

   Our objective is to make a profit, but no system is a "sure thing." There is no fail-proof system that is guaranteed to make a profit. Risk is the chance that we will lose money. "Drawdown" is a way of quantifying risk. Drawdown is the amount by which our equity declines from a peak. Suppose, for example, that we purchase $10,000 worth of stock and then the value of the portfolio falls to $8,000. This decline in value is the drawdown. It is usually expressed as a percentage, in this case 20%. Over time, the value of the portfolio might rise back higher than $10,000, and we will have a final profit. Before we commit to a system, we want to have some idea of what the risk is, or what the potential drawdown is. If we don't have a clear understanding of this, there is the chance that we will make an emotional decision when we see the declining portfolio value and prematurely exit the strategy. If we will not be able to withstand the amount of drawdown that can be expected with a system (either financially or emotionally) we should not use a system.

5. *After you explain the concept of risk to your brother, he still wants you to develop a trading system. In fact, he has done some reading and is convinced that a trend-following moving average crossover system is the way to go. He even knows what stock he wants to trade using the system—his favorite pharmaceutical company, High Profit Pharmaceuticals (HPP). You do some initial investigation, and you think that HPP is currently in a trading range. Explain to your brother why you think it would be unwise to attempt to trade HPP using a moving average crossover system at this point. (Be sure to explain the concept of a whipsaw in your explanation.)*

   It would be unwise to use any system during a trading range unless it was designed to avoid such a condition. Trend-following systems, such as moving average crossover systems, are designed to capture profits while a security price trends upward. A moving average crossover system, however, could be used if it had sufficient filters to avoid the whipsaws inherent in a trading range. Whipsaws occur when large numbers of signals occur that miss the market and produce small losses. They are particularly common in moving average crossover systems during a trading range when the moving averages, lagging price action, produce many false signals as they oscillate back and forth.

6. *Your brother, eager to develop the "perfect" system to trade HPP, has developed a system, tested it, and optimized it. His results show that he would have quadrupled his money last year trading his system! He is ready to put the system in place to trade HPP this year, expecting to quadruple his money. What questions would you have about his testing and optimization procedures, and what warnings would you want to give him?*

I would have questions about the data he was using to test his system. Was the data the same data that he is planning to use in actual trading? Did the test data include periods in which the stock price increased, decreased, and moved sideways? Did the period covered by the data generate enough trades (at least 30 to 50) to test the quality of signals produced? He wants to make sure, for example, that the profits didn't result from one long signal during a period when HPP was in a strong uptrend; he wants to make sure that the system signals downtrends properly, also. I would also want to ask about his optimizing procedures. He wants to make sure that he hasn't over fitted the historical data. Has he has run out-of-sample tests to find the absolute best parameters for trading the historical data?

7. *Two of your friends, Jennifer and Michael, have developed systems to trade IBM. During the test period, Jennifer's system had a net profit of $9,578, whereas Michael's system had a net profit of only $8,993. Explain why this information alone is not enough to determine that Jennifer's system is superior to Michael's.*

The net profit does not take into consideration the robustness of the results. In addition to net profit, robustness includes consistency of results, minimum maximum drawdown risk, and profitability in a changing market environment. Net profit alone is not a good gauge of a system's superiority.

Self-Test

1. *Ethan develops a trading system based on moving averages and sets his computer to automatically make trades based upon the system. Ethan is using*

   a. A discretionary trading system.

   b. A nondiscretionary trading system.

   c. A non-systematic trading system.

   d. A drawdown control system.

2. *An advantage of a nondiscretionary trading system is*

   a. That it gives the trader clear signals when the underlying market has changed and a new strategy should be followed.

   b. That a trader can quickly and easily respond to new market information.

   c. That it removes any decision-making responsibilities from the trader.

   d. That it removes emotions from the trading system.

3. *The amount by which your equity might fall from a peak when using a trading system is known as the*

    a. Drawdown.

    b. Nondiscretionary capital.

    c. Discretionary capital.

    d. Standard deviation of the return.

4. *Melinda has developed a system to trade MSFT. She tested the system using data for MSFT for the past five years. Initially, her system had a return of 12% a year. Her system has fifteen variables and she has fine-tuned the system so that the return for the test period data is 28% a year. Melinda must be careful that she has not*

    a. Reduced the nondiscretionary portion of the system.

    b. Removed intuition from the system.

    c. Increased the robustness of the system.

    d. Curve-fitted the data.

5. *In order to test a system effectively,*

    a. The system should generate a minimum of five buy signals and five sell signals.

    b. The data stream should be different than that which will be used in trading to make sure that the system is reliable.

    c. Up, down, and sideways trends should be included in the test period.

    d. The data should be curve-fitted.

6. *The Sharpe ratio*

    a. Is a common measure of the return versus risk of a portfolio but fails to account for drawdown.

    b. Is a common measure of the return versus risk of a portfolio that incorporates drawdown and the risk of ruin.

    c. Is the maximum drawdown from the peak in the equity curve divided by the initial capital invested in a system.

    d. Is the ratio of the average winning trade to the average losing trade.

7. *Knowing the largest winner figure for a trading system is important because it*

    a. Provides a measure of the amount of capital the trader needs to devote to the system.

    b. Provides a measure of the risk-return tradeoff the trader faces.

    c. Tells what the risk of ruin is for a system.

    d. Tells whether the system is highly dependent on finding one or two hugely profitable trades.

8. *Meredith creates a trading system which is composed of two moving averages that generate signals when they cross over each other. Meredith is using*

    a. A trend-following system.

    b. A pattern recognition system.

    c. A countertrend system.

    d. An exogenous signal system.

9. *Which of the following lists the four main categories of technical trading systems?*

    a. Discretionary, nondiscretionary, fundamental, and moving average systems

    b. Trend following, moving average, decision-based, and risk management systems

    c. Risk management, money management, trend-following, and countertrend systems

    d. Trend-following, pattern recognition, countertrend, and exogenous signals systems

10. *Which of the following is a characteristic of the necessary mindset to successful trading?*

    a. Realize that losses will occur; try to keep them small and infrequent.

    b. Do not have an opinion of the market; profits are made from reacting to the market, not anticipating it.

    c. Be organized.

    d. All of the above.

CHAPTER 23

Money and Risk Management

Chapter Objectives

After reading this chapter, you should be familiar with

▶ Definitions and measurements of risk as it relates to money management

▶ The martingale betting strategy

▶ Diversifiable versus correlated risk

▶ Methods for testing money-management strategies

▶ The use of various types of stops to manage risk

▶ Methods for determining the minimum capital needed for a system

▶ Methods for determining the percentage of capital to allocate toward one system

Chapter Summary

Risk and Money Management

Money management is primarily concerned with how to measure and manage risk of loss and financial ruin. **Risk** is the amount and probability of a loss or series of losses occurring. The essence of money management is to maximize return at minimum risk.

Testing Money-Management Strategies

You can use Monte Carlo simulation to test portfolio risk. The Monte Carlo simulation takes the trades produced by a system and scrambles them in a random manner many times. An equity curve is then created for each scrambled sequence of trades. The results from each equity curve are assembled and related to a normal distribution to see how random the system is. The less random the system is, the more likely it will be profitable with minimum risk of failure.

Money-Management Risks

The important risk consideration is the loss of capital, called a **drawdown**, which comes from losses on trades, realized or unrealized. Thus, drawdown must be controlled. The **maximum drawdown (MDD)** is the drawdown that has the highest intrapeak equity percentage loss over a period. A drawdown is usually the result of a series of losses.

You can use the **martingale betting system** in a situation where the best size can be changed but the odds are relatively even. The method is to double up on the next bet after a loss, and return to the standard bet after a win. It assumes that the payoff is the same for every bet and that the odds are even. It is thus unrealistic for trading in securities with uneven odds and different payoffs.

Position size is the amount of capital committed to a system or investment that incurs a specific risk. It is usually based on the difference between the entry price and the stop exit price multiplied by the number of shares or contracts. The three methods of determining the position size are the risk of ruin formula, the theory of runs formula, and the optimal f, or Kelly, formula. You should use all three formulas, and the formula with the smallest percentage of capital to be risked should be the one you use in a trading system.

Initial capital requirement concerns arise from the risk of a series of losses right in the beginning of a system wiping out capital and eliminating the trader from being able to reenter the system. **Leverage** is the borrowing of capital to increase the potential for gain; leverage increases risk.

Money-Management Risk Strategies

A **protective stop** is placed at the level of maximum limit of loss from entry; it is often called a "money-management" stop because it prevents the complete loss of capital. You should always place a protective stop on entry to a position, and that stop must be inviolate. After a position is entered, the position begins to profit or the protective stop is triggered. If the position is profitable, a **trailing stop** is used to lock in the gain.

Key Concepts and Vocabulary

A number of terms and concepts that might be new to you appear in this chapter. As you read through this chapter, pay close attention to the following terms and concepts. Write down a definition or explanation for each.

> Money management
>
> Risk
>
> Maximum drawdown
>
> Martingale betting strategy

Profit factor

Position size

Risk of ruin formula

Theory of runs formula

Optimal f

Leverage

Protective stop

Trailing stop

Initial capital

Monte Carlo simulation

End-of-Chapter Review Questions

1. *You have tested a system and find that it has a losing percentage of 25%.*

    a. *What is the chance of having a run of three losses?*

    b. *What is the chance of having a run of four losses?*

    c. *What is the chance of having a run of five losses?*

    a. The chance of having a run of three losses is
    $0.25 \times 0.25 \times 0.25 = 1.56\%$.

    b. The chance of having a run of four losses is
    $0.25 \times 0.25 \times 0.25 \times 0.25 = 0.39\%$.

    c. The chance of having a run of five losses is
    $0.25 \times 0.25 \times 0.25 \times 0.25 \times 0.25 = 0.098\%$.

2. *Explain what is meant by the martingale betting system.*

    A martingale betting strategy is a strategy that you can use when you can change the bet size but the odds are relatively even. For example, suppose you make a bet that if a coin lands on heads you win double what you have bet and if the coin lands on tails you win nothing. You make an initial $1 bet and the coin lands on tails (so you have lost $1). Next you double up and bet $2; if the coin lands on tails again, you have now lost $3. You double your bet again to $4; if the coin lands on tails again, you have now lost $7. Double your bet again to $8; if the coin finally lands on heads, you collect $16. You have a profit of $1; you have paid $15 total on bets ($1 + $2 + $4 + $8) and have collected $16. At this point, you would return to your original $1 bet.

3. *You have tested a system, and it has an MDD of 30%. You are willing to have a 45% draw-down. How might you use leverage with this system to maximize your return, given the level of risk you are willing to take?*

For example purposes, assume that you have initial capital of $10,000 and are willing to have a 45% (or $4,500) drawdown. If you have a system that has an MDD of 30% you can leverage your position by purchasing $15,000 worth of securities. You could expect a $4,500 drawdown when investing $15,000 in the system. However, your expected return will be higher. If you expect a 20% return from the system, investing only your $10,000 in capital would result in a $2,000 profit. Leveraging your position and investing $15,000 ($10,000 of your money and $5,000 of borrowed money) the 20% return would result in a $3,000 profit (or a return of 30% on your capital).

4. *You are employed as a money manager and know you will lose your job if your drawdown exceeds 15%. However, you have a system with a 30% MDD that you would like to use. How can you structure your strategy to use the system, but at the same time not exceed a 15% drawdown?*

Assume that you have $100,000 under your management. If your drawdown exceeds $15,000 you know you will lose your job. If your system has a 30% MDD, you don't want to invest more than $50,000 in the system. By investing $50,000 in the system, the 30% MDD would result in a drawdown of $15,000. You would want to invest $50,000 in the system and the remaining $50,000 in risk-free U.S. T-bills.

5. *A phrase heard frequently in finance is "more risk, more return." If I invest my entire portfolio in one stock, High Growth Energy Corporation (HGEC), I am taking substantial risk because "all my eggs are in one basket." Should I expect a higher return than I would if I had diversi-fied my portfolio because I am taking so much risk? Explain.*

Diversification is a basic principle of investment risk avoidance. Investing in only one stock exposes the investor to a very high level of risk because if something goes wrong with that particular investment, all of the investor's capital is exposed to that risk. The investor does not have profits from another investment to offset this loss. An investor can reduce risk significantly through diversification into securities that tend to behave differently. However, by diversifying, the investor also reduces potential return because not all investments will profit at the same rate. All investment is thus a tradeoff between potential profit and potential risk.

6. *Explain the difference in correlated (market) risk and uncorrelated (diversifiable) risk.*

Correlated (also known as market or non-diversifiable) risk is the risk generated by the over-all market. For example, a major world event can cause fear in the market that leads to an overall decline in stock prices. It doesn't really matter what stocks an investor holds when this occurs, he or she will be exposed to this market decline.

Uncorrelated risk is sometimes known as diversifiable or firm-specific risk. For example, if a pharmaceutical company announces that it is pulling a drug off of the market because of possible serious side effects, the price of the stock will decline. The reason for the decline is related to the operations of the company. If an investor was holding only the stock of this company, he or she would face a substantial loss. However, the investor can reduce this risk through diversification. If the investor is holding a number of stocks, the loss on the pharmaceutical company's stock may be offset by gains in other stocks not affected by this event. On the other hand, if his pharmaceutical company announced a new miracle drug for Alzheimer's, diversification would have reduced his profit because the other stocks would not perform as well as the drug company stock. In that case, diversification reduced return at the expense of being cautious.

7. *Explain how each of the following items would affect the percentage of capital you would want to allocate to a particular system:*

   a. *Average winning trade amount*

   b. *Average losing trade amount*

   c. *Percent of trades that are profitable*

   The average winning trade amount is the dollar amount of gain on average from profitable trades. The average losing trade amount is the dollar amount of loss on average from losing trades. Dividing the average winning trade amount by the average losing trade amount results in the payoff ratio. The larger this payoff ratio (because of either a larger winning trade amount and/or a smaller losing trade amount), the more capital you would want to allocate to a particular system. Also, the higher the percent of profitable trades, the more you would want to allocate to a system. Thus, the less likely you are to have an unprofitable trade and the smaller the average loss when that does occur, the more capital you can allocate to the system without a fear of losing all of your capital.

8. *In the words of a Kenny Roger's song, "You've got to know when to hold 'em, know when to fold 'em." How could these words be applied to money management?*

   Exit strategies are the most important decision in a system. You need to know when to hold (or remain in) your position. You can choose at your convenience when to enter a position, but once you commit to an investment you must make an exit at some time. You may have a gain, but if you exit your position too soon, your gain won't be as large as it could have been. If you have a loss and close the position prematurely, holding the position longer may have resulted in a profitable trade. However, you need to know when you have made a mistake and exit a position at a loss at times. Many investors who are unwilling to admit that a trade was not a good decision and hold on to the position waiting for a profit may suffer even a larger loss in capital.

9. *Explain how stops are an important part of risk management.*

   Before entering into a position, investors should determine the maximum amount of loss they can allow on the position. This amount will be determined by the level of risk an investor is willing to take in one position on one trade. When entering into the position, the investor places this "money-management" stop. This will protect the investor from complete loss of capital. Investors in long positions who have sell stops in place know the maximum amount they may lose if the stock price begins falling.

10. *Explain the meaning of the phrase, "Entry strategies carry no risk until executed."*

    If you have $10,000 in cash there is no risk to your capital until you actually enter into a position. Suppose that you say you will purchase XYZ stock when the price reaches $30 a share. This strategy carries no risk until the entry is executed and the stock is purchased. Until that time you have $10,000 with no risk of loss.

Self-Test

1. *You are managing $300,000 and have a system that you would like to use that has a 30% MDD. If you are willing to have a 20% drawdown, you should*

    a. Borrow $100,000 and invest $400,000 in the system.

    b. Invest $200,000 in the system and $100,000 in T-bills.

    c. Invest $150,000 in the system and $150,000 in T-bills.

    d. Invest $100,000 in the system and $200,000 in T-bills.

2. *The payoff ratio is calculated as*

    a. The ratio between the percentage of winning trades and the percentage of losing trades.

    b. The ratio between the average winning trade and the percentage of winning trades.

    c. The product of the probability of a winning trade multiplied by the likelihood of a winning trade.

    d. The ratio between the average winning trade and the average losing trade.

3. *An investor can reduce _____ risk through diversification.*

    a. Market

    b. Correlated

    c. Uncorrelated

    d. All of the above

4. *A system has a 50% chance of a loss. The probability of having a run of three losses is*

    a. 12.5%.

    b. 25%.

    c. 37.5%.

    d. 50%.

5. *Which of the following would be an example of correlated risk?*

   a. Global Oil's profits drop as oil prices fall.

   b. American Motor Works has falling revenue as a result of an automobile recall.

   c. The stock of Gamma Corporation falls on news of accounting irregularities within the company.

   d. Prime rate rises as the Federal Reserve raises the target fed funds rate in an attempt to curtail inflation.

6. *The idea behind the martingale betting system is that*

   a. By doubling up on a bet after a loss, a winning bet will eventually cover all the previous losses and return a profit on the original bet.

   b. By doubling up on a bet after a win, the bettor takes advantage of winning trends.

   c. The probability of a second loss decreases after an initial loss, but increases after an initial gain, if outcomes are independent.

   d. The probability of a second loss increases after an initial loss, but decreases after an initial gain, if outcomes are independent.

7. *A protective stop*

   a. Should be determined after a position has begun to profit.

   b. Should be placed after an occurrence of the maximum drawdown that occurred in the testing of the system because the basic market conditions might have changed since the system was designed.

   c. Only needs to be used if a trader has not protected against loss of capital through diversification.

   d. Should be placed upon entry and should be inviolate.

8. *Jeremy has placed an entry order to purchase 100 shares of a stock at a price of $73 a share. He also has a protective stop placed at $70 a share. Jeremy's position size is*

   a. $300.

   b. $700.

   c. $730.

   d. $1030.

9. *In order to determine the position size, the risk of ruin formula, the theory of runs formula, and the optimal f should be calculated. Then,*

   a. The formula with the largest percentage of capital to be risked should be used.

   b. The formula with the smallest percentage of capital to be risked should be used.

   c. The average of the three formulas determines the percentage of capital to be risked.

   d. Add the three percentages together to determine the percentage of capital to be risked.

10. *A general rule of thumb for initial capital is to have*

    a. At least two times the amount of the MDD plus the initial margin for stocks.

    b. At least ten times the margin required for a single contract for each contract traded.

    c. One-half of the amount of the MDD for stocks.

    d. No more than two times the position size for each contract traded.

APPENDIX A
Basic Statistics

Appendix Objectives

By the end of this appendix, you should be familiar with

▶ The difference between descriptive and inferential statistics

▶ How to calculate common measures of central tendency and dispersion

▶ The process of regression

▶ The basic premises and statistics related to MPT

Appendix Summary

Probability and Statistics

If two events are **independent** then the outcome of the first event does not affect the probability of the outcome for the second event. **Descriptive statistics** characterize data in a shorthand manner, whereas **inferential statistics** tries to infer various statements about data based on observed outcomes or assumptions about outcomes.

Descriptive Statistics

Measures of **central tendency** describe a set of data by determining what a typical outcome is. The **mean**, **median**, **mode**, and **geometric mean** are measures of central tendency. **Variance** and **standard deviation** are the two main measures of volatility or dispersion.

To determine how two variables vary, the **covariance** and **correlation coefficient** are used. A correlation coefficient of +1 indicates that two variables are perfectly correlated; a correlation coefficient of –1 indicates that two variables are perfectly negatively correlated. A correlation coefficient of 0 indicates that no discernible relationship between the two variables exists. Squaring the correlation coefficient results in the **coefficient of determination** or **r-squared**.

Linear regression least-squares fit involves drawing a **line of best fit** through a set of data points. The line is drawn such that the sum of the squared differences between the actual data points and the line are minimized. The variable being explained is called the **dependent variable**, and the variable doing the explaining is called the **independent variable**. **Multiple regression** refers to the use of more than one independent variable.

Inferential Statistics

The **normal distribution** is the most well-known of all probability distributions. It is a bell-shaped curve, with its peak in the center. It is symmetric about the mean, and the left and right tails asymptotically approach the horizontal axis. Approximately two-thirds of the outcomes lie within one standard deviation of the mean. Approximately 99% lie within two standard deviations of the mean.

Modern Portfolio Theory

The mean return of a portfolio is a simple weighted average of the mean returns of the individual stocks, but the standard deviation of a portfolio is less than a simple weighted average of the individual stock standard deviations. Because stocks are not perfectly positively correlated, there are significant benefits to diversification.

Performance Measurement

One simple method of assessing performance is to measure reward per unit of risk. The **Sharpe ratio** is calculated by subtracting the risk-free return from the average return from the investment and dividing by the standard deviation of the returns over the period of measurement. The **Treynor measure of performance** and **Jensen's alpha** are measures of excess return based upon beta.

Key Concepts and Vocabulary

A number of terms and concepts that might be new to you appear in this appendix. As you read through it, pay close attention to the following terms and concepts. Write down a definition or explanation for each.

Return

Random

Deterministic

Independence

Permutation

Combination

Descriptive statistics

Inferential statistics

Mean

Median

Mode

Geometric mean

Measures of central tendency

Measures of dispersion

Variance

Standard deviation

Correlation covariance

Coefficient of determination

Linear regression least-squares fit

Independent variable

Dependent variable

Multiple regression

Normal distribution

Nondiversifiable risk

Beta

Sharpe ratio

Treynor measure of performance

Jensen's alpha

End-of-Appendix Review Questions

1. *Explain the difference between descriptive and inferential statistics.*

Descriptive statistics describe or characterize data in a shorthand manner. Descriptive statistics describe things such as what a typical outcome is (such as mean, mode, or median) and how much variability occurs (such as variance or standard deviation). Inferential statistics refers to the use of observed data to infer things about general characteristics of the observed data or characteristics of additional observations.

2. *The monthly closing prices for VLO and TSO for the year 2005 are given in Table A.2 [in the Technical Analysis textbook and included here for reference]. (The closing prices are adjusted for stock splits and dividends.)*

	VLO		TSO	
Date	Adj. Close	Volume	Adj. Close	Volume
3-Jan-05	25.89	6,327,590	31.71	1,156,805
1-Feb-05	35.49	11,433,242	36.78	1,283,473
1-Mar-05	36.5	14,312,645	36.87	1,496,781
1-Apr-05	34.14	19,363,771	37.79	1,944,952
2-May-05	34.24	15,281,285	43.48	1,586,209
1-Jun-05	39.47	11,828,418	46.39	1,481,663
1-Jul-05	41.3	11,438,900	48.09	1,213,225
1-Aug-05	53.2	18,753,469	57.69	1,948,447
1-Sep-05	56.48	24,614,095	67.12	3,366,504
3-Oct-05	52.57	23,972,552	61.04	3,137,700
1-Nov-05	48.1	17,303,419	55.07	2,545,585
1-Dec-05	51.6	11,718,461	61.55	1,698,647

Source: http://finance.yahoo.com

a. *Calculate the monthly return for each of these stocks.*

The monthly return for each of the stocks is calculated as shown in the following table:

	VLO		TSO	
Date	Adj. Close	Monthly Return	Adj. Close	Monthly Return
3-Jan-05	25.89		31.71	
1-Feb-05	35.49	0.3708	36.78	0.1599
1-Mar-05	36.5	0.0285	36.87	0.0024
1-Apr-05	34.14	-0.0647	37.79	0.0250
2-May-05	34.24	0.0029	43.48	0.1506
1-Jun-05	39.47	0.1527	46.39	0.0669
1-Jul-05	41.3	0.0464	48.09	0.0366
1-Aug-05	53.2	0.2881	57.69	0.1996
1-Sep-05	56.48	0.0617	67.12	0.1635
3-Oct-05	52.57	-0.0692	61.04	-0.0906
1-Nov-05	48.1	-0.0850	55.07	-0.0978
1-Dec-05	51.6	0.0728	61.55	0.1177

b. *Calculate the following for each of these stocks:*

i. *Arithmetic mean of the monthly returns*

The arithmetic mean for VLO is 0.0732 or 7.32%; the arithmetic mean for TSO is 0.0667 or 6.67%.

ii. *Median monthly return*

The median monthly return for VLO is 0.0464 or 4.64%; the median monthly return for TSO is 0.0669 or 6.69%.

iii. *Geometric mean monthly return*

The geometric mean monthly return is calculated as

| | VLO | | | TSO | | |
Date	Adj. Close	Monthly Return	1 + Monthly Return	Adj. Close	Monthly Return	1 + Monthly Return
3-Jan-05	25.89			31.71		
1-Feb-05	35.49	0.3708	1.3708	36.78	0.1599	1.1599
1-Mar-05	36.5	0.0285	1.0285	36.87	0.0024	1.0024
1-Apr-05	34.14	-0.0647	0.9353	37.79	0.0250	1.0250
2-May-05	34.24	0.0029	1.0029	43.48	0.1506	1.1506
1-Jun-05	39.47	0.1527	1.1527	46.39	0.0669	1.0669
1-Jul-05	41.3	0.0464	1.0464	48.09	0.0366	1.0366
1-Aug-05	53.2	0.2881	1.2881	57.69	0.1996	1.1996
1-Sep-05	56.48	0.0617	1.0617	67.12	0.1635	1.1635
3-Oct-05	52.57	-0.0692	0.9308	61.04	-0.0906	0.9094
1-Nov-05	48.1	-0.0850	0.9150	55.07	-0.0978	0.9022
1-Dec-05	51.6	0.0728	1.0728	61.55	0.1177	1.1177
Product of Monthly Returns			1.9930			1.9410
11th Root of Product			1.0647			1.0621
11th Root of Product - 1			0.0647			0.0621

The geometric mean for VLO is 0.0647 or 6.47%; the geometric mean for TSO is 0.0621 or 6.21%.

c. *Explain why the mode is not a meaningful statistic for this data set.*

The mode is the return that occurs most often. There are no two months in which the returns for VLO or TSO are identical. So, each of the 11 monthly returns occurs only once. Even if there were two months in which the returns were identical, that information would not be relevant for the investor. Investors would not care that the exact return occurred in two different months; investors are more concerned with the overall return and not which exact returns occur most often.

3. *Calculate the standard deviation of the monthly return for both VLO and TSO using the data provided in Question 2. Explain how the standard deviation relates to risk.*

The standard deviation for VLO is 0.1460, and the standard deviation for TSO is 0.1019. The standard deviation is a measure of risk because it is a measure of dispersion around the mean. The larger the standard deviation is, the larger the difference from the mean return that could be expected in any given month. For example, the 0.1460 standard deviation for VLO indicates that the return for VLO could be expected to be between −0.0728 and 0.2192 about two-thirds of the time.

4. *What is the correlation coefficient for VLO and TSO? Explain what the correlation coefficient means.*

The correlation coefficient for VLO and TSO is 0.7199. This means that VLO and TSO are positively correlated to a reasonably strong degree.

5. *Plot the monthly returns using TSO as the dependent variable and VLO as the independent variable.*

The plot of monthly returns for TSO and VLO looks like the following graph:

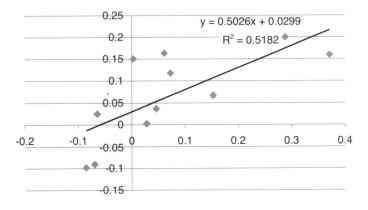

a. *Calculate the least-squares regression line.*

The equation for the least-squares regression line is y = 0.5026x + 0.0299

b. *What is the r-squared for the regression line? How is this number interpreted?*

The r-squared for the regression line is 0.5026. This means that variation in VLO's return explains 50.26% of the variation in TSO's return.

c. *If the monthly return for VLO was 3.4%, given the regression equation, what would be your best estimate of the monthly return for TSO?*

If VLO's return for the month was 3.4%, the best estimate for TSO's return for the month would be 0.5026(0.034) + .0299 = .047 or 4.7%.

Self-Test

1. *Sean is calculating the average return of his portfolio over the past 10 years and the variability of that return. Sean is using*

   a. Inferential statistics.

   b. Deferential statistics.

   c. Descriptive statistics.

   d. Dependent variable statistics.

2. *The mean return for a portfolio is _____ the weighted average of the returns of the individual components, and the standard deviation for a portfolio is _____ the weighted average of the standard deviations of the individual components.*

   a. Equal to; equal to

   b. Equal to; less than

   c. Less than; equal to

   d. Less than; less than

3. *Which of the following is a list of measures of central tendency?*

   a. Mean, variance, r-squared

   b. Variance, standard deviation, degrees of freedom

   c. Mode, variance, standard deviation

   d. Mean, median, mode

4. *Systematic risk is also known as*

    a. Diversifiable risk.

    b. Nondiversifiable risk.

    c. Efficient frontier risk.

    d. Industry risk.

5. *The Sharpe performance measure is calculated using the*

    a. Average return of the investment, the standard deviation of the investment, and the risk-free return.

    b. Average return of the investment, the beta of the investment, and the average return of the market.

    c. The mean, median, and mode of the investment.

    d. The alpha of the investment, the beta of the investment, and the correlation coefficient.

6. *Bethany has determined that the correlation coefficient between the returns on investment A and investment B is −0.8955. Which of the following would be the best explanation of this correlation coefficient?*

    a. The returns on the two investments are not related to each other.

    b. Whenever the return on investment A is positive, the return on investment B will probably be negative.

    c. Whenever the return on investment A is positive, the return on investment B will also be positive.

    d. The return on investment B will usually be 89.55% of the return on investment A.

7. *Darren is looking at the weekly returns for CAT over the past year. Which of the following statistical measures is Darren LEAST likely to be concerned with?*

    a. Standard deviation

    b. Geometric mean

    c. Median

    d. Mode

8. *If the outcome of one event does not affect the probability of the outcome of a second event, the two events are*

    a. Permutations of each other.

    b. Negatively correlated.

    c. Positively correlated.

    d. Independent events.

9. *The typical correlation coefficient between two stocks chosen at random is*

   a. 0.

   b. Between 0.2 and 0.5.

   c. Between 0.5 and 0.7.

   d. 1.

10. *In a regression,*

    a. The variable being explained is called the dependent variable, and the variable doing the explaining is called the independent variable.

    b. The variable being explained is called the explanatory variable, and the variable doing the explaining is called the dependent variable.

    c. Adding additional explanatory variables will reduce the r-squared.

    d. As many explanatory variables as possible should be included to increase the amount of multicollinearity in the model.

Answer Key

Chapter 2

1. c
2. a
3. b
4. a
5. d
6. a
7. d
8. c
9. a
10. d

Chapter 3

1. b
2. a
3. d
4. a
5. a
6. d
7. a
8. b
9. a
10. b

Chapter 4

1. d
2. c
3. a
4. d
5. a
6. a
7. b
8. d
9. b
10. a

Chapter 5

1. b
2. c
3. b
4. d
5. a
6. d
7. a
8. b
9. d
10. a

Chapter 6

1. a
2. c
3. d
4. c
5. a
6. a
7. a
8. a
9. b
10. a

Chapter 7

1. c
2. b
3. a
4. d
5. a
6. c
7. a
8. b
9. d
10. a

Chapter 8

1. d
2. a
3. a
4. d
5. a
6. d
7. a
8. c
9. b
10. a

Chapter 9

1. d
2. d
3. a
4. a
5. a
6. c
7. a
8. c
9. a
10. b

Chapter 10

1. b
2. d
3. b
4. c
5. d
6. d
7. a
8. a
9. d
10. b

Chapter 11

1. a
2. b
3. a
4. c
5. b
6. a
7. a
8. c
9. d
10. a

Chapter 12

1. b
2. a
3. d
4. a
5. a
6. b
7. a
8. b
9. d
10. a

Chapter 13

1. b
2. a
3. d
4. a
5. a
6. d
7. a
8. c
9. a
10. c

Chapter 14

1. c
2. b
3. b
4. a
5. c
6. c
7. a
8. d
9. a
10. b

Chapter 15

1. d
2. d
3. a
4. b
5. a
6. b
7. a
8. c
9. d
10. d
11. a
12. a
13. c

14. d
15. c
16. d
17. b
18. d
19. b
20. a

Chapter 16

1. a
2. d
3. b
4. c
5. a
6. d
7. d
8. a
9. d
10. c

Chapter 17

1. d
2. a
3. d
4. a
5. b

6. a
7. a
8. d
9. b
10. d
11. b
12. b
13. d
14. a
15. a
16. d
17. d
18. b
19. c
20. c

Chapter 18

1. a
2. c
3. a
4. d
5. a
6. d
7. a
8. a
9. d
10. a

Chapter 19

1. a
2. d
3. c
4. a
5. a
6. b
7. d
8. b
9. a
10. b

Chapter 21

1. d
2. b
3. c
4. b
5. a
6. c
7. a
8. d
9. a
10. a

Chapter 23

1. b
2. d
3. c
4. a
5. d
6. a
7. d
8. a
9. b
10. a

Chapter 20

1. a
2. d
3. a
4. b
5. a
6. c
7. d
8. a
9. a
10. a

Chapter 22

1. b
2. d
3. a
4. d
5. c
6. a
7. d
8. a
9. d
10. d

Appendix

1. c
2. b
3. d
4. b
5. a
6. b
7. d
8. d
9. b
10. a

Press

FINANCIAL TIMES

In an increasingly competitive world, it is quality
of thinking that gives an edge—an idea that opens new
doors, a technique that solves a problem, or an insight
that simply helps make sense of it all.

We work with leading authors in the various arenas
of business and finance to bring cutting-edge thinking
and best-learning practices to a global market.

It is our goal to create world-class print publications
and electronic products that give readers
knowledge and understanding that can then be
applied, whether studying or at work.

To find out more about our business
products, you can visit us at www.ftpress.com.